One More Story and I'm Out the Door

A Life, With Recollections About Jimmy Hoffa, the Mafia, G. Gordon Liddy, and Guardian Angels, Among Others

Thomas A. Kennelly

iUniverse, Inc.
New York Lincoln Shanghai

One More Story and I'm Out the Door
A Life, With Recollections About Jimmy Hoffa, the Mafia,
G. Gordon Liddy, and Guardian Angels, Among Others

iUniverse books may be ordered through booksellers or by contacting:

iUniverse
2021 Pine Lake Road, Suite 100
Lincoln, NE 68512
www.iuniverse.com
1-800-Authors (1-800-288-4677)

ISBN-13: 978-0-595-38358-0 (pbk)
ISBN-13: 978-0-595-82731-2 (ebk)
ISBN-10: 0-595-38358-0 (pbk)
ISBN-10: 0-595-82731-4 (ebk)

Printed in the United States of America

Among the people that I admire and respect,
I can find no common denominator. Among the
people I love, I can. They all make me laugh.

—W.H. Auden

The Irish don't really think about writing,

it is just a natural extension of what we do

all the time, which is talking.

—Maeve Binchy

A man's children slip through the net of his death,
Their bodies leave his body, and bear his life
Back into life, with his name and fame.
His memories are alive in their bones.

Like the corks that buoy up the net of the fishermen
A man's children buoy up the weave of his life.
They buoy up the warp and weft of all he achieved.
Without them it sinks, lost in the depth of ocean.

—Electra, in *Choephori (The Libation Bearers),*
by Aeschylus

To Patrick, Tim, and Katy

Special thanks to my wife, Susan, for her editorial guidance and proofreading; to Rosie Calabrese for her research assistance; and to my daughter Katy and my patient son-in-law, Douglas Olds, without whose computer-savvy assistance this thing would never have got into print.

CONTENTS

INTRODUCTION

There comes a time in every man's life when his wife and children and even his closest friends—especially his closest friends—grow tired of hearing about the people and events that together have made up the woof and weave of his life. They refer to these adventures, not derisively but with a bit of a sigh, as "Dad's old war stories." Just as he's getting warmed up and feeling mellow, usually after a few drinks and a hearty meal, someone's remark reminds him of a fascinating experience from his own career. Not long thereafter he detects a slight rolling of the eyes, a stifled yawn or two, and notices that he is being edged graciously but firmly toward the door.

It is then that he decides to write his memoirs. He figures that if he puts it all down on paper he will find a new audience. He hopes that his grandchildren, his grandnieces and nephews, and perhaps new friends and acquaintances, will find, as he did, that all in all his life was pretty interesting. And so he begins.

The historian Arthur Schlesinger, Jr. says that the generic title for all memoirs should be *Things I Remember...and Things I Think I Remember*. In recounting the events told herein I have tried to be as accurate as possible. I'll leave it to others to determine where my memory differs from reality. I just hope they won't tell me about it.

1.

ORIGINS

Have you ever met anyone who has ridden in a real steam locomotive hauling a real freight train across the country? Well, say hello to Tom Kennelly.

It was like riding the back of a great black beast at sixty-five miles an hour, high up in the cab of that magnificent locomotive, with the engineer directly behind, shouting instructions through the din—when to blow the whistle, when to ring the bell—and the fireman just below, shoveling huge quantities of coal into the great blazing belly of the beast, as we roared across the plains of Illinois and up into Wisconsin. And before the day was over I was riding the tail, the rattling caboose, at the end of a long line of loaded freight cars. Alone with the conductor, I was lulled by the clickety-clack, clickety-clack of the rails, and I envisioned us as a team, the engineer, the fireman, the conductor and I. When they dropped me off in Platteville, Wisconsin, and my parents picked me up for the ride back to my hometown of Dubuque, Iowa, I was pretty sure that someday I would be a locomotive engineer.

It was one of the great thrills of life, and I was nine years old, that summer of 1939.

It's as good a place as any to begin the story of my life.

That memorable train ride was arranged—in violation of all regulations, I'm sure—by my uncle Jim Kennelly, my father's brother, who lived in Chicago and who was a conductor with the Chicago,

Milwaukee, St. Paul and Pacific Railroad. Uncle Jim worked his way up from call boy to passenger train conductor during his fifty years with the "Milwaukee Road." He was called the "Mayor of Union Depot," and when he died Mayor Richard J. Daley sent a telegram of condolence to my Aunt Sadie.

Uncle Jim—James Francis Kennelly—was the eldest of four sons, each two years apart, of John Patrick Kennelly and Mary (Walsh) Kennelly, my paternal grandparents.

John Patrick Kennelly was born in Listowel, County Kerry, Ireland, on March 7, 1858. As a young man he made his way to Chicago, where other Kennellys were located, and thence 180 miles west to Dubuque. He apparently got a job in the local mattress factory where he met Mary Walsh, who at age 26 was a forelady in the same factory. Mary, the daughter of William Walsh and Ann (Concannon) Walsh, was born February 24, 1860, in Rickardsville, a village just a few miles west of Dubuque.

John and Mary were married at St. Patrick's church in Dubuque on November 9, 1886, John then being 28 and Mary 26. Sometime thereafter they moved to Chicago, where John obtained a job in another mattress factory. Family legend has it that John had something to do with the invention of the coil spring; if so, there is no evidence of any financial rewards therefrom. It was in Chicago that their four sons were born: James Francis (8/4/87), John Michael (5/5/89), William Edward (6/15/91—died at age one), and George William, my father (3/31/93).

John Patrick Kennelly died of a heart attack at age 37 on August 19, 1894, leaving Mary and the three boys, ages 7, 5, and 1. Thereafter Mary returned to Dubuque where she opened a candy store at 2026 Couler (now Central) Ave. She thus supported herself and her three sons until they were old enough to become wage earners, *i.e.* in their early teens. In those days there was no social security.

Mary Walsh, my grandmother, died at age 73, on February 18, 1933, when I had just turned three. I have vague memories of visiting her home, an upper duplex on White Street in Dubuque. She had white hair and always dressed in black, but she was also quite lively and pleasant. What is seared in my memory most as a three-year-old is the wake held in our home. Her body in the coffin and the black crepe bow on our front door is an image that will always remain with me.

George Kennelly, my father, graduated from eighth grade at St. Patrick's school in Dubuque and then went to work. His two older brothers had gone with the Milwaukee Road, Jim with a train crew and John in the shops as a machinist, but George was looking for a career with a more exciting future. Today that would be computers or high technology, but in the early 20th century it was electricity. He became an apprentice electrician, then a journeyman working for the E.P. Smith Electric Co., and then at age 19, went into business for himself, just before the outbreak of World War I.

In 1917 he entered the Army and was assigned to a searchlight engineers battalion. His unit was sent to France and attached to the French Army, where he engaged in combat, aiding anti-aircraft batteries by shining searchlights on German bombers.

George returned from the war unscathed, except for an exposure to German mustard gas, and resumed his career as an electrician, employed by the United Electric Company in Dubuque. He lived with his mother and brother John at 2140 Central St., in the "north end," where most of the residents were of German descent. Most of the Irish lived in the "south end." My dad walked to and from his job, and that is how he first encountered Olive Hildegarde Bitter. My father said he saw this beautiful girl, knew she lived in the neighborhood, but did not know exactly where. One day he was called to do some wiring at 2250 Washington St. When he emerged from the basement, there she was in the kitchen, this brown-haired beauty.

Olive was 19 at the time, having been born on September 10, 1900, the daughter of Henry and Emelia (Schmidt) Bitter. Henry and Emilia were born in this country, but their parents were from Germany and had migrated to the U.S. via New Orleans, eventually making their way up the Mississippi to Dubuque. Olive had two older sisters, Amelia and Irene, and two older brothers, Henry and Alfred. Olive complete two hears of high school, where she leaned shorthand and bookkeeping. She was fond of reminiscing that her father and five his brothers were tailors and her mother and six of her sisters were seamstresses, but she never could learn to sew a stitch, and had no interest in it. But she must have had a very good business head, for she was secretary to the president of the bank. In later years she did all the bookkeeping for my father's electrical contracting business.

When Olive first saw George Kennelly in his work clothes, she was not at all impressed, but when he dressed up and took her dancing, it was a different story altogether. She loved to dance until the day she died.

Her parents were not overjoyed that she was dating an Irishman seven years older, but after four years of courtship they were married at Sacred Heart church in Dubuque on May 19, 1924.

Their marriage produced three living children, Patricia Ann (2/3/27), Thomas Anthony (2/11/30), and Mary Lu (5/30/37). (A first daughter died at birth.)

My childhood years—in fact our whole family life—can best be divided into the **Dubuque Years** (prior to 1940) and the **War Years** (1940 and thereafter).

2.

DUBUQUE YEARS, 1930-1940

Prior to World War II (and for a long time thereafter, for that matter), Dubuque was a town of 40,000. It is located in northeast Iowa on the Mississippi River at the exact junction of Iowa, Illinois, and Wisconsin. An old town, it was founded in the early 1830's and named after the French explorer Julien Dubuque. When I was a child it was about 85% Roman Catholic, predominantly German and Irish, with nine Catholic parishes. It is an archdiocese, the smallest in the nation. Its residents like to brag that Dubuque, like Rome, was built on seven hills, each with a Catholic institution, be it a church, monastery, convent, or college.

In addition to being a river port for the surrounding agricultural and dairy area, the city had a few industries—meat packing, a brewery, a furniture factory, a clothing manufacturer (supposedly the locale for the musical *The Pajama Game*), and plants producing gloves and coffins. Nor was it bereft of culture; theatrical groups performed at the Grand Opera House en route from Chicago to the Twin Cities. My father, in his younger days as an electrician, ran the spotlights for many of those shows, and thus developed a love for the theater.

Dubuquers were mostly white, middle class, and Democratic. All in all, Dubuque was the quintessential "nice place to raise a family." Few would call it cosmopolitan. When I was a boy my parents frequently talked about moving to somewhere more exciting, like California. In the 1930's California was—and still is for many—a symbol of hope and aspiration. In the words of the essayist Richard Rodriguez, "Restless lives are the point of California."

The Great Depression of the 1930's hit Dubuque hard, but ironically they were good years for my father's business, the George W. Kennelly Electric Company. He was awarded the street lighting contract for downtown Dubuque. He installed the new electric signals at railroad crossings, did the wiring for the High Bridge, and put electricity into convents, monasteries, and churches throughout the tri-state area.

Later in the 1930's, when the Public Works Administration allocated funds for new schools, my father did the wiring for two elementary schools in Dubuque (Marshall and Fulton), as well as schools in other towns in Iowa.

Thus in 1931, when Patricia was 4 and I was 1, my parents purchased a new Chevrolet pickup truck and a sedan, and built a new house at 1515 Atlantic St. It was not a grand house by modern standards (construction cost: $9000), but he put into it a number of features not ordinarily found in houses of the time. There were outside yard lights, and roll-up screens on all the windows. He put the garage underground, with a driveway into the basement, so the car would be warm all winter. (Backing it up the driveway in the snow and ice was an unforeseen problem.)

Most interesting of all, he created a niche in the living room wall above the fireplace. He said—in 1931, almost twenty years in advance—that some day there would be television, and this is where it would be installed. In the meantime, it was covered with a painting. In 1998, my wife Susan and I revisited that house, still in excellent condition, and I was able to explain to the owners the reason for that niche, to their amazement.

My parents were a good match. They worked well individually and together as a team. My father operated his electrical contracting business from an office in the home. My mother, in addition to being the homemaker, did all of his office work. In the 1930's a large part of his work was obtained by competitive bidding on public contracts. There was many an anxious moment in our household, waiting to see whether Kennelly Electric was the low bidder on a big school or public works project.

They also seemed to have enough time for fun. They had many friends and lots of parties. I can remember my father saying that you meet the most interesting people in the world after two in the morning. [In his later years he mused that his health might be better if he hadn't spent quite so much time time meeting such people.]

My father belonged to a for-men-only club euphemistically called the "Dubuque Service Club," which in reality was a place for men to gather for meals, drinks, camaraderie, and a little gambling. I suspect it was created as a speakeasy during Prohibition, judging from the locked door and peephole. My dad would take me there for lunch or after work every so often, and I always had a wonderful time. I would sit up at the bar, and he taught me to play the punch boards and the nickel slot machines. One could usually find a few members sitting around playing poker and they always greeted me as one of the boys. In the back room was a blackboard with the names of horses and a lot of numbers, and a man in a green eye shade who was almost always on the phone. I never quite figured out what that was all about, and no explanation was offered. The Service Club was a very special place to me, because my sisters could not go there. Neither could my mom, and occasionally we kids would hear some disgruntlement expressed about the amount of time Dad spent there.

Mom, being of German descent, kept a clean and orderly house, and we kids did the chores that kids everywhere do. Mom loved flowers, a trait she passed on to me. Each spring I helped her plant pansies and petunias, and together we tended the plants in the rock garden.

She also looked after our cultural development. Patricia took dancing lessons at Miss Plamondon's Dance Studio, but I favored music. Piano lessons were arranged, and a piano was purchased. I began lessons at age 7 and continued until I was about 15. I could read music well and became a reasonably proficient pianist, but I always had trouble improvising. Nevertheless, the skills developed in those early years enabled me to help pay my way through high school and college, playing in dance bands.

One September when I was eight or nine Miss Edith Grof, my stern and humorless piano teacher at the Dubuque Academy of Music, strongly urged me to attend the monthly Saturday afternoon lecture series offered to all music students, studying the lives of the great composers. The incentive was that if a student attended every one of the nine sessions throughout the school year, there would be an awards ceremony at which one could select a lapel pin of his or her musical instrument, to be proudly worn for the rest of one's life. So I did it, boring as it was, at the sacrifice of some good Saturday afternoon baseball.

When the great day arrived, all the students assembled, and at the front of the room was a table containing boxes of each of the various instruments, lapel-pin size. When my name was called, I floated to the front in a complete fog, and with a sweaty hand retrieved my prize. When I returned to my seat I opened my fist and discovered that I had selected—a violin!

Too shy to rectify my mistake, I had no satisfactory answer when for months thereafter people asked, "Tommy, why are you wearing that violin on your lapel?"

It was our mother who attended to our spiritual development. She taught us our evening prayers (which I still remember), enrolled us in Nativity parish school, taught us the five decades of each of the three mysteries of the rosary, and prepared us for First Communion. Mom's faith was strong and unwavering throughout her 92 years. She firmly believed, and taught us, that God would never impose heavier burdens than one could bear. In time of trouble she would say, "Jesus, Mary and Joseph, help me," and this perseverance, coupled with her Germanic tradition of resoluteness, carried her through many a crisis in the years that were to follow. She was not one to complain. Whatever the situation, she accepted what had to be done and then did it. Her "Just Do It" attitude was many years ahead of the Nike slogan.

Daddy, as we called him, went through some shaky periods in his spiritual life, due in no small measure, said Mom, to his business dealings with church pastors. But he would never miss Mass. Confession and communion maybe, but never Mass.

During the Dubuque years, my father spent a lot of time with us children. He took us on hikes, along the river to Julien Dubuque's memorial, or along the railroad tracks so we could walk on the rails and when a train came by, see how the engine would flatten a penny. On Sundays we would often take drives in the country to places like Guttenberg to see the dam and locks on the Mississippi, or over to Galena, Illinois, to visit the birthplace of Ulysses S. Grant. Another Sunday favorite, especially during the steamy summer months, was dinner at Kretz's Cafeteria, followed by a movie in the air-conditioned Grand theater, one of the few cool places in town.

When the weather was nice, in the late afternoon I would often sit on the curb at the corner of Atlantic and 14th St. (now Loras Blvd.), a block from our house, waiting for my dad to come home from work in his truck. He would let me ride on the running board—or sometimes sit on his lap and steer—for the rest of the way home.

In my kindergarten year and later in the summer months he would often take me with him to his out-of-town job sites, usually schools under construction. I would take toys—little cars or trucks— and busy myself in the dirt piles outside or watch the cement mixers or the bricklayers. Then my dad would take me to lunch in a restaurant, or if it was an overnight trip, to dinner and a night in a hotel. It was always an adventure.

Once each year my dad and I would attend the golden glove boxing matches held in the Columbia College gym. Frank Deluhery would usually go with us. Frank was an electrician in his late twenties, a bachelor, who worked for my dad; he was also a great family friend and a wonderful story teller. We will hear more of Frank later. At the fights we would take turns predicting the winner of each bout—the white trunks or the black—and I believe there was always a small wager involved. It was great fun.

Prize fighting was a very popular sport in those days, and one Christmas at about age nine I received a pair of boxing gloves and a punching bag. My father thought it was time for me to learn the manly art of self defense. "Move in close," was his advice, "take a few short jabs, and try to get in the first punch." The very next day I ran down to the home of my best friend, George Weitzel, called him out, moved in close, took a few short jabs, and knocked him flat. Poor George was as perplexed as my father was vexed when I gave him the triumphant news that evening. It was then and there that I learned that self defense does not necessarily justify a preemptive strike.

Patricia and I got along reasonably well, except that she was a girl and three years older, and I liked to tag along with her and her girl friends, much to their dismay. But in addition to paper dolls, which I found boring, they also played jacks and hopscotch, which I did like. Then too, there were other kids in the neighborhood, and we all played tag and kick-the-can and roller skated and took sadistic pleasure in frying ants with our magnifying glasses. And many a summer afternoon was spent sitting on the curb watching and listening for the approaching sound of Mr. Koppel's horse-drawn ice cream wagon.

I enjoyed school and was almost always at or near the top of my class. The only noteworthy event during those first four years at Nativity parish school was winning second place in a school poetry contest, for which I was awarded a candy bar.

We had great times with our cousins. My mother and her siblings were a close family, and they all married and had children of similar ages. Here is the lineup:

Amelia married Ed Graff. They had Mary Janet.

Irene married Al Schiltz. Their children were Delores, Jimmy, and Betty Ann.

Henry married Mildred Conwell. They had Jim and Ann.

Alfred married Patricia Conwell (a cousin of Mildred), and their four children were Jack, Sheila, Patrick, and Joe.

All thirteen children, including we three, were born within about a dozen years, and all the families lived within ten or fifteen minutes of each other. Some of us were in the same schools. We played and fought and competed with each other almost like brothers and sisters.

There was many a family picnic at Eagle Point Park, with many games, tons of food, and at the end, the adults singing old German drinking songs.

The best time of all was on the Fourth of July. After the picnic at the park we would all retire to the home of Uncle Ed and Aunt Amelia Graff. There were no public displays of fireworks in Dubuque at that time, but Uncle Ed was a traveling salesman, and every year he would bring home from some big city or other great quantities of spectacular fireworks. Their back yard dropped off into a ravine, which was perfect for shooting off roman candles, sky rockets, and pinwheels, not to mention sparklers and cherry bombs. Such fun would never be permitted today.

Every Christmas Eve was spent at one of the family homes, and every Christmas dinner at another's, on a rotating basis. On Christmas Eve, Santa appeared in person. Each child, before receiving a small bag of candies and nuts from Santa, was required to perform in some manner of his or her own choosing—to sing a song, recite a poem, dance, play the piano, etc. It was an opportunity (or obligation) to display our newest talents. After Santa's departure, gifts were opened by all the children. It was rollicking chaos. Christmas Dinner the next day was a little more subdued, but it was another chance to break bread and celebrate together.

Whenever Christmas Eve was at our house the designated Santa (I learned years later) was always Fred Schroeder, a family friend and loyal Service Club member. Fred was a jolly fellow but one who found it necessary to fortify himself for the task at hand. One Christmas Eve, after some delay of the start of festivities, it was announced to us kids that although Santa had indeed delivered the gifts, he was in such a hurry this year that he had to rush away without greeting us. This was a terrible disappointment, but some us thought we caught a glimpse of Santa heading into the sky with his reindeer. In reality, poor Fred had been sequestered in the basement, drunk as a coot.

Easter was also a special time in our family. Holy Thursday Mass was always at 6 AM, and the pain of getting up at the crack of dawn made us feel very holy indeed. There were the Good Friday devotions from noon to 3 PM, followed on Saturday by 6 AM Mass again, but then the bells would ring out joyously and organ music would be heard for the first time since Holy Thursday. At noon on Saturday Lent was officially over, and we could gorge ourselves with the candy we had given up for Lent. On Sunday morning we would all find Easter baskets under our bed, filled with goodies. All except my father, who invariably would find nothing but an old hat filled with toilet paper, pieces of coal, an onion, a potato, and maybe a rutabaga. I'm sorry to report that the same fate later befell me as a father, except for the coal.

In the summer we would often drive (or ride the Burlington Zephyr) to Chicago for vacations with Uncle Jim (of Milwaukee Road fame), Aunt Sadie, and their son Bill Kennelly. They lived at 2537 Cullom Ave. on the north side. Aunt Sadie was a lively woman with a wonderful wit. She and my mother were great friends. Cousin Bill was five years older than I and treated me like his kid brother. When he was 14 and I was 9 he had a job delivering groceries and he would take me around on his errands. I would ride on the handlebars of his bicycle and it seemed as though we rode all over Chicago.

While in Chicago we would also spend a day with the Misses Railton, my father's first cousins. Dorothy, Mae, and Adeline Railton were spinster ladies who lived in the family home at 1744 Byron St., along with their seldom-seen brother Walter. [Some in the family say that Walter had a drinking problem and the sisters hid him in the attic.] The Railton ladies would always take Patricia and me (before Mary Lu was born) to the Lincoln Park Zoo, and upon our return would treat us to ginger ale and cookies.

There would also be a visit to the home of Aunts Daisy and Nell. Daisy Bridget Kennelly and Helen "Nell" Kennelly were my father's aunts. Daisy was married to Solomon Landauer, who was referred to in the family as "a very nice man even if he is Jewish."

It is necessary to digress here for a bit of family lore. In 1947 one Martin Kennelly was running for mayor of Chicago, to replace the deceased legend of Chicago politics, the infamous Edward "Boss" Kelly. Kennelly was running as the Democratic party's reform candidate who was going to clean up corruption in the city. Martin was thought to be distant relative of our clan, and the name alone made everyone proud supporters of cousin Martin.

Now it so happened that Uncle Solly, husband of Daisy, was a city employee under Boss Kelly—inspector of water works, if I'm not mistaken. Solly had only one leg, and so he was provided with a car and chauffeur to perform his public service. The fact that Uncle Solly also used the car and chauffeur on weekends and holidays was of no consequence in Boss Kelly's Chicago.

In due course and no doubt after a fair campaign, Martin Kennelly was indeed elected mayor of Chicago, a proud day for the Kennelly clan. However, as the reform mayor, one of his first official acts was to take away the car and chauffeur from poor old Uncle Solly. From that day forward his name was no longer spoken, except in vain, at family gatherings.

After two terms Martin Kennelly was replaced by Richard Daley, and Chicago politics returned to normal.

One summer day in 1936, when I was six, a great milestone occurred in our lives. We took our first ride in an airplane. My father announced that a 14-passenger plane was coming to Cedar Rapids the following Sunday and was selling rides to all comers. Dubuque had an airport too but its dirt runway could not accommodate such a monster craft. Mom was opposed, but decided that if the rest of us were going to die she might as well join us. Sunday finally arrived, and with great excitement we drove the 57 miles to Cedar Rapids. Though the waiting line was long it moved quickly because the ride was only twenty minutes. At last the great moment arrived, and we were aloft. Obviously we had never been so high before, probably a couple thousand feet, and we couldn't believe how small the cows and barns and cars were. Why, you could hardly even see the people below. My mother was predictably terrified; it was a classic stocking-shredder for her. As we flew over the Cedar River, she said she now knew how Charles Lindbergh felt when flying over the Atlantic.

Another great event occurred on My 29, 1937, when I was seven. My mother and father went off to the hospital and brought home a new baby girl. This came as a complete surprise to me. I made it known that I would have preferred a baby boy. They said the hospital was all out of boys, but as a consolation prize I could name the baby. I name her after Mary Lou Kessler, the prettiest girl in my first grade class. My mother changed only the spelling, to Mary Lu.

My baby sister became the most important person in my life. She was a beautiful child, as a formal portrait of her at age one attests. We became very close, and have remained so throughout our lives. In her formative years, especially when our father was away in the hospital for long periods and our mother was working, Patricia and I did our best to help care for her and look out for her, and this brought us all close together. I tried to be a role model for Mary Lu during those years, not always successfully, given that I was a high school student, but she grew up to be a fine young woman. We have always had a special relationship, and even in our senior years we have done a number of volunteer projects together.

There were a great many changes taking place in the world in the mid-1930's. I was interested in current events because my parents were. Since television had not yet been invented, we got our news from the newspapers and from the built-in radio in the living room, supplemented by the Movietone Newsreels which were shown in every movie theater, following the feature film.

My parents read and listened with apprehension and concern the news of the rise of Adolph Hitler in Germany. My first recollection is of the *Anschluss* in 1938, when Hitler took over Austria. We watched his rantings and ravings on film in the newsreels, and occasionally heard him live on a neighbor's shortwave radio, and thought he sounded like a madman. But not everybody felt this way. Dubuque was a heavily German town, and many people, including some friends and neighbors, were in sympathy with Hitler's arguments and with his virulent anti-Semitism. The Reverend Charles E. Coughlin, "the radio priest," preached every Sunday afternoon from Royal Oak, Michigan, on what he called a Christian solution of our nation's economic difficulties. He was also a blatant Jew-baiter, blaming most of our troubles on the "Jewish bankers." He had a radio audience of ten million people, including many Catholics in Dubuque, and his weekly journal, *Social Justice*, sold briskly at the church door following all the Masses.

On September 1, 1939, the world was plunged into war with Hitler's invasion of Poland, and from then on I followed the war closely, keeping track of the battle lines from the maps in the newspapers.

At about this time things started going downhill for my father's business. The projects started by President Franklin D. Roosevelt to stimulate the economy had pretty much been completed, and no new business was coming in. The depression was far from over and business was terrible for everyone. There were a few house-wirings, which my father bound boring and unchallenging. There were rumors of "defense plants" going up around the country, and my parents began to look upon this as an opportunity to get out of the business and out of Dubuque. Dad's chief assistant, Frank Deluhery, had already secured work constructing an aluminum plant in Clinton, Iowa.

In August 1940 my parents heard of a gunpowder plant being built near Memphis, Tennessee, by the giant E.I. duPont deNemours company, and the two of them decided to drive to Memphis to take a look. They had never been south of Illinois in their lives.

To put this in historical context: By June 1940, France had fallen to Hitler's armies, and all indications were that England would be next. Italy had also entered the war on the German side. Winston Churchill was beseeching Roosevelt for help. England desperately needed ships, planes, and munitions. Roosevelt recognized that the U.S. could not remain aloof, but was faced with strong public sentiment against any intervention in another European conflict. A leading isolationist spokesman was Charles A. Lindbergh, the celebrated and highly admired pilot. Finally, on June 10, 1940, Roosevelt proclaimed that "we will extend to the opponents of force the material resources of this nation," and it would be done "with full speed ahead." Included in the plan was the expansion of our capacity to produce gunpowder. Although it was described as "powder for England," Roosevelt was also building up our defense capability.

In Memphis, my father was hired on the spot, on August 15, 1940. This being the feast of the Assumption, my mother took it as a good sign. However, it did leave her in the position of having to drive the 700 miles back to Dubuque alone, then sell the business and the house, have the furniture packed and shipped by barge down the Mississippi to Memphis, care for three children aged 13, 10, and 3, generally uproot herself from her family and friends and the life she had lived for her entire 40 years, and then drive the three of us back down to Memphis to begin a new life. It was a severe challenge to her belief that God never gives us more burdens than we can handle.

She accomplished it all in less than three months. By early November we were on our way, just at about the time that Franklin Roosevelt was defeating Wendell Wilkie for an unprecedented third term in the White House. (A campaign slogan: "We rose with Roosevelt; why wilt with Wilkie?")

Our lives were about to change dramatically.

3.

THE WAR YEARS: TENNESSEE, CALIFORNIA, KENTUCKY, ALABAMA, MINNESOTA

Tennessee

It was the first time any of us had ventured into the Deep South, nor did we know anyone else who had ever been there. My mother said we would see cotton growing in the fields, and we did. We stopped to pick up a few bolls, and were amazed—so that's where cotton comes from! It was November, near the end of the harvest season, and we saw black people, men, women, and children, each dragging a long burlap sack into which they stuffed the cotton bolls. We also saw where they lived, in decrepit wooden shacks right there in the fields, without electricity, running water, or window screens. We also learned a new term: "sharecropper."

Memphis was a pleasant enough city, and after staying for awhile in our very first motel (a newly coined term)—the Alamo Plaza—we rented an apartment in a fourplex at 1099 North Parkway (later demolished to make room for a highway) in a nice middle class neighborhood. But when we went downtown we discovered something else: water fountains labeled "white" and "colored;" movie theaters in which the main floor was for "whites only," with a separate entrance to the balcony, for "colored only." We noted that on the buses all the black people had to go to the rear, and if all the seats in the rear were occupied, they had to stand, even with empty seats in the front. The train station and the bus station had separate waiting rooms for "white" and "colored." We were encountering for the first time a new way of life: segregation.

I cannot honestly say that we were appalled or outraged. We had no basis for comparison; I cannot recall ever seeing a black person in Dubuque. Segregation just seemed to be the norm where there were people of two races. Obviously the black people were the underprivileged class, and they were generally considered inferior to whites. It may be hard to realize now that we accepted this so easily, but in 1940 our social consciences had not yet been raised, and concepts like "civil rights" and "equal opportunity" had not yet entered the public lexicon. Oh, we had read about the good works of men like Booker T. Washington and George Washington Carver, but they were considered commendable because they were endeavoring to improve the lot of their people; they were not asserting any fundamental civil rights or any claim of equality for members of their race.

My mother enrolled Patricia and me in a Catholic school, of which there were very few in Memphis, but it was within walking distance of home. I had not started the fifth grade in Dubuque in September because of a polio scare, but I had no trouble catching up.

I did experience for the first time a phenomenon which would repeat itself in several new schools for the next two years (five of them): the Encounter With the Class Bully. It is (or was in those days) a rite of boyhood that the kid who considers himself the toughest in the class must assert his dominance over any new kid who enter his domain. This is accomplished rather simply. On the second or third day he approaches the newcomer in the school yard, at recess or just after the closing bell. He makes sure the other boys are watching. He accuses the new kid of violating some sacred playground rule, then snarls an epithet, and knocks him to the ground. The newcomer has of course forgotten his father's instructions about moving in close, taking a few short jabs and landing the first punch, so he slinks off, holding back the tears as best he can. It is not smart to challenge the Bully, who has attained his title honestly; he is bigger and tougher than everybody else. The next day all is forgotten and the new kid is accepted by all as a fellow classmate.

That year we experienced our first Christmas away from Dubuque, but my father's two brothers, bachelor Uncle John and Uncle Jim, along with Aunt Sadie and cousin Bill, came down to Memphis to celebrate with us. And in January 1941 our good friend Frank Deluhery brought his bride, Lucille, to visit us on their honeymoon.

Our family took time to visit the surrounding countryside, including a visit to Shiloh/Pittsburg Landing, site of one of the first great battles of the Civil War. It was my first introduction to Civil War history.

In Memphis I also resumed my piano lessons, with a gentle retired piano teacher, Mrs. Larned, who lived in the apartment directly below. I was her only pupil. From below she could hear me practicing, and if she detected any deviation in dynamics or tempo, there would come a rapping on our floor with a broom handle.

Mrs. Larned was determined to make me into a concert pianist, but alas, the time was too short. By February construction of the defense plant was nearing completion, and it was time to move on.

California

My father heard that there was work in the shipyards at Mare Island near Vallejo, California, just across the bay from San Francisco. In early 1941 as war was raging in Europe, our merchant ships were being sunk by Nazi submarines, and new ships were being built at Mare Island as fast as possible. For my parents, this was the long-awaited opportunity to head for California. As for me, I had enjoyed studying geography in the 5th grade, and was eager to see more of this country. So the furniture was placed in storage, and on February 12, 1941, the day after my eleventh birthday, we headed west in our 1940 Chevrolet.

Well, not exactly. First we headed southeast. "As long as we're going to California," said my parents, "we might as well take a look at Florida." Traveling down through Alabama to Pensacola, we got our first glimpse of the Gulf of Mexico. We then drove along the Gulf coast to New Orleans where we stayed for a couple of days, thence into Texas and our first thrilling sight of operating oil wells, en route to Houston. My dad took a job at an oil refinery in Galveston for a few days, to pick up some extra cash but mostly, I think, to have the opportunity to stay at a place right on the beach. He loved watching the surf roll in, a new experience for all of us.

Then it was the long, long drive across Texas to El Paso, where we spent a day in Ciudad Juarez for our first look at Mexico, tourist style.

This first journey across the western United States was one adventure after another. I kept a journal, which I still have, and it is filled with the wonders observed for the first time by a young boy: oil wells; longhorn cattle and cowboys; buying a Mexican sombrero; awakening in the morning in Arizona for a first-ever view of the mountains; the barren desert with sagebrush and tumbleweeds just like in the movies; crossing the Colorado River at Yuma and entering California at last; orange and grapefruit orchards; the old Spanish mission at San Diego; the "homes of the Stars" in Hollywood; the Golden Gate bridge. Looking back, now having traveled over most of the world, it's still fun to think of the joy and excitement of that first cross-country trip with my parents and sisters.

Needless to say, we loved San Francisco. We visited the Ira and Mildred Neil family, cousins of my mother, and they showed us around the city.

As anticipated, my father was hired as an electrician in the shipyards at Mare Island. But housing in the area had not yet caught up with the tremendous influx of new workers. The only place we could find was a small "tourist court" just outside a little town about 15 miles away, called Napa. I believe it is still there, at the intersection of Highways 121 and 116, now all gussied up and with a fancy name like "The Vineyard Inn." In those days Napa was mostly surrounded by pastureland, with very few vineyards. Little could I know that 53 years later my wife and I would be retiring to this same Napa, and that my sister Mary Lu and her husband would have preceded us there by several years.

However, in 1941 our tenure in Napa was to be short. Out motel expenses were about equal to my father's daily pay (about $12) and there simply was no family housing available anywhere in the area. In addition, my father was not very happy in the shipyards. The work was grueling, noisy, and dangerous, and he was overqualified for the work assigned. Reluctantly, therefore, they decided to leave California and head back east.

Kentucky

DuPont was building another defense plant near Louisville. Frank and Lucille Deluhery were already there, and the company was eager to rehire its experienced electricians.

This time from California we took the northern route east, through Reno, Salt Lake City, Denver, and St. Louis, new territory for all of us. Again my journal is excitement-packed, including an account of the car sliding off the road in a March blizzard in the Rocky Mountains, requiring a snow plow to pull us out, which I got to ride.

It was late March when we arrived in Louisville, and my father was immediately hired as a foreman at the gunpowder plant construction site. I had thoroughly enjoyed being out of school for six weeks, but as soon as we got settled I was enrolled in a Catholic school, to finish out the 5th grade. For Patricia, it was her third high school in her freshman year.

We enjoyed Louisville, and the state of Kentucky has a great deal to offer. The blue grass country around Lexington, with its green rolling hills, grazing thoroughbreds, and white board fences, was stunning. (On a return to Kentucky in 1985, for the finals of the NCAA basketball tournament, I was dismayed to see the fences now painted dark brown.)

Relatives from Dubuque came to visit us in the summer of 1941. We kids were delighted to see and play with our cousins again. We visited many of Kentucky's famous sites: Mammoth Cave National Park; a fort built by Daniel Boone in Bardstown; the plantation where Stephen Foster wrote "My Old Kentucky Home;" and the boyhood home of Abe Lincoln near Hodgenville, among others.

Louisville also had a Triple A baseball team, just a notch below the big leagues, and my mother and I would often attend the Tuesday Ladies Night games. We saw a lot of players on their way to—or just back from—the Boston Red Sox.

One weekend we drove up to Cincinnati, about a hundred miles north, and my dad took me to a Reds—Pirates game at Crosley Field. Built in 1912, Crosley Field was torn down in 1970 to make way for Waterfront Stadium, which in turn was demolished and replaced by another new ball park in 2002. A sure sign of aging is remembering a ball park that has since been replaced twice.

We also looked up some distant cousins on my mother's side in Louisville, Louis and Susan Rogge and their son, Louis Philip. "Phil" was born just one day after me, but he was twice my size. Later, in 1947, Phil and I enrolled as freshmen at the College of St. Thomas in St. Paul. Phil's uncle, Lloyd Rogge, was the chief financial officer at the college. After our freshman year Phil entered the Carmelite seminary. We have kept in close touch with him through all these years. In 1955 I was privileged to serve Mass for "Father Louis" in my new Marine Corps lieutenant's uniform for the nuns at the Carmelite convent in Niagara Falls, Ontario.

In 1998 Susan and I had the good fortune to join Father Louis and others on a pilgrimage to the Holy Land at Easter time. Together on Good Friday we trod the Via Dolorosa in old Jerusalem, following the footsteps of Jesus; and on Easter Sunday we visited the church of the Holy Sepulchre. At all the holy sites Father Louis' profound knowledge and insightful commentaries brought the New Testament to life, making this one of the great experiences of our lives. Father Louis, as of this writing, is still very active, dividing his time between Rome and a Carmelite house in Joliet, Illinois. And he is still twice my size.

Back to Louisville in 1941. I enjoyed finishing the fifth grade, once I got past the bully-on-the-first-day episode, but the best part of my school was its location, just a couple of blocks from Churchill Downs. The racing season was in April and May. Kids were admitted free if accompanied by an adult, so after school we boys would frequently head over to the track to catch the last two or three races. We could almost always find adults to take us through the entrance. We were well behaved, so nobody bothered us, and our parents knew where we were. We would pick our horses and pretend to bet, then tote up our wins and losses. It was great fun, and we got to know the place pretty well. The names of all the Derby winners for the past 74 years were posted on the walls, and we practically had them memorized.

The 75th running of the Kentucky Derby took place on the first Saturday of May, 1941. I had heard of a way to sneak in, and so was up bright and early that morning and took the streetcar to Churchill Downs. Sure enough, beyond the backstretch and behind the stables, along the perimeter fence, there was a guy with a ladder who, for a nickel, helped his customers over the fence. Churchill Downs attracts over 100,000 fans on Derby Day; I spent the day in and around the stables, watching the horses and trainers come and go with each race. It seems amazing in today's high-security world that this could have been possible, but in 1941 nobody noticed an 11-year-old kid who didn't draw attention to himself. I sat in a stable window facing the backstretch to watch the big race. There was a deafening roar as the horses galloped past. From fifty feet away the sound of thundering hooves cannot adequately be described; it must be experienced. For a good replication, see the film "Seabiscuit."

My favorites were Our Boots and Porter's Cap, but Whirlaway came from behind in the home stretch to win the Derby, setting a track record. Whirlaway, it turned out, was a great horse and he won the Triple Crown that year, 1941. You can look it up.

It was at this time that I set as my career goal to be a jockey. For one thing, I was small for my age. Further, I had ridden several ponies, and a farm horse once, and had liked it. Granted I had never been on a racehorse, but they seemed to be very well trained so probably all that was necessary was to hold on and steer. Besides, about half the boys in my class also planned to be jockeys.

But alas, another aspiring career was cut short. By November 1941 the defense plant was completed, and it was time to move on again.

Alabama

This time it was Birmingham. My father again was hired as foreman on the construction of a DuPont powder plant. The Deluherys and several other of my dad's co-workers made the move at the same time, so it wasn't as though we were all alone once again. Besides, it was fun exploring a new city and its environs as a family.

In later years I have had many conversations with other parents about the relative merits of children growing up in the same house, in the same bedroom, on the same tree-lined street, versus moving from place to place, as military kids do, as children of professional athletes and coaches do, and as we did. I can see the advantages of life in one place, but in no way do I feel that I was cheated or disadvantaged in my growing-up years. In fact, our adventures together kept us close as a family, perhaps more than most. We learned to rely and depend upon one another, and that prepared us, I believe, for the difficult times a few years hence when my father was hospitalized for long periods of time.

Birmingham was indeed the deep, deep South. Not only was there the embedded racial segregation and inequality with which we had become familiar; we detected a general hostility toward northerners in general, and Catholics in particular. Priests did not go out in public wearing their Roman collars. Only 1% of the population of Alabama was Catholic, which at that time was less than China. On one occasion my mother was checking out an apartment for rent, and inquired whether there was a Catholic school in the area. "Oh, you are Catholics?" said the landlady. "I met some Catholics once, and they were very nice people." But suddenly the apartment was no longer available.

We found a furnished apartment, a fourplex, at 1618 16th Ave. So., on a hill just below the famous state of Vulcan (Birmingham being a steel mill city). My mother then went to visit the bishop at the cathedral, which seemed to be the only Catholic church in Birmingham, in order to enroll Patricia in the diocesan high school and me in the sixth grade. The bishop said there would be no problem with Patricia, but the elementary school was completely filled and there would be no room for me. Mom pleaded with him, saying that she had never put her children in anything but Catholic schools, and his diffident reply was, "Well, there's a first time for everything."

Undaunted, my mother began to search about and discovered, to her amazement, another Catholic parish and school, which the bishop had not bothered to mention. It was a very poor parish in a depressed part of town, but it was within walking distance of our apartment, a few blocks beyond the bottom of our hill. Located between our home and the Catholic school was a school for black children, a dilapidated frame building perched on cinder blocks with dirt for a schoolyard. Through some unspoken agreement the two schools had different opening and closing times so that the two groups of students would not encounter each other.

The parish school was staffed by four Sisters of Mercy, and there were four classrooms, each with two grades. The principal, Sister Laurentia, was a spirited woman who presided over the 7th/8th grade. The parish was located in an ethnic neighborhood of mostly Italians and Syrians, and most of the students were children of immigrants.

Although I had started the 6th grade in Louisville, Sister Laurentia persuaded my parents that I would be much better off in her classroom, and so I advanced to the 7th grade. It was an interesting class, to say the least. My classmates included a boy, 17, a girl, 19, and another "boy'" age 21. I was not yet 12. At recess these kids did not play kickball or hopscotch; they pitched pennies, engaged in a few boy-girl activities, and from them I learned to shoot craps. But they were friendly kids and for once nobody offered to beat me up. To add to the mix, Sister had also recruited a few other newcomers from construction families like ourselves, including twin boys from Tulsa and a brash but funny kid from the Bronx. I must say I enjoyed the school.

Since it was impossible for the nuns to survive on the dollar or so per month they charged (and sporadically collected) for tuition, they held an annual parish spaghetti dinner and raffle. They accepted my mother's offer to take them around after school in her car to collect the necessary foodstuffs and raffle items. Most of the parents were small shopkeepers, with little cash but willing to make in-kind donations.

According to my mother, the routine was as follows: Sister Laurentia would engage in suppliant conversation Tony in his delicatessen or Hamid in his grocery store, negotiating for a few pounds of hamburger, a couple jars of tomato sauce, or a package or two of pasta. Meanwhile Sister Immaculata would busy herself about the store, surreptitiously removing from the shelves anything that would fit into the deep pockets of her habit—a bottle of wine, a carton of cigarettes, a box of candy. Returning to the car, they would count up their loot, then on to the next victim. Eventually they collected enough for both feast and raffle. Times were tough, and these good nuns had to be resourceful, in addition to being holy women and selfless teachers. One wonders whether Tony and Hamid were on to the caper all along, and had a good chuckle to themselves.

One weekend as we were visiting Montgomery, Alabama's capital city, someone heard on the radio that the Japanese had bombed Pearl Harbor. Pearl Harbor—where's that? In Hawaii. A big naval base has been bombed. Lots of ships sunk and people killed. It looks like war. It was Sunday, December 7, 1941.

The next morning, back in Birmingham, we listened to President Roosevelt's "Day of Infamy" speech, and Congress declared war on Japan. Within two days we were also at war with Germany and Italy.

Construction of the powder plant was accelerated, and my father and the others went on a 10-hour, 7-day schedule. It was extremely grueling.

In the city of Birmingham, with its steel mills, there was great anxiety and uncertainty. Would we be bombed? The Aleutian Islands off Alaska had been invaded, and a lone Japanese plane dropped a bomb somewhere on the coast of Oregon. Air raid wardens were appointed for each block, buckets of sand were distributed, and practice blackouts were held. This was occurring in many other cities, I'm sure.

The news grew steadily worse. Wake Island and Guam fell, the Japanese invaded the Phillippines, the final battle at Corregidor was lost, and this was followed by the infamous Bataan Death March by our captured troops. At the same time, fierce naval battles were being fought and we were losing more ships and men. The Japanese seemed unstoppable in their march through the South Pacific, and Australia was in danger.

In the midst of the gloom, there was some happy news. My mother told me that Lucille Deluhery as going to have a baby, and she and Frank wanted me to be the godfather. Though not yet twelve and not yet quite sure where babies came from, I was naturally thrilled.

Patrick John Deluhery was born January 31, 1942. As I held him in my arms at the christening, I could not have imagined that he would some day be a college professor of economics and a state senator from Iowa. Nor that on August 9, 2003, Susan and I would attend the wedding of Patrick's daughter Allison, who is also my goddaughter.

In the late spring of 1942, the plant was completed, and it was time to move on again. This presented a problem. DuPont had plans for an additional plant near the Twin Cities in Minnesota, but construction would not begin until the summer. So my dad and Frank Deluhery and some others found work on the expansion of a steel mill in Gadsden, Alabama, about 60 miles away. To move again, and subject Patricia to her fifth high school in two years, was out of the question. So it was decided that my dad would take a room in Gadsden and come home on whatever weekend days he might be lucky enough not to be working. As soon as school was out, I happily accepted his invitation to spend a few days with him.

Gadsden was a quintessential mill town. Nearly everybody worked at the steel mill, lived in company houses (little better than shacks), and—just as in the folk songs—every worker "owed my soul to the company store." Even at my age I could see that this was a pretty grim life, and created a dog-eat-dog atmosphere, the effect of which was to exacerbate the hostility between poor whites and poor blacks. Gadsden would become the scene of several incidents during the civil rights struggles in the 1960's.

Minnesota

By late June 1942 it was time to begin our trek northward. After stopping in Dubuque for a welcome reunion with all the cousins, we arrived in the Twin Cities in early July. Meanwhile the war raged on. Hitler had invaded Russia in the spring of 1942, and Germany and the Soviet Union were locked in a deadly struggle at Stalingrad. U.S. tanks were battling German armor in the North African desert. In the South Pacific the Japanese had been stopped short of Australia. America was building up its arsenal and preparing at last to go on the offensive.

DuPont's new powder plant was located in Rosemount, about twenty miles south of St. Paul. Once again there was a housing shortage, as in any locale where a huge new war plant was being built. While awaiting new housing construction in South St. Paul, we were able to get accommodations in an apartment hotel in Minneapolis.

Then a wonderful thing happened. Uncle Henry and Aunt Mildred Bitter in Dubuque invited me to join them for a vacation at Whitefish Lake in northern Minnesota. I was overjoyed. My cousin Jim was 14 and his sister Ann was my age, 12. We were very good friends as well as cousins.

Northern Minnesota—the North Woods—is spectacularly beautiful in the summer, with its pine forests interspersed with sparkling blue lakes, seemingly around every bend in the road. Scientists may claim that this is the result of receding glaciers, but the locals know better. They know that it is the work of the giant Paul Bunyan and his faithful companion, Babe the Blue Ox, stomping around the area. You can see their monumental statues in Bemidji. Anybody who uses a pine tree for a toothpick is bound to create a new lake with every footstep.

Whitefish Lake is just the right size—about five miles across and ten miles long—large enough to be interesting and small enough not to have whitecaps. It is irregularly shaped, like a leaping fish with its back arched, which makes it interesting for exploration. It was populated by just a few resorts and private homes.

For six idyllic weeks we lived in a cabin at Arnold's Black Pine Beach Resort on the shores of the lake. Aunt Mildred was a great cook, the fishing and swimming were wonderful, and in the evenings we played cards while out on the lake the loons could be heard calling softly to each other.

Early most mornings, Uncle Henry, Jim, and I would go out trolling for walleyes and great northerns. The walleyes made succulent meals and the northerns, though bony, were fierce fighters. Rare was the day we came back empty handed.

Uncle Henry was an unusual person. In France in 1918, two days after the Armistice, Corporal Henry Bitter's unit was engaged in a training exercise. One of the soldiers "froze" after pulling the pin on a hand grenade. Corporal Bitter, then 22, tried to pry it from his hands, but it exploded. Corporal Bitter was blinded and lost both hands.

It was a very difficult recovery period for the whole family, but eventually Henry met and married Mildred, had two children, and developed amazing skills, considering his handicaps. Although he had to be fed, he dressed himself (except for the buttons), tended his own garden, played a mean harmonica, and educated himself in innumerable subjects through "talking books." He was an optimistic man.

He was also an expert fisherman. In the boat, Jim and I operated the motor and baited his hook, but he could handle the rod *and* reel as well as anybody. And he had an uncanny sense of where the fish were.

During the long days out on the water, Uncle Henry would tell us about the books he had read. We heard stories from Rudyard Kipling in India, Jack London in Alaska, and Richard Halliburton in Africa. Among our very favorites was the story of Captain Ahab and his search for Moby Dick, the Great White Whale.

Sometimes when things got a little dull, Jim or I would tug violently on Uncle Henry's line. "I got one!" he'd shout, and then would pretend to be miffed when he discovered he'd been tricked. Perhaps it was cruel, but he had a great sense of humor, and we all had a wonderful time. He also chain-smoked, and Jim, after lighting his father's cigarette, would sometimes also light up, and taught me to do the same. His parents of course never knew.

Leisurely afternoons were spent on the beach, and Jim and Ann taught me to swim. Sometimes Ann and I would row over to the lily pads and catch sunfish and bluegills; other times we would all go over to a sandbar on the far side of the lake and with a seine catch live minnows for the next few days' fishing.

Good news came over the radio one evening. The U.S. Marines had invaded Guadalcanal, a strategically located Japanese-held island in the South Pacific. At last we were on the offensive!

On one of our last days at Whitefish, an overcast day with intermittent rain, we had been fishing all morning without any success and were feeling cold, wet, and discouraged. Suddenly I felt a terrific yank on my line. After a battle that lasted probably ten minutes but seemed an eternity, Jim helped me bring an a 9 pound great northern. To this day I can feel the excitement and elation, and it shows in the picture which I still have. It was a large fish in those parts, and we were instant celebrities at Arnold's Black Pine Beach. We even got a mention in the local paper.

But Uncle Henry summed it up best of all. "You did it," he said. "You got Moby Dick."

All too soon, it was the end of August and time to return to the Twin Cities.

Just before school started, we moved into a new rental house in South St. Paul at 650 7th Ave. So., and the furniture was shipped back up the Mississippi from Memphis. I entered the 8th grade at St. Augustine parish school; Mary Lu was enrolled in the kindergarten; and Patricia entered St. Joseph's Academy in St. Paul for her junior year.

South St. Paul, with a population of about 15,000, was a twenty minute streetcar ride from St. Paul, but it was not a bedroom community. It was a stockyards and meatpacking center—the largest between Omaha and Chicago—and therefore had its own distinctive character and—er, flavor. The stockyards were right off the main street (Concord St.), extending for many blocks, and directly behind them were the packing plants of Swift & Co., Armour, and Cudahy.

Most of South St. Paul's residents were employees of either the stockyards or the packing plants, and the ethnic makeup of the town was primarily eastern European. The social centers of South St. Paul were—and perhaps still are—the Polish Hall, the Serbian Hall, and the Croatian Hall. Parties, dances, and weddings always were held at one of the three, and the three nationalities did not mix particularly well. Incidentally, in the memorial museum at Ellis island today one can find a picture of the Croatian Hall in South St. Paul.

I quickly made friends with my classmates at St. Augustine's and did reasonably well academically, except for "shop," a weekly class in woodworking for boys. (The girls did dressmaking.) Although playing the piano required a certain amount of manual dexterity, I discovered that I had no skills whatsoever with hand tools. Our first project was a broomholder. This provided experience in sanding, planing, and use of the circular saw. One then moved on to bigger projects. At semester's end some boys proudly carried home piano benches, bookcases, even desks. I sheepishly slunk away with my finally-approved broomholder—for which my mother professed great admiration. I have had no reason thereafter to doubt my incompetence in the manual arts.

I graduated from the 8th grade in June 1943 and spent that summer earning money for the first time, caddying at the Southview Country Club.

4.

SOUTH ST. PAUL HIGH SCHOOL, 1943-1947

By September 1943 the plant at Rosemount was completed. The next project, gigantic in size, was in eastern Washington, in a vast desert along the Columbia River, and it was known as the Hanford Project. It was in an unpopulated area, about 80 miles from Yakima, the nearest city. Once again there was no family housing yet available, and so although my dad began work there, the rest of us were not scheduled to move west until spring.

The project was top secret. None of the workers flocking there could have imagined that they were building the site for the world's first production of plutonium, the explosive element in the atomic bomb. Until 1943, only a tiny bit of plutonium had ever been made by man, and the element does not exist in nature.

There were signs that Germany was moving fast in the field of atomic research, and the nation that won the race would probably win the war. My father was an electrical superintendent, supervising 200 men, and all he knew was that it was to involve the generation of a tremendous amount of electrical power. Only the superintendents were allowed to see the blueprints, and then only a small portion at a time.

In all, nine nuclear reactors would be built at Hanford, churning out plutonium for the bomb dropped on Nagasaki and for most of the nation's nuclear stockpile for the next forty years.

The history of the construction of the Hanford Project has been written, and the numbers are staggering. New construction included more than 130 barracks, and 900 hutments. The men were fed in eight huge mess halls which served from 50 to 60 tons of food per meal. A bus system to transport workers from their barracks to widely scattered jobs inside the area required 900 buses with a seating capacity of 30,000. There were few if any social amenities; not that there would have been time anyway, as everybody worked twelve hours a day, seven days a week.

My mother went out to visit my dad for a few days around Thanksgiving. She came back appalled at the living and working conditions, and worried about his health. The unobstructed desert wind, in addition to the dust and sand kicked up by the construction work, was a constant threat to the health of the work force.

Dad could not get home for Christmas 1943, and in fact there was no opportunity even to purchase Christmas gifts or cards. I remember his sending a "get well" card for Christmas, with apologies, because it was the only thing available.

He did come home in February 1944, broken in health and suffering from tuberculosis. For the second time and second war in 25 years, he had given his all for his country. At age 50 he was admitted to the Veterans' Hospital in Minneapolis.

In those days there were no wonder drugs for the treatment of tuberculosis, which is highly contagious. In 1943 the only "cure" for TB was isolation and prolonged bed rest. If the patients did not die sooner, and many did, they would eventually recover, but always with damaged lungs. My father would spend the next two years in that hospital.

It was a turning point in our lives. My parents had little savings, having spent most of their reserves on the frequent moves from city to city. DuPont provided no benefits for its subcontractors. My father received a small Social Security disability pension, far from enough to support the family. So at age 43 my mother took a job as a secretary with the Internal Revenue Service in St. Paul. She worked five and a half days per week. She sold the car to get cash; gas rationing did not justify the cost of upkeep.

She accepted this new challenge with her usual determination, commitment, and faith. On Sundays she rode the streetcar for more than an hour each way (two transfers) to Minneapolis to visit my father. She went alone because the hospital would not admit anyone under 18. Occasionally we would accompany her, and my father would wave to us from the second floor window.

At home Patricia and I were mature enough to recognize the gravity of the situation, and we worked reasonably well together, helping with the cooking and the household chores and taking care of Mary Lu, who was then six and starting school.

At about this time our rental house was sold, and we moved to an upper duplex at 128 6th Ave. North. Luckily, this was directly across the street from the South St. Paul Public High School, which I had entered the previous September.

The high school had about 800 students. Although most came from stockyards and meatpacking families, they were the sons and daughters not only of cattle drivers but of cattle traders and commission agents, of managers as well as assembly line workers, and with a sprinkling of children of shopkeepers, doctors, and lawyers.

The school was not exactly loaded with cultural opportunities, but every once in awhile there would be an "assembly" in the school auditorium, for the presentation of visiting musical groups or entertainers. One such group was billed as the "von Trappe family of musicians, refugees from Austria," earning a meager living traveling from school to school across the country. They were a father and mother and several children, who dressed in odd clothes and sang and played several instruments. They sounded pretty amateurish—"corny" was our expression at the time—and were not well received. This of course was long before they became famous as the subjects of the hit Broadway musical and film, The Sound of Music.

South St. Paul High School was known in the Twin Cities area for a) its football teams and b) its forensics teams. The "Packers" were good on the gridiron because the players got summer jobs at the packing plants, with ample time to practice slamming into sides of beef.

The forensics program owed its success solely to the charismatic leadership of its director, Raymond J. Happe. "R.J.," as he was affectionately known to his students, founded the speech and debate program in 1937, in his early thirties, and when he retired in 1971, 34 years later, his teams had won eight state debate championships and numerous speech championships—more than any other school in Minnesota. Nearly all high schools with forensics programs belong to the National Forensic League, and during several years So. St. Paul was the leading NFL school in the nation.

Each of us, if we are lucky, meets maybe half a dozen truly "unforgettable characters" in our lives; persons, in addition to our parents, who have inspired and guided us or taught us our lifetime skills. R.J. Happe was the first such person in my life. He showed me, and hundreds of others, how to gain self confidence through public speaking, how to think logically, argue persuasively, articulate smoothly—and have fun at the same time. R.J. was upbeat and amiable but intensely competitive, and he instilled those qualities in his students. He also truly loved his students, and his affection was reciprocated. He was witty, compassionate, and genuinely proud of all the kids in speech and debate, who comprised about one of every five students in the school.

During my freshman year I did not participate in extracurricular activities, but at the beginning of my sophomore year I decided to try out for the debate team. Speaking in front of a class was frightening at first, but I soon learned to enjoy my newly discovered self confidence, and I also found that I was pretty good at it, in spite of my small stature and somewhat squeaky voice, at age 14. I learned that a tremendous amount of research is required to become thoroughly familiar with all aspects of both sides of the year's debate topic, such as universal military training, creation of a federal world government, or socialized medicine. This training in meticulous preparation stood me well in my later career as a trial lawyer.

Debating was my coming-of-age vehicle. I loved it, worked hard at it, and it enabled me to interact with fellow students, male and female. By representing our school at tournaments all around the Midwest, each of us was able not only to establish our own identity but to experience the thrill of working together, just like the football and basketball guys.

Public speaking brought me just the confidence I needed as a small person, younger than most of my peers, in a new community. It was at this time that I decided I wanted become a trial lawyer, and if possible, a district attorney. I never wavered from that desire.

Studying debate topics as well as doing research for orations brought me into closer contact with the great social issues of the day. Coming from a Democratic household, I was comfortable as a liberal, and have been all my life.

My knowledge of current events was also enhanced by competition in extemporaneous speaking, which involved giving a three minute speech on a current topic drawn at random one hour in advance.

Great opportunities for research opened up when, at 16, I got a job as a page at the James J. Hill Reference Library in St. Paul, one of the Midwest's preeminent libraries. I worked one afternoon per week after school and Saturdays, and also a couple of summers, retrieving and shelving books for patrons, at 35 cents per hour. When not busy I had dozens of magazines and thousands of books at my disposal.

In my senior year, my debate partner was Hartland Schmidt, a 6'3" genius, who later became a brilliant physicist in Los Angeles. We advanced to the Minnesota state championships, where we lost in the finals by one point to Duluth Denfeld High School, the other big power in the state. Eventually a member of that team became my debate partner in college.

The National Forensic League awarded points for participation in each competitive event, with bonus points for high rankings. The names of point leaders were published each month in the NFL national magazine, and when I graduated I was among the top ten in the country. This gave me great satisfaction, having done it in three years.

Like most teenagers today, my other great interest was music. It was the Big Band era of the 1940's. All the big bands came to the Prom Ballroom in St. Paul for one night stands. My best friends were Dick Vasatka, Dick Taylor and his brother Chet, a year older, and Larry Patterson. Whenever one of the famous bands came to town—Tommy Dorsey, Jimmy Dorsey, Duke Ellington, Harry James, Benny Goodman, Woody Herman, and especially Stan Kenton—we were there. Not to dance, but to stand in awe and admiration with the crowd directly in front of the bandstand, for the whole evening. We knew the names of nearly every sideman in every band and we could recognize their solos when we heard them on juke boxes or the radio. (LP's, tapes, and CD's had not yet been invented.)

South St. Paul's own little "big band" was called the Downbeats. The band consisted of guys in their late teens to married men in their thirties. They played standard big band arrangements, but they were pretty good musicians, and they played for dances and social events around the suburban Twin Cities area. They invited me to sit in once in awhile, and when Ralph Swanson, their piano player, went off to the navy I was asked to join them, at age 17. I did not have Ralph's skills, but since we played standard big band arrangements, the pianist was not required to do much more than play chords, with a rare brief solo.

We had great fun, played on weekends for some fancy proms and at some seedy road houses all around our part of Minnesota, and averaged around $15 each per gig, which wasn't bad in those days.

When Ralph Swanson returned from the navy I joined my friend Dick Vasatka's band, which he formed at about that time, and which lasted for the rest of our college years.

On April 12, 1945, en route home from a successful speech and debate tournament at Mankato, MN, riding in Mr. Happe's car, we heard on the radio the shocking news of the sudden death of President Franklin Delano Roosevelt. After twelve grueling years in office, through the Depression and recovery and the war years, he suffered a massive stroke and was gone in an instant. The nation's grief was profound. He was clearly the most admired man in America. For us young people, he was the only president we had ever known.

Less than a month later, on May 8, 1945 Germany surrendered and the war in Europe was over. The celebration of V-E Day was sub-dued, as the war was only half over. Looming ahead in the Pacific was the invasion of Japan, with a prediction of one million American casualties.

Then on August 6 the United States dropped the first atomic bomb on Hiroshima, killing hundreds of thousands of Japanese civilians. On August 9 another was dropped on Nagasaki. In the ensuing days we learned for the first time what the Hanford Project as all about.

On August 14, 1945 Japan surrendered. The decision of whether or not to use the atomic bomb must have weighed heavily on our new president, Harry S. Truman, and the ethics of the decision is debated to this day. But there is no doubt that he had the overwhelming support of the American people at the time.

On the evening of the day of surrender, called V-J Day, I went with my friends to downtown St. Paul. It was pandemonium. The nation erupted in joyous celebration. People were drinking and dancing in the streets. Everyone has hugging and kissing everyone else. At age 15, I kissed more women, young and old, that night than on any other day in my life.

V-J night aside, I had only minimal success with girls in my high school years. This is not to say I was not interested in them. In fact, I cannot remember a time in my life when I did not admire the beauty and enjoy the company of females. Beginning in the first grade, there was always some pretty girl that I secretly admired. But in high school, when I first wanted to express these feelings, I was not making much progress. I worked hard at compensating for my lack of physical attraction by developing a pleasing personality, or so I believed. I was popular with girls as a buddy, and perhaps even admired for my forensic and musical talents, but not romantically. I think I was the typical teenage "nice guy," with no sex appeal.

For one thing, I was shorter than most. Entering my junior year, I was 4'10" and weighed 75 pounds. High school girls are not generally attracted to boys six or seven inches shorter. (At graduation, I had grown to 5'7" and 120 lbs.)

Most importantly of all, I had not yet learned the first rule of courtship: If you want to charm a woman, ask her a lot of questions and get her talking about herself. At the end of the evening she will regard *you* as a caring, compassionate and wonderful, not like those *other* guys who talk only about themselves and seem to have only one thing in mind. Of course this is worth the effort only if she turns out to be a really interesting person, but what better way to find out? This is a lesson I did not learn until my more mature college years.

In the spring of 1946 my father was released form the VA hospital in Minneapolis. It had been a long two years. Following many months of recuperation at home, he took a job as a maintenance electrician at the First National Bank Building in St. Paul. He was obviously overqualified, but the work was light, the hours were regular, and the pay was steady. He was 53. My mother had left the IRS after the war and had become the secretary to "Martha Logan," the nutritionist at Swift & Co. in South St. Paul. Swift, in addition to being the country's largest meat producer at that time, produced many other products related to cooking and baking, and Martha Logan was for Swift what Betty Crocker was for General Mills. Many a product of Martha Logan's experimental recipes found its way to our kitchen table.

During my senior year, 1946-47, the U.S. Navy announced its Naval Reserve Officer Training Corps (NROTC). The Navy would provide to college entrants who passed stiff mental and physical tests, full college scholarships at certain colleges, plus $50 per month, in exchange for two years' service as a commissioned officer in the Navy. One of the colleges was Notre Dame. It sounded like a terrific deal to me.

My classmate Chuck Pearson and I applied. We passed the written exam, and Chuck had no trouble passing the physical. But I was rejected because I was seven pounds underweight. "However," said the medical officer, "if you can gain seven pounds in two weeks, we'll give you another physical and you'll be in."

For the next two weeks I gorged myself on all the weight-inducing foods I could find. The next exam, two weeks later, was at 7 AM in Minneapolis, and on the way I stuffed down four more bananas and a milk shake.

This time I was placed in the dentist chair first.

"Sorry," said the medical officer. "You're rejected. Malocclusions."

"Malocclusions? What the hell are malocclusions?"

"Overbite." Another reason I wasn't sexy.

And they didn't even put me on the scale.

Malocclusions kept me out of Notre Dame and the Navy. But they didn't keep me from becoming a lieutenant in the United States Marine Corps seven years later. Go figure.

Chuck Pearson got an NROTC scholarship to the University of Minnesota. He graduated in 1951, entered the Navy, and was sent to Korea where he was killed in action. There but for the grace of God....

In June 1947 I graduated from high school, 6th in my class of 200.

Before moving on, notice must be taken of my thespian experience. In the Junior Class play, *You Can't Take It With You,* I was Donald the butler, played in black face (true to the original production, but there were no African Americans in So. St. Paul). In the Senior play, *My Sister Eileen,* I had the minor role of Frank Lippincott, a suitor of Eileen. After graduation, in the So. St. Paul Community Theater production of old-timey melodramas, I was the offstage piano player who provided the sound effects after such immortal lines as "No, no, a thousand times no; I'd rather die than say yes! and "Lips that touch liquor shall never touch mine!"

The culmination of my acting career came in *Arsenic and Old Lace,* in which I played the body in the window seat. Thus endeth my time on the boards.

5.

ST. THOMAS COLLEGE, 1947-1951

When I graduated from high school, I did not really want to go to St. Thomas in St. Paul. I wanted to go to the University of Minnesota—the "U"—where most of my friends were going. But my mother insisted that having missed a Catholic high school, I should get a Catholic college education, financial burden or not.

There *was* a financial problem. My father requested a meeting with the Rev. Vincent J. Flynn, the president of St. Thomas, and explained that we could not afford the full $350 annual tuition. Father Flynn was a compassionate priest and awarded me a one-half tuition scholarship. (Things were simpler in those days—no lengthy financial aid form to complete.) During the next four years I got to know Fr. Flynn better, as I became more involved in student government, and I developed an increasing admiration for his abilities as an administrator and as one deeply interested in the welfare of both students and faculty.

I will be forever grateful to my mother for her firmness. I cannot think of any four year period in my life when I learned as much, had as much fun, and made as many good friends, many of whom remain close to this day.

Most important for me, it was at St. Thomas that I came to a much broader and deeper understanding of my Catholic faith. Prior to St. Thomas, Catholicism had meant prayer and the sacraments, the ten commandments, and regular attendance at Mass, all of which is good, but it was mostly on the level of God & Me. My faith was individualistic.

At St. Thomas I discovered the length and breadth of the Catholic tradition, particularly in Catholic social thought. From the classic themes of social and political theory developed by Plato and Aristotle, including the concepts of moral commitment, ethics, and promotion of the common good, St. Thomas Aquinas argued that God's own self is the highest good we can attain, and that right relation to God requires a commitment to the common good of our neighbors and of all creation.

This idea of promotion of the common good is central to the Catholic intellectual tradition, and the College of St. Thomas had a number of faculty who had long been active in the field of Catholic social thought. Dr. Heinrich Rommen, professor of political science and a refugee from Nazi Germany, had authored the classic study *The State in Catholic Thought*. During his five years at St. Thomas, before he was lured to Georgetown University, he had a profound influence on his students, including myself, and on his colleagues. He emphasized that the tradition of Catholic social teaching calls for social (beyond merely personal) responsibility, regard for the common good, and the promotion of social and economic equality. In other words, as another professor put it, "We need to work to create a society not marred by the present divisions between privileged suburban enclaves and despairing inner city ghettos." It was no longer God & Me.

Another renowned professor of political science was Dr. G.W.C. Ross, a 1902 graduate of Harvard Law School and an unforgettable character in his own right. Dr. Ross taught constitutional law, and he brought to life all the great Supreme Court cases interpreting the Constitution and the Bill of Rights through which we have come to define the respective rights and duties of both our government and its citizens. Dr. Ross and other professors led me to a greater understanding of the concept of justice—both man's relationship with his government (distributive justice) and man's relationship with his fellow man (commutative justice). I became ever more sure that a career somewhere in justice is what I wanted.

Interest in the Catholic social tradition of the common good naturally leads to political activism. One of the young faculty colleagues influenced by Dr. Rommen was Eugene J;. McCarthy, a sociology professor at St. Thomas. McCarthy, along with other Minnesota college professors and some older veteran students, had been engaged from 1946 to 1948 in a struggle to wrest control of the Democratic Party (in Minnesota the Democratic Farmer-Labor Party) from its left-wing Marxist elements.

The consequence was an abrupt redirection of McCarthy's career. He was nominated to Congress in 1948, at age 32, in a hard-fought victory against the left wing. He was thought to have no chance against a respected Republican incumbent in a year in which the national Democratic party was itself badly split. President Harry Truman, who took office upon FDR's death was running against not only the formidable Republican governor of New York, Thomas E. Dewey, but against two former Democrats. Henry Wallace had been dumped as vice president by FDR in 1944 and was now the candidate of the left-wing Progressive party. The other candidate was Strom Thurmond, governor of South Carolina, who had led the southern delegation out of the Democratic convention that summer over civil rights issues (promulgated by Hubert Humphey, Minnesota's candidate for the Senate), and now headed the Dixiecrat Party. Few would have predicted that Truman, Humphrey, and McCarthy would all win.

McCarthy's nomination to Congress generated a tremendous amount of enthusiasm among young people, particularly among us students. Eugene McCarthy was a man of unimpeachable ethics. At one point in the campaign, a group of us who were distributing his literature door-to-door found that someone just ahead of us had left his opponent's literature on the same porches. So we gathered up the latter's materials and triumphantly brought them back to Prof. McCarthy. He was incensed, and made us retrace our steps and return all the materials.

This small incident is indicative, I think, of the high moral standards he maintained throughout his illustrative political career. He was considered one of the moral and intellectual leaders of the Congress, which he served for five terms, and of the Senate, which he served for two.

Minnesota political life was very vibrant in those days. There were good leaders and excellent young future leaders in both parties. Walter "Fritz" Mondale, very active among young Democrats, was a student at Macalaster college in St. Paul and a powerful speaker, against whom I once debated, long before he became Minnesota's attorney general, a U.S. Senator, vice president under Jimmy Carter, and the Democratic nominee for president in 1984. The debate coach at St. Catherine's, the sister college of St. Thomas, was a Republican candidate for governor. Harold Stassen, a native of South St. Paul, had become Minnesota's Republican governor at age 32, before going off to fight in World War II. In short, Minnesota was a great place for young people interested in politics.

While in college I read *Confessions of a Congressman*, a memoir by Jerry Voorhees, a Californian of the highest moral character, who was defeated by Richard Nixon. Nixon's gutter tactics in that campaign launched his political career. Voorhees described the high calling of public service in such glowing terms that I began to think seriously of some day running for Congress myself. Although that never materialized, my interest in politics has never abated. I have not always agreed with some of the leaders and policies of the Democratic party, but I have always considered myself a liberal Democrat.

Enrollment at St. Thomas when I entered in 1947 was 2300 men, of whom more than half were World War II veterans. We neophytes learned a great deal from the veterans. Their life experiences and worldview enriched our campus life.

St. Thomas had a rich tradition in forensics, and I entered the debate program immediately. Among my debate partners in a moderately successful freshman year were Bob Treanor, a veteran ten years older than I, whose wise counsel and wry commentaries on the foibles of human life I have enjoyed for the past 50 years; and Tom Ticen, then president of the All-College Council, who got me interested in student government. In my senior year I was elected president of the All-College Council. The ACC served a dual purpose; it was a link between the student body and the administration; and it coordinated the activities of all the campus student organizations. It was a 72-member body of veterans and individualists, termed by Father Flynn "the organization that really runs the Institution." I had to become thoroughly familiar with Robert's Rules of Order to keep the meetings from getting out of hand. The ACC was a given a great deal of autonomy by the administration, and it was an enjoyable experience, well worth the time and effort. At the end of the year the faculty moderator wrote: "As Pres. of ACC, very tactful and able to handle any situation. Always very fair." I really appreciated that.

In my second year my debate partner became Jim Rooney, a newly arrived freshman from our high school rival Duluth Denfeld. We were partners for the next three years. We became great friends and a successful team. We won the Minnesota State Collegiate Championship (26 colleges and universities) all three years. Our overall tournament record was 104-25. In 1951 we competed in a national speech and debate tournament at Oklahoma A & M (now Okla. State) against 132 other colleges and universities from 35 states. Some schools sent several representatives to compete in the different events: debate, oratory, extemporaneous speaking and discussion. Due to limited funds, Jim and I were the only St. Thomas participants. Between us we entered all the events and finished among the top ten schools overall. I was third in extemporaneous speaking.

In that year the national debate topic was "Resolved, that the United States should nationalize its basic industries." The United Kingdom just after WW II had nationalized its mining, utilities, and transportation, and serious thought was being given to doing the same in this country. Jim Rooney and I were researching the concept that nationalization might help to level out our recurrent business cycles and prevent another Great Depression, but we needed to know more about the economics of business cycles. Our coach recruited a new young professor of economics to tutor us. Charles Schultze, then 27, tutored us for hours on Keynesian economics and the theory of business cycles. He was brilliant, lucid, witty, and extremely helpful.

It seems that we were taught by the best in the business. Charley Schultze went on to an outstanding career in both academia—at the Universities of Indiana and Maryland—and in public service. He served as Director of the Bureau of the Budget under President Lyndon Johnson and as chairman of the Council of Economic Advisors under Jimmy Carter.

A highlight of our forensics experience was the West Point tournament. Each year in May the U.S. Military Academy sponsored a national debate tournament, by invitation only. College coachs in eight national regions were asked to select the top four teams in their region to attend the tournament. In 1950 Jim Rooney and I were selected from the Upper Midwest region. It was an honor all college debaters coveted, and we were thrilled, not only to be selected, but to be making our first trip to New York. Dick Krueger, our coach, secured tickets for a tour of Manhattan, a Broadway play (Maurice Evans in Shaw's *Man and Superman),* and the Rockettes show at Radio City Music Hall.

We did not do well at the tournament, winning two and losing two in the preliminary rounds, not good enough for the quarter finals, but we thoroughly enjoyed our time at West Point. We lived on campus, dined with the cadets in the mess halls, and gained an appreciation of the rigors of their training.

Tom Nesbitt, a high school friend cum cadet, introduced us to a number of his classmates, all of whom were about to graduate and become Army lieutenants. We spent one evening with ten of them, drinking beer and talking about their and our futures. Less than two months later, on June 24, 1950, the Korean War broke out, and all of these young men were rushed into combat as platoon leaders. Tom later informed me that, of our ten drinking companions, seven had died in action by the end of the summer.

My own military experience began in 1948, when because of increasingly hostile Cold War relations with the Soviet Union, the military draft was reinstated. A college student could obtain a deferment by joining a college ROTC unit or a local military reserve unit, both of which required a commitment to active duty upon completion of one's education. My closest friends from So. St. Paul, Dick Vasatka and Dick and Chet Taylor and I joined the Navy Reserve. Every Tuesday evening we spent two hours at Wold-Chamberlin Naval Air Station in Minneapolis, the closest installation. We were taught close order drill, basic seamanship, how to tie knots, and not much else. We were issued sailor suits, given the rank of seaman recruit, and were paid a small amount for each drill meeting. There was also an obligatory two-week summer "cruise" (not necessarily on a ship), but this was not strictly enforced.

Later the training station was moved to an island in the middle of the Mississippi river in St. Paul. There I was assigned training as an Electronic Technician's Mate, which involved, as far as I could tell, plotting the location of ships on a big board during simulated battles. The Russian navy was in no danger based upon my skills. As my buddies worked up to seaman apprentice and seaman, I remained a seaman recruit. I was finally compelled, at age 22, to undergo a two week "boot camp" at the Great Lakes Naval Training Station, along with a bunch of foul-mouthed 17- and 18-year-olds. In 1953, having agreed to join the Marine Officer Candidate program after law school, I received an honorable discharge from the Navy, with five years' longevity as a seaman recruit.

At home, my sister Patricia had graduated from high school in 1944 and was working as a legal secretary when she met Frank Thibault, an instantly likeable and warm hearted man, one of eight siblings in an equally congenial family in St. Paul. Frank, a navy veteran, was two years ahead of me at St. Thomas, planning to become a high school English teacher. In addition, his creative mind has enabled him to become a life-long and successful inventor of board games and toys. Frank's creations have provided fun and entertainment not only to his family and friends, but have been sold to countless gamesters in this country and abroad.

On September 17, 1949, Patricia and Frank were married in St. Augustine's church in So. St. Paul, and I was an usher. Frank had graduated in June and had become an English teacher at Hastings High School, about 20 miles south of St. Paul.

On September 28, 1950, Michael Francis Thibault was born, and I had the honor of being his godfather. As with Pat Deluhery, I could not have imagined that this beautiful child in my arms would one day be seen on national television as a successful coach in the National Basketball Association and the Women's NBA. Mike is shorter than six feet and was not a great player himself, but his love of the game and extraordinary coaching skills, together with his knack for handling athletes with varying personalities, has brought him great success and respect in his profession.

The Maintenance Man and the Chief Justice

Like most college kids, I needed summer employment. Upon completion of my first year at St. Thomas, I was hired as a maintenance man at the First National Bank Building in St. Paul, where my father was an electrician. Pay was 85 cents an hour and a number of college students were hired for the summer. Mostly we worked on remodeling offices. The most fun was knocking down interior walls, which involved flailing away with a sledge hammer until the wall was down. It was very noisy and raised a lot of dust, which invariably brought complaints from nearby tenants, thus gave us a feeling of great power.

It was in this job that I learned that there is a most efficient way of doing every task, even such menial ones as swinging a sledge hammer, pushing a broom, or mopping a floor, and those who do it as a career take great pride in their skills.

Sometimes we would be assigned to the night shift, which required cleaning offices and rest rooms. Dusting and vacuuming and emptying waste baskets was easy; cleaning toilets was less enjoyable. Three years at this task provided incontrovertible evidence that women, generally speaking, are *much* messier than men.

One of the offices assigned to me for regular cleaning was the law firm of Brown, Bear, Burger & Wolf. In addition to its intriguing name, the Burger in the firm was Warren Burger, who eventually became Chief Justice of the Supreme Court of the United States.

A digression must be made here. Fast forward 25 years. One day when I was practicing law in Washington, DC a young woman in her twenties walked into my office and identified herself as Margaret Elizabeth Burger, daughter of the Chief Justice. She had been referred by Beth Markey, a friend of our family. Elizabeth had recently become a Catholic, and she wanted to officially change her name to Margaret <u>Mary</u> Elizabeth Burger, in honor of the Blessed Virgin. I explained that this could be done with a simple petition to be presented to the court, supported by her affidavit. I would prepare the papers and have them delivered to the Burger home in suburban Virginia the following Saturday morning.

I asked my fellow lawyer, Oliver Dibble, who often handled matters for me in Virginia, to make the delivery.

When Oliver arrived at the Burger home, he found the Chief Justice raking leaves on the front lawn. When Oliver informed him of the purpose of his visit, Mr. Chief Justice became incensed, shook his rake at Oliver and literally chased him off the property, shouting that they had a family lawyer who would handle any and all legal matters involving his daughter. We never heard form the poor young woman again.

To California and Back by Thumb

During the summer of 1950, upon completion of my junior year in college, I began making post-graduate plans. Since my second year in high school I had wanted to be a courtroom lawyer. Also, I wanted to live in California, something my parents had talked about for years. If I was going to practice law in California, it seemed prudent to look into California law schools.

In those days there was no Law School Aptitude Test, at least not to my knowledge. It was simply a matter of sending in an application, along with a one's college transcript. But I thought it would make sense to visit the law schools first, to see which I might like, and which might be willing to accept me.

I did not have the funds to go by plane, train, or bus, and in fact I wanted the experience of hitchhiking my way across the country. In those days hitchhiking was common. Most of the roads, even the so-called major highways, were two lanes only, and hitchhiking was not prohibited as it is on the interstate highways today.

So in mid-August 1950 I quit my job with the maintenance crew at the bank, packed my suitcase (the era of the backpack had not yet arrived) and hit the road.

As I think back, it must have been worrisome for my parents, especially my mother, to see their 20-year-old son heading off, alone on the highway, on a 2000 mile trip to California and back. I think that in later years if any of my own children had suggested this I would have been extremely concerned. Maybe my parents were, too. But if so, they hid their concern and expressed only their complete confidence and trust that I was right in wanting to visit these schools, that I would have a wonderful time, and that God would watch over me. Those were indeed safer times.

It was easy to get rides because I was always well dressed and clean shaven. In fact, when I left home I was wearing a suit and carrying a new Samsonite suitcase.

My first destination was Omaha. As it turned out, making my way through Iowa en route to Omaha was the most difficult part of the trip. There was, and still is, a small town every six miles in that agrarian state, and at that time the major highways went through every one of them. It was my custom to affix a sign on my suitcase with taped letters designating my next big city destination—OMAHA and later DENVER and SALT LAKE, etc.—in the hope of attracting the long distance driver. But in Iowa this was ineffective, either due to the inherent friendliness of the people or because nobody ever traveled far in Iowa. The typical ride was from Farmer Haystack who would say, "I ain't goin' as far as Omaha, but can drop you off at my farm three miles up the road." I got rides in trucks, tractors, and farm wagons and heard a lot about the year's corn crop and hog prices, but it took me at least two full days to cover the 400 miles from the Twin Cities to Omaha.

Once there, I was greeted warmly by John and Margaret Oertel, distant cousins on my father's side, with whom I stayed for the weekend. They were extremely gracious and introduced me to many other cousins, young and old. Little did I dream that fourteen years hence I would be introducing them to my future bride from Omaha at my engagement party in their city.

The rest of the trip west went much faster, due to the longer distances and wide open spaces between the major cities: 500 miles to Denver, another 500 to Salt Lake City, then 525 to Reno. Nearly every city of medium size or larger had a YMCA, where one could get a clean bed and shower for fifty cents or a dollar. There were also Tourist Homes, whose owners would rent a room or two for a couple of bucks a night. I think these had their origin in the Depression years, providing their owners a little extra income in tough times. These Tourist Homes were the forerunners of today's B&B's, without the breakfast.

I met some interesting people along the way, and from the locals one could with a little effort learn something about the geography, history, the political views, and even the gossip of the local area. For good writing in this genre, I recommend John Steinbeck's *Travels With Charley* and William Least Heat Moon's Blue Highways.

Heading west from Salt Lake City I was picked up by three young men from Mexico, driving an old clunker with a leaky radiator. Its top speed was about 40 mph and we were forever stopping to let the engine cool off, then adding water from cans and bottles they carried. But they were delightful *compadres,* friendly and exuberant. They spoke little English, so it was my first opportunity to practice my high school and college Spanish. We shouted to each other over the *mariachi* music on the radio. That night about ten o'clock the driver suddenly swerved off the highway, drove straight into the desert, and parked. I became apprehensive. They all jumped out, opened the trunk of the car, and extracted a double mattress—the only item in the trunk. They invited me to join them, and there we slept, the four of us on that mattress, under the stars. In the morning, after breakfast in the next town, I bade them farewell, mainly because I needed faster transportation if I was ever to get to California. But I was grateful to these men who had nothing, yet shared with me their car, their merriment, and a place to sleep.

Leaving Utah on old Highway 40 and entering West Wendover, Nevada, there was a 30-foot high neon sign of a cowboy, waving his arm and beckoning the weary traveler to the Stateline Casino. It was a beacon in the night, could be seen for miles, and it meant that you were entering the only state in the union permitting legalized gambling. At that time the Stateline was an oasis in the desert. Today the old cowboy is still there, but one has to drive off Interstate 80 to see it on old #40; and West Wendover is a glittering mini-metropolis of luxury hotels and casinos. We have stayed there several times in recent years en route back from the Sundance Film Festival in Utah. Each time I see that old neon cowboy I remember the first time he waved to me in the desert night.

In Reno, I had a problem. Arriving at night, I found that because of a convention, there were absolutely no rooms available anywhere. I went to the police station and asked the desk sergeant if he had any suggestions. He looked me over and said, "Well, we do have one empty cell. If you can be out by 6 AM before my replacement arrives, it's yours." So if you ask if I know Reno, the Biggest Little City in the World, my answer is yes, I do; I once spent a night in jail there.

Finally, just west of Reno, the California state line! Though it had taken me about ten days, I thought about the pioneers in their covered wagons, traveling for six months, beginning from St. Joseph, Missouri, only to be confronted by the very formidable High Sierras. Highway 40, as does Interstate 80 today, passed the very spot where the ill-fated Donner Party was stranded in the terrible winter of 1847.

I got a ride over the mountains and was dropped off a few miles west of Sacramento. I remember making my way by foot to a rise in the road, and just over the crest, near what is now Fairfield, there opened a vista of the Great Central Valley, surrounded by the golden hills of California. A feeling of exhilaration came over me. I felt that this was truly the beginning of a new phase of my life. Today whenever I pass that crest I still remember that moment.

In San Francisco I was greeted with much enthusiasm by the wonderful Neil family, cousins on my mother's side, who lived at 738 10th Avenue, a block from Golden Gate Park. Mildred Bitter Neil was my mother's first cousin; her father, Joseph, and my mother's father, Alfred Bitter, were brothers. They are the same family we had met in 1941, on our first trip to California.

Uncle Joe had since died. Mildred's husband Ira was away on an 18-month assignment with the Bechtel company in Saudi Arabia, building an oil pipeline. Mildred was managing the family alone, which consisted of eight children, ranging from Joe, about a year older than I, down to Susie, about 4. The kids accepted me as one of their own and were great fun. We explored Golden Gate Park, went sailing in the bay, and took in a 49-ers pre-season game at Kezar Stadium, my first professional football game. It was pretty heady stuff for a kid from Minnesota. I stayed about a week.

Then I began my law school visits. I liked the University of San Francisco because it was Jesuit and only ten blocks from the Neil home in a great city. Little did I realize that 50 years hence I would be enrolling in courses with my wife on that very campus, at the Fromm Institute for Lifelong Learning.

I liked Stanford because it had the most beautiful campus I had ever seen, with its Spanish mission style architecture and Romanesque arches and the golden mosaics on the administration building. As for the law school, I thought the dean was a bit pompous, had never heard of St. Thomas, and gave me little reason to think that I would qualify for *his* school.

I was very pleased with Santa Clara. The town, with of population of 11,000, was in a beautiful valley of fruit orchards. Its neighbor, San Jose, 95,000, was a quiet residential city. Santa Clara University was Jesuit with an enrollment of 1200 men. Dean Edwin J. Owens had founded the law school in the 1930's, and still taught Contracts. The law school was small, only about 50 students (all men, of course), mostly all from the west coast. Dean Owens took a personal interest in me and expressed delight that someone from Minnesota was interested in his school. All in all, Santa Clara impressed me as a wonderful place to live and study.

Then on to Los Angeles. I visited the law schools at Southern Cal, UCLA, and Loyola. I was impressed by the UCLA campus at Westwood. UCLA had just created a law school, with a new building, and the dean was actively recruiting students. But the idea of living in Los Angeles did not appeal to me. Even then it was sprawling and smoggy, and a bit overwhelming for someone of my background.

As one can tell from the above, my investigation of law schools was not at all scientific or professional. My likes and dislikes were for all the wrong reasons, mostly having to do with location and little to do with the quality of the schools. I had not thought of inquiring into such important factors as reputation of the school, quality of faculty, or strength of a school's placement service—very important to securing employment. I doubt if I even knew what the bar passage rate was for any of the schools. My main thought was that if I wanted to be a California lawyer I should go to a California law school (not essential, I later learned), and I might as well do it in a pleasant place.

Heading back east from Los Angeles by thumb, I encountered Las Vegas for the first time. What is today the Strip was in 1950 a two-lane road with three casinos: the Flamingo (owned by mobster Bugsy Siegel), the Thunderbird, and El Rancho. Though I was not permitted to enter the casinos because I was under 21, I was told they offered free lunches to gamblers.

On my way out of Las Vegas the next morning I was picked up by a driver who also picked up another passenger two blocks up the road. The other hitchhiker was man in his 30's named Fred Wagstaff, from Boston. Fred was a stand-up comic who had been performing in one of the casino lounges. However, explained Fred, he had this terrible addiction to gambling. Not only had he gambled away his earnings, he had sold his car and then lost the proceeds as well. Thus he had joined the ranks of the hitchhikers, and was heading for his brother's place in Chugwater, Wyoming.

We stopped for lunch in a hot, dusty little town in southern Utah called Beaver City. As we were finishing lunch, our driver said he would get some gas at the corner station and wait for us there. When we arrived ten minutes later the car was gone. He had taken off with all our belongings! This was confirmed by the gas station attendant. It being a very hot day, I was wearing only a T-shirt. Gone were my suitcase, all my clothes and toiletries, a camera, and my sister Patricia's wedding pictures, which I had carried to show to the Neils. Fred was in the same fix.

Once the shock wore off, we were able—not without some difficulty—to roust the local sheriff out of a pool hall. He made some perfunctory phone calls to other counties and the highway patrol, then returned to the billiard table. We waited until the next morning with no results. In the meantime I called home and my parents wired me some money with which I purchased a red sweatshirt, underwear and toiletries, which I carried in a paper sack. Then Fred and I were back on the highway.

Fred turned out to be a delightful traveling companion, regaling me for the next day and a half with every routine in his night club act. More than fifty years later, I am still getting some yuks out of Fred's old jokes. We parted company in Cheyenne, he heading north to Chugwater, and I pointed east to the Twin Cities. The rest of the trip was, by contrast, uneventful.

The trip was a wonderful adventure, but it was great to be home again. My mother was greatly relieved but somewhat dismayed, having seen her son leave in a new suit, carrying a new suitcase, and return in a sweatshirt carrying a paper sack.

Soon it was time to return for my final year at St. Thomas, to assume my duties as president of the All College Council, prepare for a final year of forensics, and take some additional courses in history, political science, and theology.

Proof of the Existence of Guardian Angels

Late one afternoon during my senior year I received a call from a man identifying himself as Jay Burke.

"I hear you play the piano, and I need a pianist for an event this evening," he said.

"Is it with a dance band?" I asked.

"Not exactly," said he. "You'll be playing singleton—background music for a couple of hours for a private affair at Fort Snelling." The pay would be $25, a rather handsome sum at that time. Playing background dinner music is an easy gig, so I accepted.

Jay picked me up at home, wearing a tuxedo. "Must be a fancy banquet," I commented as I climbed into his car. Jay then casually explained that it wasn't exactly a banquet. It was in fact a fund raiser for the postal workers' union for their trip to the annual convention in Florida. The event was a stag show, with Jay as the M.C., and I was to play the piano for the strippers. Though dumbfounded, I shrugged my 20-year-old shoulders as if to suggest that this was old hat for a man of my experience.

Upon arrival, Jay took me directly to the ladies dressing room where he introduced me to "the girls." We worked out the musical numbers appropriate to their artistry and my limited practice in this field—including old standbys like "Harlem Nocturne," "Hawaiian War Chant," and "Back Beat Boogie."

I had seen a few burlesque shows in downtown Minneapolis in my day, but I venture to say that this show exceeded anything ever seen on a public stage. I speak with authority, having had the best seat in the house. Suffice it to say that if there is a corresponding noun for "raunchy," this show defined it.

The next morning I told my father about the previous evening's adventure. He thought it was hilarious, but we deemed it prudent not to tell my mom.

A week or so later Jay called again. He and his "actresses" were revving up for another show the following Friday evening right there in my own town of South St. Paul, at the Serbian Hall. The ladies had been very pleased with my musicianship, and could I join them again?

I told Jay that I was Catholic, in my senior year in a Catholic college, and had just been elected president of the student council, and therefore I didn't think it was appropriate. I would have to decline. Jay allowed as how he too was a Catholic but with him it was just a matter of supply and demand, but said he understood and would look for a substitute.

The following Saturday morning I picked up the St. Paul newspaper and emblazoned on the front page of the metro section was the headline: STAG SHOW RAIDED. Included with the extensive story were pictures of Jay, the ladies, *and* the hapless accompanist.

To make matters worse, they hired an ambitious young lawyer who challenged the constitutionality of the city ordinance prohibiting such nefarious activities, alleging a violation of terpsichorean expression, a form of freedom of speech. He took the case all the way to the Minnesota Supreme Court, generating further and protracted publicity.

Eventually the law was upheld, justice was done, and Jay, the ladies, and the pianist were all sentenced to thirty days in jail.

So don't try to tell me that guardian angels are a myth.

Speaking of the postal service, college students in those days were hired to help carry the mail during the Christmas rush. I was hired that Christmas, to deliver mail in South St. Paul. We walked door-to-door, carrying a leather bag, unlike the motorized carriers of today. It was cold but enjoyable work, as everybody was happy to see the mailman come with Christmas greetings from far and near. I did the same thing for two Christmases while in law school, and carrying the mail in the warmth and sunshine of Santa Clara was more enjoyable than in frigid Minnesota.

Romance at Last, and Making Tracks

I was slowly gaining confidence and maturity in college, as well as physical stature, and I had more success with women than in high school. In my sophomore year I met a girl named Dolly Carley. Dolly was my age and a debater at the University of Minnesota. She was blond, cute, very bright, and had a good wit, and we shared similar interests. She lived on a lake, wore a fur coat, her family owned seven cars, and she genuinely liked me and took my arm as we walked down the street. This was a new and heady experience for me. I felt a little like F. Scott Fitzgerald. Dolly and I enjoyed each other's company for our next two college years, but as we approached graduation, Dolly—understandably—began to talk in terms of marriage and starting a family. This was the farthest thing from my mind, as I was leaving for law school in California at the end of the summer. So we separated, amicably but also with a few tears.

In June 1951 I graduated from St. Thomas, *magna cum laude*, ranked 6th in my class. It was a great four years, during which I made lifelong friends. Chief among them is my classmate George Ebling, a longtime Sacramento resident, who keeps me up to date on the machinations of the California legislature and the governor's office.

The summer after graduation, desiring a job outdoors and one that paid more money, I was hired at $1.44 an hour as a section hand with the Minnesota Transfer Railroad, a small line which shuttled boxcars between St. Paul and Minneapolis. A section hand is part of a gang that repairs old track and lays new track. It is heavy labor, but it is outdoor work and great for building up the body, for which I felt a great need, and they hired summer help to augment the regular crew of old timers. There was a lot of new track to be laid that summer.

I took a certain pride in learning how a railroad is constructed, and being a part of it. It was all done by hand then, just about the same as it was in the 1860's when the transcontinental railroad was built.

After the road bed was surveyed, we section hands began the digging and leveling with picks and shovels. Then with tongs we lifted the ties, covered with creosote and stacked nearby, two men to each tie, and spaced them evenly along the road bed. Then we placed square steel plates ("tie plates"), with holes for the spikes, on each tie.

Then came the rails, each 39 feet long and weighing 700 lbs., carried by ten of us with tongs that resembled giant pliers, one man on each handle. The rails were placed at a width of exactly 4'8". Each rail had two holes at each end and we bolted the rails together by means of rectangular steel connecting pieces ("angle irons") with wrenches about 4 feet long.

Next came the spikers. Four spikes were hammered through each tie plate, two on each side of the rail, in such a manner that the head of the spike is attached to the rail. This was skilled work, as two spikers worked in tandem, facing each other and swinging sledge hammers, three strokes to a spike. One man was in the downstroke while the other was in the backswing. Once in awhile the boss would give us college kids a shot at spiking, mostly I think for the amusement of the old timers, to see if we would get out of sync and hit each other in the head; also, if we hit the rail instead of the spike, which often happened, the hammer would go flying off in space and our arms would sting for an hour.

After the rails were bolted together and spiked to the ties, they would have to be aligned. This was done by all hands using giant crowbars, with the straw boss sighting down the line and giving orders. Finally, an engine and dump car would dump gravel all along the track, and it was the job of us section hands to shove the gravel under the ties to provide stability. Each of us stood with one foot on a tie and other on the shovel, tamping the gravel under the next tie. This was known as "gandy dancing," and thus laborers in a railroad section gang were traditionally called gandy dancers.

We college guys took a lot of ribbing from the old timers, but at the end of the summer one old fellow said to me, "Y'know, Tom, for a college kid you're not bad." It was a compliment I'll always treasure.

6.

SANTA CLARA UNIVERSITY LAW SCHOOL, 1951-1954

Santa Clara was my first choice, and I had been accepted, but I needed financial help. By good fortune, Fr. Flynn, the president of St. Thomas, was acquainted with Fr. Gianara, the president of Santa Clara, and so a letter from Fr. Flynn on my behalf resulted in a scholarship to the law school.

Leaving St. Paul in late August 1951, I was driven as far as Denver by my mother, my sister Mary Lu, and cousin Delores Schiltz from Dubuque, who joined us for a little vacation. From Denver I arranged to drive a car to Pasco, Washington, ironically within the Hanford Project area where my father had worked, and then hitchhiked to San Francisco, this time without incident.

In Santa Clara I secured a room in a house at 930 Bellomy St. rented to law students. There were eight of us, including one other first year student. They were great guys, but unfortunately not the most serious students. I thoroughly enjoyed myself, but we partied too much. It was my first experience living away from home, and I readily joined the fraternity house atmosphere.

The law school had fewer than 60 students (compared to 900 today) and since each class had only about 15, each student got plenty of individual attention. The professors were competent but journeyman-like; certainly not like the big stars of the major law schools who simultaneously mesmerize and terrorize their students. The emphasis was not to ponder the great legal issues of the day, but to qualify its students to pass the California bar exam, and at this it was achieving about the same rate of success as the big schools. We were offered the courses that were covered in the bar exam and not much more. No big-concept courses like "Major Trends in Human Rights Legislation" or "Conflicting Theories of Environmental Regulation."

I had no quarrel with this philosophy. However, I found the case method of instruction tedious and boring—reading case after case to determine the present status of the law, including majority view, minority view, and weight of opinion. In addition, I had no burning interest (except to pass the bar) in such fields as contracts, real property, and corporations. I envisioned myself as a future criminal trial attorney, not in civil practice drawing up contracts or leases or wills. I did enjoy and paid close attention to criminal law, constitutional law, and evidence, and in these subjects I got A's and B's; in the others I got mostly C's. To my amazement I also got an A in taxation, a subject I despised. As a result, I have felt compelled to do my own annual tax returns to this day.

In my letters home I gave glowing and enthusiastic reports about the wonderful weather in Santa Clara, and how pleasant it was to live in that valley, in a small town surrounded by orchards and low mountains. The severe Minnesota winters were taking their toll on my father's fragile health, and my letters rekindled my parents' long-simmering desire to move to California. They decided to make the move the following January, 1952.

That Christmas I got a ride home to Minnesota with some other Bay Area students, and returned to California via a Greyhound bus, an experience I hope never to repeat. The bus arrived in the Sierras in the middle of The Great Blizzard of '52. As we came through Truckee on old Highway 40 I saw the proprietor of a gas station digging *down* through the snow to reach the *top* of his pumps. The following day the westbound transcontinental train heading for San Francisco was marooned and snowbound for three days. [The Sierras can get six feet of snow in

24 hours. It has happened many times, including the winter of 1995-96, and my daughter Katy and I tried to ski in it, without much success. That winter the Lake Tahoe area received a total snowfall of 870", more than 70 feet!]

Upon returning to Santa Clara I realized that through profligate living I had already spent all the money I had saved up for the entire school year. So, it was off to look for a part time job again. I got a job in a gas station (before the era of self serve) for about 15 hours per week, which carried me through the rest of the school year.

I did not bring a lot of expertise to the gas station business. I did not own a car and had very little knowledge or interest in them beyond knowing the location of the gas tank and the places to add oil and water. [Nor has my knowledge greatly expanded in the ensuing 50 years.] But I was enthusiastic and friendly to the customers, and therefore the kindly manager overlooked more than one opportunity to fire me on the spot. Once in attempting to change a customer's oil I mistakenly drained his transmission fluid. Another time a customer coasted in with an empty tank and therefore could not start the engine even after filling the tank. I remembered someone once saying that the solution was to put a little gas in the carburetor. Not realizing that you have to remove the air cleaner first, I managed to set the front end of his car on fire. When I was on duty it was a thrill a minute for all concerned.

In January my parents decided that before leaving for California they would make a final trip to Chicago and Dubuque. They had given up the lease on their home, effective the end of the month, and had everything packed and ready to go upon their return. Mary Lu, a freshman at St. Joseph Academy, stayed home. Near DeKalb, Illinois, they were involved in a head-on collision with a truck. My father had only minor injuries, but my mother suffered a broken hip. After a week or two in the hospital, she was transported to Dubuque where, in a body cast, she recuperated for about six weeks at the home of Uncle Henry and Aunt Mildred.

As a result, they postponed the move to California and returned to St. Paul. They rented a duplex in West St. Paul at 728 Winslow Avenue, and made new plans to move to California at the end of the summer.

I received the news of the accident in the middle of studying for semester exams in January, the final straw in a disastrous first semester of law school. I received preliminary D's in both Contracts and Real Property, and was warned by Dean Owens that my scholarship was in jeopardy.

It was a good wake-up call, and thereafter I settled down to a routine of study and work and a minimum of partying at 930 Bellomy. By the end of the year I had pulled up my grades to a respectable level and salvaged the scholarship.

Upon returning unexpectedly for another summer in Minnesota, I was able to rejoin my old gang of section hands on the railroad. In late July the work petered out and several of us students were laid off. In a day or so I got a job at Armour & Co. in So. St. Paul, making corned beef hash.

Love Blooms Anew

Having severed all ties the previous summer, upon my return to Minnesota I asked my friend Dick Vasatka to fix me up with a blind date. Dick was dating (and later married) a lovely So. St. Paul girl named Carol Lamphere, who had just completed her sophomore year at St. Catherine's College, the sister college of St. Thomas. The following Saturday I was introduced to Carol's classmate and best friend, Jacqueline Horner. Jackie was 20, had short brown hair, sparkling brown eyes, and a great smile. We were instantly attracted to each other, fell into romantic love, and were inseparable for the rest of the summer.

Jackie introduced me to world I had never known, the world of art. I had never taken an art course, and did not grow up in a family that visited art galleries or art museums. I knew nothing about the Impressionists, not to mention classical or Renaissance art. Jackie was an artist, and she opened my eyes to the wonders and beauty of paintings and sculpture, and for this I will be forever grateful to her. We looked at art books together, she instructing me, and visited the Walker Art Institute in Minneapolis. Titian and El Greco were my instant favorites. And like most people, I became fascinated by the Impressionists, and also developed a strong liking for the works of Franz Marc and Georges Rouault. We both especially liked Marc's *Blue Horses*. [Forty years later, while studying for a Master's in Liberal Studies at Georgetown University, I did a long paper comparing the spiritual aspects of the works of Marc and Rouault.] Jackie also sculpted for me a fine ceramic crucifix, which I still have.

It was an idyllic summer, and I departed again for California with mixed emotions. It was great to be leaving this time with my parents and Mary Lu for our new home in Santa Clara; at the same time, leaving Jackie was difficult. Fortuitously, her older sister and husband had recently moved to Redwood City, just 25 miles up the peninsula from Santa Clara, so we made plans for her to visit them the following Easter, and for her to spend the entire following summer (1953) as a nanny for their young children. Meanwhile we maintained a steady and fervid correspondence, in the days when people still wrote long letters to each other.

Our family had a leisurely and delightful drive west, remembering our earlier voyage in 1941. Once arrived, we rented a small but new house on the east side of San Jose, at 14515 Jerilyn Drive. Mary Lu enrolled in the local Catholic high school for girls, and eventually both my parents secured employment at the Westinghouse plant in Sunnyvale, Dad as an electrician and Mom as a secretary.

For spending money, Mary Lu and I set up a baby sitting service in the neighborhood. One of our clients operated a side business as a children's photographer, and he asked me to be a door-to-door advance man for him, setting up appointments. In that era when most women were stay-at-home moms, door-to-door salespersons were quite prevalent, but they were about as popular as today's telemarketeers. After a gazillion irate turn-downs, I got an idea. I bought up all the "No Solicitors" signs I could find in the local hardware stores at 25 cents each. I then knocked on doors, asked "Lady, are you tired of people like me? Then buy my sign for a dollar." I got a lot of laughs, made some money, and then ended my sales career.

After several months my parents purchased their "dream house" in Santa Clara, at 2247 Serra Ave. It had a nice backyard with an outdoor grill and fruit trees. It was their home until my mother sold it in 1969, a year after my father's death.

In my second year of law school I became involved in local politics. The 1952 election which put Dwight Eisenhower in the White House was also a sweep for Republicans in California. The Democratic party was fragmented and in disarray up and down the state. At that time California permitted cross-filing in the primaries, which meant a candidate could file for election in both parties. Since the Republicans were generally the incumbents and thus better known, and the Democrats would field seven or eight candidates, the Republicans would often win both primaries, thus ensuring election.

Alan Cranston, a state assemblyman from the Bay Area, conceived the idea of forming a statewide grass roots organization called the California Democratic Council. The purpose was for Democrats, organizing at the local level, to gather together in a state convention each year to endorse a single candidate for each statewide and national office, thus unifying financial and human resources to combat the Republicans. I became a charter member of the Santa Clara chapter, and attended the state conventions in 1953 and 1954. Although the fights among the candidates for endorsement were lively and acrimonious, and therefore great fun, the CDC did become an effective force and eventually carried Alan Cranston to the U.S. Senate and Edmund G. "Pat" Brown to the governor's office. The CDC ultimately became obsolete with the elimination of cross-filing.

In the summer after my second year of law school I got a job with the Pacific Gas & Electric Co. maintenance crew, digging ditches. The work was not all that bad, the pay was pretty good, and the best part was getting a chance now and then to operate the jack hammer for breaking up concrete. What power! It was especially fun at 8AM in a quiet residential neighborhood.

After a few weeks I heard that one could get a job selling fireworks for the two weeks before the 4th of July, for the princely sum of $25 a day, so I ended my career at PG&E and Mary Lu and I signed up. We were given a load of fireworks which completely filled my car, a 1941 Dodge which I had purchased for $195, and were assigned to a roadside stand at the corner of Bayshore Highway and Embarcadero Road in Palo Alto. There was an infinte variety of incendiary devices for sale, and nearly every customer—especially kids—wanted to know what each one "did." Not having tested any of them, it was an opportunity to use our creative imaginations. "It sends up multicolored showers of fire" or "red, white, and blue stars" or "orange and green rockets" or anything else that came to mind. Actually, California law prohibited any device from rising more than three feet, a fact we normally omitted.

We were resupplied regularly, and at the end of each day we had to load up and take everything home. Though I was a smoker, I was careful to abstain during the commute.

At the end of the evening on the 4th, we gathered with a group of other vendors in a vacant lot and set off all remaining inventory. It was a wonderful conflagration, albeit only three feet high.

By this time the orchards were being harvested and annual canning season was on. I got a job with Del Monte in Santa Clara, dumping crates of grapes into a large revolving cylinder like a big cement mixer which shook the grapes from their stems, on their way to becoming fruit cocktail. We worked six days a week, 6 AM to 4 PM, and then after a nap and a quick dinner I would head up to Redwood City several times a week to visit Jackie. Often we would go up to San Francisco or Sausalito, or on a Sunday, to Santa Cruz or Carmel.

By the end of the summer Jackie and I agreed that we would be married sometime after we both graduated the following year.

It was a memorable but exhausting and expensive summer, at the end of which I had not saved enough for the school year, so I went on the night shift at the cannery, working midnight till 8 AM, loading cases of canned fruit onto pallets, for the first month of my final year of law school.

1953 was not a good year for my father. His tuberculosis flared up again in the fall, and he had to spend another year in the Veterans Hospital in Livermore, about an hour away. Mom got a job as a secretary at Willow Glen High School in San Jose, closer to home than Sunnyvale. We visited my dad on Sundays, and later when school was out and I was studying for the bar, I would frequently visit him on weekday afternoons. He was discouraged but determined to recover, and never tired of hearing about our various activities.

By the fall of 1953 the So. St. Paul draft board was breathing down my neck. The Korean war had scooped up most of their eligible manhood, and I was no longer in the Navy Reserve, so they denied my deferment for my final year of law school and were about to draft me into the Army. I applied to the Board of Appeals, explaining that I planned to apply for a commission in one of the military services upon graduation. The Board granted the deferment on the condition that I apply to at least three services, and that I sign up with whichever branch accepted me first. And that is how I eventually became a United States Marine.

The final year of law school was uneventful. Whereas the four years of college were among the most enjoyable of my life, the three in law school were among the least stimulating. In later years, when people asked how I did in law school, I would say that I finished 6th in my class, failing to mention that there were only 12 in our graduating class.

Language and the Law

One interesting aspect about the development of our Anglo-Saxon judicial system from its earliest days is how our language has been influenced by various sources down through the centuries. In the 12th century, after the Norman conquest, the courts of England were using a combination of Old English, French, and Latin. Thus there was the famous case in which a town's residents were suing a candle manufacturer. Making candles from tallow caused a terrible odor, and the residents sought an injunction to abate the nuisance. The factory owner countered that candle-making was an essential industry. The court decided in favor of the owner, holding that "Le utility del chose excusera le noisemness del stink."

Courts are also called upon from time to time to decide when the use of language can be harmful to another. Consider the following case coming out of Minnesota. Mr. A called Mr. B and said, "I'm thinking of hiring Lawyer Brown as my attorney and I understand that he once represented you. Can you tell me what you think of him?"

B replied, "Well, if you want the truth, Lawyer Brown is an incompetent asshole."

Lawyer Brown got wind of this and sued B for slander.

The case went all the way to the Minnesota Supreme Court, which decided that it *is* slanderous to call a lawyer incompetent, but it *is not* slanderous to call him an asshole.

So when talking about your lawyer, choose your words carefully.

Tales from Mariani's

In the spring of 1954 a new restaurant opened in Santa Clara. Mariani's was a large and upscale restaurant featuring Italian cuisine. But the owners were two Serbians and a Hungarian: Nick, Joe, and Joe's sister Ann. I applied for a job as a busboy and was hired, starting opening day, and worked 25 hours per week until the bar exam in October.

Nick and Joe hired as waiters only longtime professionals, all men, of many nationalities, who had worked all over the world. Professional waiters are a peripatetic and volatile breed, men of great pride whose only aim is to satisfy their customers and thereby enhance their tips. They do not take kindly to temperamental chefs who in any way obstruct this mission by providing less than perfect dishes, or not at the perfect temperature, or not at just the right moment. On the other hand, chefs take a dim view of waiters who interfere with *their* perfect creations by not ordering or picking up at precisely the right time. All in all, a good kitchen is a shouting, jostling, chaotic place. The tranquility of order in the dining room belies the pandemonium in the kitchen.

Opening day is the worst. Never, ever, patronize a restaurant in its first week or so. Eventually these things settle down to a sort of rhythmic disorder.

At Mariani's, things hardly ever settled down at all. What with the Hungarians, the Serbs, the Greeks, the Italians, and the Turks, nearly every day presented a fascinating episode. Several are etched forever in my mind. One Saturday evening a waiter emerged with a roar from the kitchen, hotly pursued by the sous-chef wielding a meat cleaver. Through the dining room they raced, and into the bar where the avenging chef was finally subdued by the bartender and several burly customers. He was relieved of his weapon, perhaps even of his job, and sent home. Thirty minutes later he reappeared at the back door, this time with a baseball bat. Fortunately he was spotted in time and hustled out without further commotion.

One evening there was seated for dinner at one of my tables the famous boxer Floyd "Bobo" Olson and his wife. Bobo had won the world middleweight championship the previous evening at the Cow Palace, earning several hundred thousand dollars. Bobo attracted a lot of attention, and the waiter Filipe and I provided exquisite service, anticipating Bobo's largesse.

Bobo left of tip of exactly seventy-five cents.

"The sonovabitch," said Filipe, "I hope he loses his next fight."

One day a new waiter, Angelo, arrived on the scene. It developed that Angelo had preciously worked for twenty years at Ernie's, one of the very finest restaurants in San Francisco. I asked Angelo how come he was no longer at Ernie's.

"Well, it's this way," he said. "You see, I'm from Turkey, and I had my own little way of greeting customers. I would bow low and say to them in Turkish, '*Appapiso!*' and they would say '*Appapiso* to you Angelo.' This was my trademark.

"One evening," he continued, "The Turkish consul, unknown to me, was brought to my table, and I gave him my usual greeting. But you see, it was my own private joke. In Turkish *Appapiso* means kiss my ass."

"And that is why I am no longer working at Ernie's."

Today, more than fifty years later, Mariani's is still in operation at the same location. I doubt if it's still as exciting.

At the end of the school year I skipped my own graduation in order to attend Jackie's at St. Catherine's in St. Paul. I had become some-what concerned about our relationship. She had had surgery for a tumor in the uterus the previous winter and was apprehensive about having children. When I arrived for her graduation, it became clear for a number of reasons that her priorities had changed. She was no longer interested in planning a wedding, and decided to do a year of graduate work in English. We did not break up, but our relationship had clearly changed.

I returned home disappointed, but it was time to begin studies for the bar exam in October. I, along with nearly everybody else in our class, enrolled in the bar review course taught in San Francisco by Bernard J. Witkin. Bernie Witkin was a legend in the bar review business. Three evenings a week for eight weeks he brought the law to life, reviewing the basic concepts of the ten or so areas of law covered in the bar exam, along with the "hot issues" likely to be covered in each subject. He was a bar exam prophet. All of this he did with great skill, charm, and levity. For the first time I really felt I understood what the law was all about. I credit Professor Witkin with getting me my license to practice law.

We used as our guide Witkin's 3-volume *Summary of California Law*. Fifty years later, when I returned to California in 1994, Bernie Witkin was still giving his bar review course; but now his *Summary of California Law* consisted of 32 volumes!

The California bar exam, considered one of the toughest in the country, was a three-day ordeal: eight hours a day of writing, identifying issues and solving problems in fact situations covering all areas of the law. When the results came out the following January, everyone in our class had passed. I doubt if any class in any school has had a 100% pass rate before or since.

After the bar exam I had time to paint the exterior of my parents' home, and then boarded a train to Washington DC to begin my new life in the Officer Candidate Corps at the U.S. Marine Base in Quantico, Virginia.

7.

UNITED STATES MARINE CORPS, 1954-1958

Lean, Mean, Fighting Machine

After a day in Washington, not believing I was really seeing the Capitol, the Washington monument, the Lincoln Memorial and the other historic sites I had read about all my life, I took the train to Quantico, 35 miles south, arriving on November 15, 1954.

The officer candidate program was eleven weeks of living hell. This was so by design, as it was the length of time the Marine Corps allotted itself to turn a bunch of useless, worthless, pampered, soft, vermin-like college boys into rough, tough, disciplined fighting leaders of men. We were given the rank and pay of Pfc. and addressed always as "candidate."

From reveille at 5:30 AM to lights out at 10 PM, seven days a week, including Christmas and New Year's, we were herded, hounded, shouted at and driven, to become United States Marines. It worked. By drilling and marching, by learning to clean, dismantle, and shoot a rifle, through the obstacle course, through long, arduous hikes with full pack, through endless hours sitting in classrooms learning military history and military tactics, by putting them into practice with field maneuvers, by digging and huddling in foxholes through cold rainy nights, and by learning, sometimes the hard way, the importance of instant, unquestioned obedience to commands, we were becoming part of a great military organization. We gradually came to see in ourselves and our comrades qualities and strengths that we never knew we had. And we were proud. Each of us was a member of the BEST squad, the BEST platoon, and the BEST company in the BEST military service, the Marine Corps.

As in all such situations, we came from diverse backgrounds—farms and small towns and big cities. There did seem to be a disproportionate number of Irish Catholics from Boston, much to my liking, and I developed lifelong friendships with some of them. Also, in the two companies (about 200 men), seven or eight of us were law school graduates and thus three years older, which created a special comradeship among us.

The day I graduated and received the gold bars of a second lieutenant in the United States Marine Corps in February 1955 was probably the proudest day of my young life. At 5'10" and 134 lbs., I viewed myself as the personification of the lean, mean, fighting machine.

But we could hardly consider ourselves officers equipped to lead men into battle. That would come in the next phase of our training. The Marine Corps views every officer, no matter what his ultimate specialty, as first and foremost an infantry officer, starting as a platoon leader commanding 44 troops. Thus the next phase was five months of infantry training, called Basic School.

First we were given ten days of liberty, and I got a military hop back to California for a joyous reunion with my parents and Mary Lu, and also Pat and Frank, who naturally expressed pride in seeing me in my second lieutenant's uniform. It was also an opportunity to be sworn in to the California bar, as I had missed the group ceremony in January.

In Basic School we were still not treated as officers but as students, and continued to live in barracks and take our meals in mess halls. But we were permitted to have cars (I bought a 1948 Dodge for $400) and were given liberty from Saturday noon until Sunday evening. Most of us spent our weekends in Washington trying (with limited success) to meet girls, or as summer came on, surfing, drinking, and looking for women at Virginia Beach.

In Basic School we received further training in military history and tactics, at the platoon, company, battalion and regimental levels. Again there were long hot days in the classroom (during which I developed the art of sleeping without nodding), followed by field exercises under simulated combat conditions. Rotating positions of leadership were assigned to all students during these maneuvers.

There were of course the occasional screw-ups. One night I was put in charge of a night compass march. This involved leading my platoon several miles through the Virginia wilderness on a moonless night, using only the compass for guidance. It was a terrible trek. We thrashed through the underbrush, fell over dead trees, and stumbled into a creek. When we finally reached our destination I discovered to my dismay that we had followed the correct route, but were twenty yards off line; just to our right was a dirt road.

On the firing range, I qualified as s sharpshooter on the rifle (one notch below expert) and as an expert with the pistol.

One of the best things about Basic School was learning to use the many weapons employed by the Marine Corps. We fired mortars, artillery, and bazookas. Operating a flamethrower was the greatest feeling of power since the jackhammer at PG&E. Whenever I got fed up with the rain and muck of the red Virginia clay or the heat and humidity, I would say to myself, "But when else in life would I have the opportunity to operate a machine gun or ride in a tank?"

Basic School finally came to an end with the traditional Three Day War, during which everything we had learned was to be applied in one gigantic moving battle. Actually it mostly involved marching for 72 hours in the oppressive heat and humidity of a Virginia August. I did learn one thing in this experience, even though it was just simulated combat: As just one of the troops in line, you never know just what the hell is going on up front. All the action takes place only at the head of the line, and mostly it's just confusion and blindly following orders. I have heard this observation made many times by soldiers and journalists who have been in combat.

Another rule of combat seems to be that the smallest guys get to carry the biggest weapons, and vice versa. In our company it seemed that all the small and wiry guys like myself were assigned machine guns. Marching with a full pack and a machine gun meant carrying about 90 lbs. The jocks on the other hand, many of whom had been excused periodically during the summer to play baseball with the Quantico team, got to carry pistols. We further noted, with some bitter satisfaction, that many of them collapsed from exhaustion during the three days and had to be carted off, while all of us smaller guys made it to the end. Perhaps the jocks were just smarter after all. We all graduated.

Just before graduation, each of us received orders for our permanent duty assignment. I was overjoyed to be assigned to the 1st Marine Division Legal Office at Camp Pendleton, California. My very close friend, Stu Land, whom I had first met on the train from Washington to Quantico, was also assigned to Camp Pendleton, to the Base Legal Office.

But first all the lawyers were assigned to the Naval Justice school at Newport, Rhode Island, for seven weeks of training in military law.

Jackie came to Washington for a short visit, and we toured all the sights and took a brief trip to Ocean City, MD. At the end of her visit we agreed to remain "good friends." She was about to begin her high school teaching career at White Bear Lake, a suburb of St. Paul, and I was about to embark upon my military legal career at last.

Leaving Basic School meant the end of barracks life. Living in a quonset hut with 43 other men for nine months creates a wonderful spirit of camaraderie, but it also causes a desperate longing for some privacy. I felt like a free man again.

Marine Lawyer

The Naval Justice School was a wonderful experience, and we all felt especially fortunate to be there during September and October, to witness the autumnal splendor of a New England leaf season.

During the seven weeks, we learned the Uniform Code of Military Justice from cover to cover, and received hands-on experience in mock trials and appellate procedure. Military courts, especially general courts-martial, operate pretty much like civilian courts, with a few exceptions. The counterpart of a civilian jury is a "court," composed of a minimum of five and maximum of nine officers, selected by the commanding general of the Division or of the Base. In most places, at least in the Marine Corps, court members are selected at random from a pool and serve for a fixed period, much like civilian jurors. Any member who has knowledge of the defendant ("accused" in the military) or of the crime(s) charged is automatically excused. If an accused is an enlisted man he is entitled to have one-third of the court composed of enlisted men. This option is rarely exercised, because enlisted court members are likely to be senior sergeants who are believed to have less tolerance for military infractions than officers.

Every accused has the benefit of the presumption of innocence, and his or her guilt must be proved beyond a reasonable doubt. However, a conviction is obtained by a vote of two-thirds of the court, rather than a unanimous verdict as is required in civilian courts.

In general courts-martial, a fully qualified military lawyer is appointed to represent every accused, who in addition may retain civilian counsel if he so desires and has the necessary funds. Every GCM is presided over by a Law Officer (the equivalent of a civilian judge) who must be an experienced trial lawyer and hold the rank of major or above. Being a Law Officer is a full time duty assignment.

Crimes charged can be all of those commonly recognized in civilian life, plus a few others specifically related to military life, such as absence without leave, desertion, disobedience of an order, conduct unbecoming an officer, and specific conduct "prejudicial to good order and discipline."

If an accused is convicted, the court then reconvenes to determine the punishment, with maximums set in the UCMJ, also by a two-thirds vote.

Before sentencing, every accused has the right, through his counsel, to present evidence of extenuating circumstances ("he is a Native American who could not adjust to military life and went directly back to his reservation without attempting to hide out"), or in mitigation ("he has no prior offenses and is a good auto mechanic/tank driver/mess kit repairman"). The accused also has the right to make a sworn or unsworn statement on his own behalf.

Penalties may include reduction in rank, forfeiture of pay, a punitive discharge, and a prison term ("confinement at hard labor"), as set forth in the code section describing the crime.

Though much has been written and said about "command influence" in the military, I can say that in my almost three years of prosecuting and defending Marines in general courts-martial, I never saw an example of a commander attempting to influence the outcome of a case. It is true that certain commanders put special emphasis on going after certain types of crimes, such as drug dealing, drunk driving, or even sexual misconduct. But the same can be said of local and federal district attorneys and all the way up to attorneys general, governors, and presidents. The public is forever being galvanized into some "war against crime," and the enemy varies with time and circumstances—from street crimes to drugs to organized crime to terrorism.

Concerning the "fairness" of military courts vs. civilian courts: Looking back now, after some 35 years of participating in both, and on both sides of the courtroom, I have concluded that if I were guilty I would rather be tried by a civilian jury. But if I were really innocent, I would rather rely on a military court. This is why: I believe a civilian jury can be more easily swayed by an able defense counsel using sympathy or emotion or powerful oratory, or even by extraneous factors such as an overbearing prosecutor; thus a guilty defendant has a better chance of getting off in a civilian court. But military officers are more likely just to examine the hard facts to arrive at the proper verdict. On the other hand, I believe that if I were really innocent and had a valid defense, the military court could be more likely to examine it carefully and rationally, and less likely to have the civilian juror's common view that "he wouldn't be here if he hadn't done *something* wrong." Perhaps that's just another way of saying, if you're innocent, you're better off with a more intelligent jury, and if you're guilty, hope to get a gullible one.

However, for a juror good common sense is more important than brilliance. I once had the privilege of hearing two of the greatest final arguments ever heard in a criminal trial. The scene was the U.S. District Court in Washington, DC in the early 1970's, and the defendant was Bobby Baker, Secretary of the U. S. Senate, whose mentor was Lyndon Johnson. Bobby Baker was a powerful figure in Washington who because of his position was able to dispense favors and influence legislation. He was charged with accepting bribes from lobbyists for doing just that.

Baker was represented by Edward Bennett Williams, by all accounts one of the country's greatest trial lawyers ever. The Department of Justice prosecutor was Bill Bittman, in his early thirties, a friend of mine, who had just successfully completed the trial of Jimmy Hoffa.

It had been a long and fiercely contested, high-profile case. On the last day the courtroom was packed with journalists and with other lawyers, who knew this would be a historic moment. The final arguments lasted several hours. Williams met all expectations as an orator, but Bittman was every bit his match. The jury hung on every word from both advocates. When it was over, everyone in the courtroom was drenched with perspiration, simply from the tension.

Baker was convicted on all counts. The point of the story is this: The foreman of the jury was a mail clerk, a lowly GS-2 government employee. After the trial, when asked by the press to comment on the eloquence of Mr. Williams, he replied, "It was one of those stirring speeches—a gem of a speech—but we weren't interested in it, you see. We knew that he was trying to save his client." Here was a juror, chosen by the others as their leader, who was not highly educated or from a privileged class, but who was intelligent and possessed of common sense. Another juror commented, "Baker had nothing to go on other than he had a good lawyer. We're not lawyers, we're interested in the facts."

And that is why I have great faith in our jury system. I firmly believe that in *almost* all cases, twelve men and women, chosen at large from the community and deliberating together, will somehow arrived at the right conclusion and justice will be done.

But then I have never served on a jury.

During our seven weeks at Newport, we spent most weekends in Boston. Tim Murphy, a fellow lawyer from our class, had two lovely cousins there, the McSweeney sisters, who added considerably to our enjoyment of the city.

All too soon we finished our course in military justice and it was time to head back to California and to Camp Pendleton. I was glad that my hitchhiking days were over and I could drive my own car.

On Being Cosmopolitan

Having lived on both coasts and in the Midwest, I have found that most people think that folks from the east coast and from the west coast are more cosmopolitan than Midwesterners. We tend to think of Boston Brahmins and San Franciscans as representing the ultimate in urbane sophistication. This is a myth. Just the opposite is true. Here is the reason. If you grew up in Boston, a city so lovely and with so much history and culture, you might never see the need to travel west of the

Charles River. Similarly, many San Franciscans can think of no reason to leave their beautiful city. Anything east of the Sierras is not worth the bother.

But if you were born and raised in Kansas or North Dakota, you can't wait to get the hell out of there. You want to see what else the world has to offer, besides corn and wheat and snow! So Midwesterners, by far, travel more and thus become more cosmopolitan.

Two well known contemporary U.S. Senators, Robert Dole from Kansas and Arlen Specter from Pennsylvania, both came from the town of Russell, pop. 4696, in the middle of Kansas. Who can name two from San Francisco? How can this be? The answer is simple. Both of those guys, as soon as they could, hopped a freight out of Russell. I've driven through there, and I don't blame them.

New Yorkers are a special case. They don't leave because they believe that life everywhere is as grim as theirs.

Camp Pendleton, California

Camp Pendleton is a sprawling base with 20,00 Marines, at Oceanside, about 100 miles south of Los Angeles and 25 miles north of San Diego. It is the home of the First Marine Division. The Division is supported by the Marine Corps Base, which provides the facilities, logistics, and support staff for the Division. I was assigned to the Division Legal Office, comprised of 10-12 officers and an enlisted staff of secretaries and court reporters (all males while I was there). The Base Legal Office was similarly staffed.

When I arrived in October 1955 the Division legal office was headed by Lt. Col. Fenton J. Mee, who was not only an outstanding lawyer, but was a combat veteran in World War II, having received two Silver Stars at Iwo Jima. Only the Congressional Medal of Honor is higher than a Silver Star. Mee was a great leader of men, and morale was high in the office. The same was true in the Base legal office, to which my friend Stu

Land was assigned. Although the offices were separate, there was close coordination, and we all socialized together frequently.

Together these officers were among the finest group of lawyers with whom I have ever been associated. Many established outstanding careers after leaving the service. Stu Land became managing partner of Arnold & Porter, one of the top three law firms in Washington. Mitch Rogovin became successively general counsel of the IRS, Assistant Attorney General in charge of the Tax Division, and then one of the best criminal trial lawyers in Washington. Clem Snyder became a judge in Minnesota. Paul St. Amour presided as Law Officer in of the most prominent and complex trials coming out of the Vietnam War, involving the massacre of civilians by Marines; later Paul established a successful law practice in Boston. These and others with whom I served were, in addition to being outstanding lawyers, men of unimpeachable moral character. And they loved to have a good time too.

In the legal offices newly arriving lieutenants were assigned either to the prosecution or defense office, and were rotated every six months or so. After assisting in a trial or two, we were then solely responsible for our own cases. Thus after three years, Marine legal officers received more responsibility and had more trial work than most of their counterparts in civilian life.

Successful prosecution requires meticulous investigation and preparation, to ensure that each element of each offense, including specific criminal intent, can be proved beyond a reasonable doubt. My experience in debate preparation came in handy.

I was stimulated by the discipline required to be a prosecutor, but found defense work even more challenging and enjoyable. It requires more creativity and imagination, first to search for the weaknesses in the prosecution's case (there are few open-and-shut cases), and then to search for a plausible (but not fictitious) theory of defense. Sometimes there is none, and the client is best advised to plead guilty or attempt a plea bargain.

One of the first cases to which I was assigned illustrates the challenges faced by a defense counsel.

U.S. v. Sergeant Pimentel

Background: After an enlisted marine finished boot camp at San Diego, he was assigned to Camp Pendleton for 30 days of intensive infantry training. Much of it took place at night, requiring overnight camping. The custom was for two men to share a tent, with each carrying a "shelter half." Sgt. Pimentel was in charge of a platoon of trainees. Since he too had only a shelter half, he would select one of his trainees to share a tent.

When Sgt. Pimentel appeared in my office, he had been charged with six counts of sexual abuse and was facing a general court-martial. It was charged that over a period of thirty days he had attempted to sexually molest each of six different young tent-mates.

I was advised by experienced trial attorneys that it is easy to defend against one charge of homosexual conduct because it is the accuser's word against that of the accused. But it is virtually impossible, they said, to beat the rap when you are facing six accusers on six different occasions; therefore it would be wise to try to negotiate a plea.

But it was too early to make this determination. Besides, the sergeant vehemently denied each and every allegation. "It flat our just didn't happen," he insisted. He was not the toughest looking marine I had ever met, but he displayed none of the feminine characteristics that a court might identify as suspicious. His service record showed ten years of merely average performance but no prior offenses.

I interviewed the accusers, as well as several other men in the platoon, and the unit commander (a captain), and looked a the offense reports. Then I prepared my defense.

At the outset of the trial, things looked grim. The accusers were all fresh-faced innocent appearing young men who claimed that Sgt. Pimintel had attempted to fondle them during the night, but that his approaches had been rebuffed.

On cross-examination, I first asked each to repeat the date on which the incident occurred. I then began to develop my case. I was able to elicit from each of the young men that Sgt. Pimentel worked them very hard, that he was super-critical of their performance, that his inspections were excessively fault-finding, and so on. It became clear that they did not like their sergeant and, encouraged by me, were only too eager to voice their criticisms. All six also testified that they were close friends with each other.

The unit commander verified that Sgt. Pimentel was a stern taskmaster, but those were just the qualities he wanted in his sergeant—someone who could mold these young men into real Marines.

Sgt. Pimentel testified in his own behalf and denied each allegation of misconduct. He came across as a good witness, and stood up well under cross-examination. He acknowledged that he may not have been well liked by the men, but he was trying to do his best for the good of the Corps.

In summation I laid out our defense. This appeared to be a conspiracy by a group of disgruntled young men out to get rid of their sergeant. They were all close friends and Sgt. Pimentel had made their lives miserable. They had the motivation. None of them complained to the captain at the time of the alleged acts, which would be the natural thing to do. Instead, all filed their complaints on the same day. Given these facts, could the court conclude beyond a reasonable doubt that my client, with ten years of blemish-free service, had committed these reprehensible acts?

Sgt. Pimentel was acquitted.

Epilogue to the case: After the acquittal, Sgt. Pimentel was called before an administrative board and then handed an Undesirable Discharge as a homosexual. I represented him and objected strenuously, to no avail. Administrative boards are not bound by the reasonable doubt rule, and they booted him out of the service.

As I was to discover years later as a criminal defense lawyer in Washington, a civilian government employee can also be acquitted of a crime and then be fired for having committed it.

Gladys Towle Root

If I were to compile a list of unforgettable characters I have met, Gladys Towle Root would surely be on it. A famed Los Angeles criminal lawyer, Ms. Root was retained by the families of four young Marines charged with robbing a Post Exchange at Camp Pendleton. I was the appointed defense counsel.

Gladys was flamboyant. A tall, slender, and graceful woman in her fifties with auburn hair, she costumed herself like an aristocrat form the Gay Nineties. She wore floor length velvet gowns, with a brocaded bodice and a pinched waist. Her huge hats were of the period, and her rings were like small lanterns. He name should have been Floradora.

Imagine her walking into a military courtroom to face a court of seven Marine officers. I expected to be embarrassed for her, but she was so natural, and so good at what she did, trying cases, that instead of antagonizing the court members she absolutely charmed them. The prosecution had a strong case and the trial should have been over in three days, but Gladys managed to stretch it out for two weeks. She knew the rules of evidence inside out, and used them to gain every possible advantage. In two weeks I learned more about how to deal with evidence—how to present it, and when and how to object to it—than at any other time in my life. Gladys put on a great show, but she never acted the fool, unlike some other so-called "great" courtroom personas I have seen. She could be hard as nails one moment and soft as butter the next. At times she had the prosecutor muttering to himself and the Law Officer ready to strangle her, but she would remain calm, looking for the edge, just fighting for the constitutional rights of her clients.

The court members were not turned off by her performance, but were impressed, and said so after the trial. I think they really wanted to find some way to acquit somebody of something, just for Gladys. But the evidence was overwhelming, and the four accused were duly convicted, dishonorably discharged, and sent off to prison.

Gladys had gained her fame in Los Angeles by representing homicide defendants. I once asked her how she got into this area of the law. She said that when she came out of law school she wanted to do domestic relations work. Her first client was woman seeking a divorce. Gladys urged the woman to go home and try to work things out. The woman went home and put a butcher knife through her sleeping husband's heart. "And that is how I got into the homicide business," said Gladys.

She was most proud of the fact that in 27 years, none of her clients had gone to the gas chamber. I guess when you spend a lifetime defending murderers, you look for your consolation where you find it.

In the fall of 1956 a wonderful housing opportunity presented itself, through Chuck Getchell, a navy lawyer at the Base legal office and a good friend. Chuck was from San Marino, an exclusive area of Pasadena. In the 1920's some upscale families from San Marino had established a secluded colony of homes on the beach just south of Oceanside, which they called St. Malo. This must have been one of the first gated communities. The houses were half-timbered in the Normandy style and had large living rooms with fireplaces, three bedrooms, and charming terraces. There were winding paths and flower gardens. It was a scene out of a Thomas Kinkead painting. The San Marino families used them only as summer homes. Chuck's family knew one of the owners, a widow name Mrs. Graden, who offered the house to him for the period September through May. Chuck invited Stu Land and me to join him, and we gratefully accepted. Not only was the house captivating; the beach was secluded and there was a tennis court in the complex. Most of the parties given by the Division and Base legal offices were held at our house in St. Malo. We also arranged for friends to rent a couple of the other houses.

Forty-two years later I took my wife and children to visit St. Malo and nothing had changed, except there was a guard at the gate, and I had to talk my way in. My family could not believe that I had lived as a Marine in such delightful surroundings.

I lived at St. Malo until I left the Marine Corps in February 1958, except for the summer of 1957, when I rented a house in San Clemente with Al McGee, another lawyer, who after completing his service set up a solo practice in his home town of Atlantic City.

During this period I also taught business law at the community college in nearby San Marcos two evenings a week for a couple of semesters, during which time I gained an appreciation for the tremendous amount of preparation involved in teaching, as well as the relatively low pay.

I also had the opportunity on a couple of occasions to participate in war games at the Division level, as an umpire. I followed the progress of the troops in the field, designating casualties, determining when an objective was taken, and so forth. It also involved spending a night on a landing ship and then taking part in an amphibious landing. It was instructive and great fun.

The Strange Saga of Sergeant Owens

This was the most interesting case I had as defense counsel at Camp Pendleton. It started as another PX robbery. Three assailants held up the cashier at gunpoint, forced him to turn over all the cash, and then viciously pistol whipped him. But the MP's apprehended them leaving the scene. They were arrested, photographed, fingerprinted, and all three signed confessions that evening. All three were sergeants, and their leader was Sgt. Owens, who persuaded the others to help him carry it out. I was appointed Owens' defense counsel.

My client had been a Marine for twelve years, was a Korean combat veteran, and until this event had maintained a clean record, as had his accomplices. He had a loving wife and child and no serious financial problems (although the other two did), and there seemed to be no plausible explanation or motivation for the crime.

At our first interview, Sgt. Owens flatly denied any involvement. Shown his photograph at the scene and his signed confession, he acknowledged both, but steadfastly maintained that he would never do such a thing. I sent him to the Base hospital for psychiatric evaluation. Meanwhile the other two pleaded guilty, were convicted, and sentenced to dishonorable discharges and ten years in prison.

Owens was examined at length and evaluated by Dr. John Mullin, a Navy captain psychiatrist and one of the most competent and dedicated doctors I have ever met. Capt. Mullin uncovered a history of bizarre behavior by Owens, beginning in Korea, where it was corroborated that on at least two occasions he had gone out alone on night patrol and had returned with heads of North Korean soldiers. This being a combat situation, apparently no action was taken by his superiors.

Captain Mullin concluded that Owens was suffering from a form of paranoid schizophrenia, with two distinct personalities. Further, Dr. Mullin diagnosed Owens as having incurred traumatic amnesia in connection with the robbery, meaning that he truly did not remember those events, and therefore denied them. Mullin could not determine the motivation for the robbery by the "other self" because of the amnesia.

The bad news was that Capt. Mullin said that Owens' current condition did not meet the high standard required for a defense of insanity. He could not conclude that Owens did not know the difference between right and wrong, nor that he was unable to adhere to the right, nor that he was unable to cooperate in his own defense (the "McNaghton's Rule" for determining competency to stand trial, used in most civilian courts and by the military). On the latter point, I found Owens to be mostly lucid if sometimes vague and rambling. I could not discuss the crime with him because he did not remember it. But amnesia did not constitute a defense.

The case was set for trial. I explained to Owens that a guilty pleas would be the best course of action, since there was no defense, and if the details of the bloody pistol whipping came out at a trial, the court would likely be very hard on him at sentencing. I also explained that a guilty plea would require him to admit each and every element of the crimes, and the specific intent to commit them.

Owens agreed to do as I recommended, but said he would be lying, because he did not commit the crimes. However, if it would help him, he would be willing to lie.

This presented me with a serious ethical dilemma. It is unethical for a lawyer to permit his client to lie on the stand. In this case he would actually be telling the truth, but he would *think* he was lying. Could I permit him to do that? If I didn't permit him to tell the truth because he did not believe it to be true, the result would be a trial, to his detriment.

After a great deal of soul searching, I decided I could not permit him to plead guilty under these circumstances, and we would have to go to trial. Hopefully hie mental illness, though not amounting to a defense, could be offered in mitigation at the time of sentencing.

On Sunday evening of the day before the trial, I got a call from Capt. Mullin. He had spent most of the weekend with Owens at the hospital and had now concluded that Owens was a full-blown schizophreniac. He was ready to testify that Sgt. Owens was incompetent to stand trial, and in all probability was incompetent at the time of the offense.

On Monday morning, faced with this testimony from Capt. Mullin, who was the ranking medical officer at the hospital and whose reputation was renowned throughout the Naval establishment, the Division commander ordered that Owens be sent to the Oak Knoll Naval Hospital in Oakland for a 90-day evaluation. There a battery of psychiatrists fully supported Capt. Mullin's conclusions. All charges against Owens were dismissed. After a year of treatment at Oak Knoll, he was determined to be cured. He was released, and given an honorable discharge and a medical disability pension.

Was justice done? I believe so. In our legal tradition, a person judged mentally incompetent is not responsible for his acts, however reprehensible. What about the other sergeants? They ended up with ruined lives while the person who started the whole thing was exonerated. But they were responsible for their own actions, even though they were recruited by someone who was not. Life has strange twists and turns.

New Developments in the Kennelly Family

By 1956 Frank and Patricia Thibault had brought four beautiful children into the world: Michael, Mary Ann, Larry, and Jeanie. But in the mysterious way in which God plans our lives, both Mary Ann and Jeanie had been diagnosed with cystic fibrosis, and were not doing well. The Minnesota winters were very difficult for them, so Patricia and Frank decided to move to California, where the climate would be more conducive to their health. Naturally this delighted all of us in California, though I'm sure it was difficult for Frank to leave his large family in St. Paul.

They rented and later purchased a home in Saratoga, just a few miles from Santa Clara, at 13347 Fontaine Drive. Frank landed a job teaching English at Fremont High School, and later at Sunnyvale High School, from which he eventually retired.

Cystic fibrosis was not a well known disease at the time, and treatment was in its early stages. There still is no known cure, but medical science over the years has found methods and medications to prolong the lives of its victims, as well as improve the quality of their lives, so that today it is not uncommon for a CF patient to live well into the thirties and forties.

Such was not to be the case for beautiful little Mary Ann, who died at age 5 and adorable Jeanie, not yet 3. Their deaths were very difficult for the parents and for the whole family, and especially for my father, who was very close to little Jeanie.

Frank and Patricia subsequently had five more children, three of whom had CF. Susan died at 16, John at 19, and Ann Marie just past her 21st birthday. All were very special children, with unbelievable courage, an inner glow and warmth that seems to be a special gift of CF children, and a love for others that has been an inspiration to all who have been privileged to know them.

People have wondered how Patricia and Frank could accept the loss of five children. But anyone who knows them knows of their great personal courage and strong moral character, and knows that their strong faith has helped to sustain them. People also wonder how they could face having more children, knowing what a gamble it was. But if they had taken that attitude, they would not have had Larry, Barbara, and Jane, who along with Mike are four of the most genuinely good people I have ever known, and the same is true for all of Patricia and Frank's grandchildren, none of whom, praise the Lord, have CF.

There was also big news with my sister Mary Lu. At age 20, after two years of college and an active social life, she opted for the religious life, and entered the convent of the order of St. Joseph of Carondelet in Los Angeles. My parents drove her down, and on the night before she entered, in February 1957, my Marine buddies and I gave a big party for her at St. Malo.

During her early training and while I was still at Camp Pendleton, I was able to drive up to visit her about one Sunday a month. The convent was located on a mountain high above Beverly Hills, with views looking down on the homes of Hollywood celebrities. It was great seeing her frequently again, and she was very happy.

Plans for Civilian Life

I was due to be released from active duty in November 1957, upon completion of my three year commitment, but I was enjoying my life and my job so much that I asked to be extended, and received a 3-month extension to 15 February 1958.

This gave me some extra time to decide what I wanted to do next with my life. Going into private civil practice in San Jose sounded extremely dull; this was confirmed by visits to some Santa Clara alums who were doing just that. I had a few perfunctory interviews with big law firms in San Francisco, but they were not very interested in me because I had not come from a big fancy law school, and I was turned off by their stuffiness and elitist attitude. These senior partners were *not at all* interested in my Marine Corps trial experience, the military being an inferior class to them.

That pretty much made up my mind. What I really wanted was to spend some time in Europe, not just a short visit, but to live and work there for a period of time. My father was not happy to hear this. He thought it was time for me to settle down, find a job in some big law firm and work my way from the bottom to the top. Having to justify my flight of fancy, I told him that in my view, which remains my view today, life, even for a professional person, is not necessarily a matter of moving from the bottom to the top of a single ladder. Life can be a whole series of different professional experiences. Granted one does not have the right to waste his time and talents, particularly if his parents have sacrificed on his behalf, but those talents can be used in a lot of different ways and in a lot of different places. I assured him that I intended to find a meaningful job in Europe.

Then all I had to do was find it. I wrote to my high school buddy, Chet Taylor, who was now a lawyer with the Air Force at Chateauroux, France, and asked if he knew of any civilian legal jobs with the Air Force in Europe. As luck would have it, he did. In fact, Chet was about to be transferred to Weisebaden, Germany, and he arranged for me to take his place at Chateauroux, providing that I could get to France on my own and become a "local hire," so that I would not have to go through the civil service competitive examination process. Done. I booked passage on the *S.S. Stockholm,* sailing from New York on March 19, 1958.

[Twenty-five years later I had the opportunity to return Chet's favor. He was about to retire from the Air Force and asked if I had any contacts with law firms in Washington who might be interested in his experience. Chet had risen to the rank of brigadier general as a Staff Judge Advocate, enjoyed an outstanding reputation in the military, and probably knew more about government procurement than anybody else in the Air Force. This made him extremely attractive to large firms representing defense manufacturers seeking government contracts. I contacted my friend Gerry Gilbert, the hiring partner with Hogan & Hartson, one of Washington's most prestigious firms, and he was delighted to bring Chet in as a partner with a very nice six-figure salary. My opportunity to return Chet's favor was a fine example of the circularity of life.]

8.

LES BONS TEMPS EN LA BELLE FRANCE,
1958-1960

Chateauroux is in the very center of France, about 150 miles south of Paris. It is in the lower part of the Loire Valley, one of the most beautiful areas of France. After viewing slides of the area, I could hardly wait.

The *Stockholm*, at 20,000 tons, was a relatively small ship, but she was sturdy enough to have survived a collision just off Boston a couple of years earlier with the Italian liner *Andrea Doria*, at 82,000 tons, in which the Italian ship went to the bottom.

Our destination was Copenhagen, and the passengers were mainly comprised of old Scandinavians heading home or people of my age, Scandinavians and Americans, heading to Europe for one reason or another, and out to have a good time en route. And we did, until the storms hit. March is not a good time to sail to northern Europe in a small ship. It was supposed to be a seven day trip, but it took nine days. One day we actually lost 175 miles. There were times when only a handful of hardy folks showed up for meals. By some quirk, I was one of them, until the very last day.

Nevertheless, it was a thrill to be in Europe at last. I took delivery of my new 1958 Renault Dauphine ($850), and headed across Denmark, stopping at the home of Hans Christian Andersen. All of Denmark looks like one of his fairy tales.

The next stop was Hamburg. I was eager to see what Germany looked like 13 years after the war. Hamburg had been heavily bombed and there were large vacant areas in the center of the city, but all in all the city looked quite prosperous, with new shops and apartment buildings (thanks to the Marshall Plan which rebuilt Germany, our enemy, but not France, our ally). Out of Hamburg, I drove as far as the East German border. It was a no-man's land, with watch towers and barbed wire, and about a half-mile of ploughed land planted with mines on either side. It was my first encounter with the actual Iron Curtain.

Then on to Holland. I was thrilled to see operating windmills, and people on the street actually wearing wooden shoes. I bought a pair, in a real shoe store, not a tourist shop.

At Groningen, Holland, I visited my cousin Pat Bitter from Dubuque. He was in his first year of medical school. Having been unable to gain admission to a U.S. medical school, he was accepted at the University of Gronigen, and began his sudies without knowing a word of Dutch. He and his wife Jean Ann and two (or was it three?) children were living in a tiny apartment heated by a coal stove, and he rode a bicycle to school. I don't know how he did it. To me Dutch is a totally incomprehensible language; everything sounds like either "hoffenofer" or "offenhofer." By the time Pat finished his medical training he had five children, and ultimately nine. They eventually moved to the San Francisco Bay area, and Pat became a very successful dermatologist. Nobody deserved success more than he.

After visiting Amsterdam, with its marvelous Rijksmuseum and the spectacular tulip gardens at Keukenhof, I arrived in Brussels just in time for opening day of the Brussels World Exposition, the first postwar World's Fair, and the first to be called "Expo." A great attraction was the Soviet Union pavilion, this being the first time the Soviets had presented an exhibition of its arts and industries (mostly industries) to the outside world. Of particular interest was a replica of Sputnik, the first ship to orbit the earth, the launching of which in 1957 shocked the United States and galvanized our own space program.

Then off to France! As I approached Paris, I couldn't believe I was seeing the Eiffel Tower on the horizon. The City of Lights at last! I picked up a student hitchhiker, who invited me to join him and his friends on the Left Bank that evening. Thus I spent my first night in Paris in a bohemian restaurant, seated at a long table quaffing red wine and enjoying *steak et frites* (400 francs—one dollar—per serving) with about a dozen students from France and elsewhere. Eat your heart out, Ernest Hemingway! My French and Spanish from high school and college were not all that helpful, but my new comrades spoke some English, and by the end of the rollicking evening I was speaking and comprehending all three fluently, or so I believed.

After a few days in Paris, congratulating myself for having made the right decision in coming to Europe, I headed south through Orleans, with its famous monument to Jeanne d'Arc—"Joanie on a Pony"—and into the chateau country of the Loire Valley. The French countryside was even more beautiful than I had imagined, with its many hedge-rows marking the boundaries of small farms (later eradicated with the advent of mechanized farming), the villages of gray stuccoed houses with red tile roofs and always an old church in the town square, the omnipresent *boulangeries* and *patisseries*, the horse-drawn wagons, and the farmers and workers, each wearing the obligatory French one-piece work suit and beret, and each with a cigarette dangling from his lips. It was spring; the wheat was up and the fields of red poppies were in bloom. The country roads, as well as the village streets, where shaded by plane trees on both sides, each perfectly manicured.

Chateauroux is just a few kilometers from Bourges, which is a charming medieval city containing one of the Seven Great Cathedrals of France. Chatearoux, on the Indre river, is not quite so charming. It was named after the red chateau of the Duc du Berry, its feudal landowner. It is also the birthplace of Balzac, who labeled it the "dirtiest city in France." An exaggeration, but Chareauroux of 1958 was a working-class city of about 60,000, home of a French airbase and, after the war, the headquarters of the U.S. Air Material Force, European Area. It was here that the Air Force negotiated all contracts with European suppliers for all of its procurement needs in Europe, from jet engines to ice cream.

Chateauroux made up in location for what it lacked in charm. Located in the center of France, it was to be the jumping off place for my travels through all of France and nearly all of Europe for the next two and a half years. And incidentally, the place where I was to work.

It would take a week to complete the paper work before I could become a civilian employee of the Air Force, which gave me the opportunity to drive over to Geneva. My friend Chuck Getchell, who was released from active duty about the same time as I, and having had a similar desire to see Europe, was studying at the Graduate School of International Studies in Geneva. A few months later, I successfully recommended Chuck for another civilian lawyer position at Chateauroux, and he was happy to accept. We rented an apartment "on the economy" at 2 rue Doree in Chatearoux.

Spring of 1958 was an exciting time to be in France. The Algerian revolution was at its climax, and the splintered and powerless French government seemed paralyzed, unable to put down the revolution and unwilling to grant independence. Premiers came and went in dizzying succession, unknown and unremembered. One premier, Pierre Mendes-France, managed to gain some notoriety by launching a national campaign against drunkeness. He urged that each adult agree to consume no more than *one litre* of wine per day. He suggested milk as an alternative. *Milk.* The public was outraged—an attack upon French liberty! The campaign was disbanded and Mendes-France soon followed his predecessors into oblivion.

In May 1958 the French paratroop command in Algeria, determined to keep Algeria as a French colony and led by some politically powerful generals who appealed to French nationalists, was threatening to land in Paris and carry out a military coup. I was in Paris on Sunday, May 13, when the government ordered tanks and other armored vehicles into the streets, in anticipation of a possible invasion from the sky.

Meanwhile Parisians, inured to the crisis, lined up at the cinemas along the Champs Elysees, as was their usual Sunday afternoon custom. The following week Gen. Charles DeGaulle, hero of the Resistance, who had been waiting in the wings, agreed to take charge of the government, providing a new constitution would we written giving the executive much greater power. The deal was brokered, the crisis averted, and the Fifth Republic was born, with DeGaulle as its president. Not long thereafter, Algeria was granted its independence.

At the Chateauroux legal office, Chuck and I worked in the section which reviewed for legal sufficiency all contracts negotiated with European contractors, to determine whether they were in compliance with Air Force procurement regulations. Although not as much fun as trying court cases, it was interesting work and involved frequent interaction with contracting officers.

Having just come from the Marine Corps, it took me awhile to get accustomed to the more informal style of the Air Force. There was very little saluting and there were no spit-shined shoes. There was much fraternization between officers and enlisted personnel. I was taken aback when on introduction, the First Sergeant in charge of all enlisted persons in the office addressed me by my first name and asked that I call him "Lou." But I soon came down off my high horse and enjoyed the friendliness and camaraderie of all the staff.

There were a good many American civilians employed at the base, including a nice group of young women, recent college graduates who had come, like myself, for the adventure. Civilians had access to the Officers Club, which was at all times a lively watering hole. The French civilians who worked at the base ("foreign nationals" as our insensitive government terms them) did not have access to these facilities, and there was very little fraternization between the French and the Americans, except off the base, and only the most intrepid Americans made an effort to get to know their French neighbors or learn their language. Yet many Americans became irritated at any French person who could not speak English.

The late 1950's was a great time to be young and living in Europe. It was a time when all the world seemed carefree. We were in good health, our jobs provided enough money, and life was an adventure. In the future would be mortgage payments, family responsibilities, and long range career concerns. But for now the major decision was what new region to explore the following weekend, and life's only nagging responsibility was to write home once in awhile.

This period was long before the influx of tourists of later decades, and travel was easy and inexpensive. One could go anywhere, even the big cities, and check into a hotel without advance reservations. Excellent meals could be enjoyed in the many savory restaurants in every town, including Chateauroux, for less than two dollars, not including the one dollar carafe of local wine. Paris was a little more expensive, but I stayed in Paris on both left and right banks for as little as two dollars a night (small room w/o bath; a larger room *avec bain* might go as high as $18). By some mysterious arrangement, American government employees could purchase gasoline coupons in almost every European country for 20 cents a gallon. In my two-and-a-half years in Europe I put more than 35,000 miles on my car.

Now, nearly 50 years later, I still enjoy going to Europe, but it does require more planning and preparation, and I'm always a little nostalgic for the halcyon days of the Fifties.

In June my friend Ed Ellis, a lawyer lieutenant at Chateauroux, and I took in the famous Le Mans 24-hour road race (*Le Quatre-Vingt de Le Mans*), less than a hundred miles west of Chateauroux. Being a road course rather than a track, it takes place on a two-lane country road which meanders around and finally encircles a large forest, with various spectator viewing locations. We were seated in a grandstand noteworthy for the fact that a couple of years earlier a race car had missed a curve and ploughed into this grandstand, killing a dozen or more spectators. Notwithstanding this note of apprehension, we found the race rather boring. A couple of hours watching Formula One cars flash past, without ever knowing who's in the lead, gets pretty tedious. So we decided to do something more adventurous.

With careful timing, we dashed across the raceway and into the woods. After hiking awhile, we came upon a farmhouse. The farmer, tending to his livestock, greeted us and invited us in. It was a typical French farmhouse, with the chickens and pigs on the ground floor and the living quarters just above. Monsieur and his wife and children seemed oblivious to the international event going on around them. We had a very pleasant conversation, Ed being more fluent in French than I, and we accepted their invitation to stay for the evening meal, which was simple and delicious. As darkness fell, we all made our way out to the highway to watch for awhile as the headlights of the racers flashed past. Then Ed and I bid our gracious hosts adieu and drove back to Chateauroux, feeling pleased and satisfied that we had had a day to remember.

In October 1958 I was sent to Germany for a 30-day training session at a U.S. Army procurement school. The school was in the Bavarian Alps, about an hour south of Munich, near Bad Tolz, and had been the former training base for Hitler's ski troops. The location was idyllic, on a hillside over looking the picture-book Bavarian village of Lengriess, and the autumn foliage added to the serenity of the place.

The students were military and civilian employees engaged in procurement work, from all the U.S. military bases in Europe. Our class was greatly enlivened by two young unmarried French women, Jacqueline Herail and her friend Huguette, both of whom worked for the U.S. Army at La Rochelle, on the west coast of France. I was one of the few single men in the class, and Jacqueline and I became instant friends. She was 25, with short dark hair, flashing dark eyes, and an effervescent personality. She was fluent in English, with a charming accent, and mixed well with everybody, as did Huguette. Jacqueline was from Bordeaux, had obtained employment with the Army after high school, and she and Huguette were sharing a flat in La Rochelle.

Lengriess was a wonderful experience. Besides learning a great deal about government procurement, there was plenty of time for socializing. A couple of weekends most of us went to Munich, one of the best cities in Europe, to take in the opera and the symphony and the beer halls. One weekend we were taken on a tour to Garmisch-Partenkirchen, the leading German winter sports resort; Oberammergau, home of the famous Passion Pllay; and Berchtesgaden, to Hitler's notorious Eagle's Nest. On weekdays, after class, Jacqueline and I often took long walks in the hills around Lengriess, where she taught me a number of French hiking and drinking songs, some of which I still remember.

After Lengriess, upon our return to our respective jobs, Jacqueline and I met together one or two weekends every month. Sometimes I would drive to La Rochelle, about 150 miles west of Chateauroux, or I would drive to Poitiers, about half way between, and she would take the train from La Rochelle. Or we would meet in places like Nantes or Perigeux. Each time we would explore as much of the surrounding countryside as time permitted, as she had not traveled in France a great deal either. In this way we covered most of the western half of France, seeing it for the first time together, from the Perigord and the Dordogne to Brittany and Normandy. We always had a wonderful time, gaining an appreciation of the very diverse topography, as well as the variety of local cultures and customs that comprise the unique country that is France. And of course we always enjoyed great cuisine and wines, even (and sometimes especially) in the smallest towns and villages.

Thanks to Jacqueline's patience, my fluency in French improved greatly, though not enough to avoid some embarrassing moments. On one occasion, I was asked by French friends how Americans are able to keep their bread fresh for several days, whereas French bread goes stale after one day. In French, I tried to explain that in America we add preservatives, using the French word *preservatif*. Unfortunately, *prservatif* translates to "contraceptive." But Jacqueline, too, sometimes had her problems with English. Once when we were entering a large city she looked around and said, "This town has many tall buildings; they are almost like—how you say in English—sky crappers."

Upon my return from Lengriess I was given an additional and most enjoyable duty. I was assigned to represent the Air Force in hearings before the European Services Board of Contract Appeals on contracts that originated out of Chateauroux, wherein there was a dispute between the government and a contractor on interpretation or performance of a contract. Both sides were represented by counsel, and briefs were written and oral arguments heard, much like a court of appeals. It was not as exciting as a criminal trial, but nevertheless challenging and enjoyable, and I was solely responsible for each of my cases. The ESBCA was headquartered in Weisebaden, but it was the custom to hold the hearings in the vendor's city. Consequently, I traveled at government expense not only to Weisebaden but to Paris and other cities like Madrid, Amsterdam, Brussels, and London, and usually managed to arrange a few days of sightseeing on each visit.

In February 1959 Jacqueline and Huguette invited me to La Rochelle to celebrate my 29th birthday. They invited friends and prepared a fabulous dinner. Their third floor walk-up had a stove but no oven, so they roasted a turkey at a neighborhood bakery. Their friends brought gifts and a birthday cake and the wine and brandy flowed. Needless to say, I was very moved. Is it any wonder that I became a Francophile?

It is said that French people fall into two categories, Parisians and the rest of France. If that is so, and if Parisians tend to be rude and haughty sometimes, these friends certainly represented the rest of France. Incidentally, I once asked Jacqueline, "Why is it that the French are always criticizing Americans?" Her reply: "Don't worry; we are always criticizing ourselves too."

Sometime in the spring of 1959 Chuck Getchell met an American girl named Ann Winthrop from Ipswich, Mass. Later Ann and Chuck's sister landed jobs in Paris. They rented a five room apartment at 9 rue de Marignan, just a half block off the Champs Elysees. It became our Paris headquarters. Chuck contributed toward the rent, and I also stayed there on weekends when I was not out exploring the French countryside. (Nobody who came to Europe for fun stayed in Chateauroux on weekends.) Not surprisingly, Ann's place also became a popular hostel for relatives and friends and friends of friends who just happened to be visiting Paris, but Ann was generous with her hospitality.

There were additional opportunities for travel. As an active member of the Marine Corps Reserve, I was entitled (required, actually) to spend two weeks on active duty each year. Since there were no Marine bases in Europe, I was assigned in May 1959 to a small U.S. Naval Air Station at Blackpool, just outside of London. I took a hotel in London and rode the commuter train each day to Blackpool, where I did practically nothing, leaving me rested for the evenings and weekends to explore London. I saw lots of plays, including the original cast of *My Fair Lady*, with Rex Harrison and Julie Andrews, for which I got an orchestra seat for one pound ($2.80). That tour of duty got me promoted from first lieutenant to captain.

The following year (March 1960) I was sent to the legal office of the U.S. Navy Base at Port Lyautey, Morocco, near Rabat. There I met Jack Phillips, a navy lawyer lieutenant and his wife Kathleen, who were very gracious hosts and took me on sightseeing trips to Casablanca and Fez, both fascinating cities. Twenty-eight years later, when Jack and Kathleen were pursuing successful careers in Washington, Kathleen hired our son Tim as a fact checker at U.S. News and World Report, one of his first jobs out of college. Another example of the circularity of life.

In the summer of 1959 I was able to rent a 3-bedroom house in St. Georges-sur-Arnon, a village of maybe a hundred inhabitants, about 20 miles from Chateauroux. It was the largest and newest house in the village, built by a doctor in Paris whose parents lived in St. Georges. It was built as a vacation home, but the doctor apparently never had time for a *vacance*, so he rented it out. It was fully furnished, in a beautiful setting, and included a lovely garden which sloped down to a gentle stream (the Arnon), with a small rowboat. It also came with a caretaker. Monet would have been happy at "La Garenne." I certainly was.

At about the same time, I was given a French poodle by an American family that was relocating back to the states. Jacques was a two-year-old miniature (medium size), very intelligent, bilingual, *i.e.* he obeyed commands in two languages, and friendly with everyone. By now I really felt like a French country gentleman. Jacques became my constant companion; in France, dogs are welcome everywhere, even in hotels and restaurants.

Having secured the house, I then invited my parents to come and join me. Mom was most eager to come, but my dad was hesitant; he was 66, his health was fragile, and he was reluctant to travel so far. But he was tempted by the prospect of seeing Paris, which he had missed in World War I, and of visiting the battlefields where he had fought forty years before. He agreed to come for a few weeks.

In September 1959 they did come—and they stayed for eight months! They sailed from New York on the *S.S. United States*, the newest and fastest ship on the high seas. I met them when they docked at Le Havre. What a joy to see them after 18 months! We spent a couple of days in Normandy, visiting the D-Day beaches as well as Honfleur and the tapestries at Bayeux. An entry from my mother's diary reads: "Rates very reasonable—for example, our room in Bayeux for 3 of us, including evening dinner and breakfast, cost us about $8.00." We also stopped at Lisieux to visit the basilica and home of St. Theresa.

Then on to Paris! It was a great pleasure to show my parents this fabulous city, the old hand escorting the new tourists. Needless to say, they were thrilled. Another entry from Mom's diary: "What a city! Indescribable! I was so impressed and so excited driving down the Champs Elysees I cried." We stayed a few days, covering everything from the Tour Eiffel to High Mass at Notre Dame to Versailles to attending a concert by the New York Philharmonic, Leonard Bernstein conducting.

They loved the house in St. Georges and settled in very nicely. We made several more visits to Paris. Sometimes I took them with me on business trips, *e.g.* to Wiesbaden. They purchased a new Pougeot, just like the one I had recently purchased, and frequently went off for a week or two on their own, following itineraries I helped plan for them. We also visited, as promised, the battlefields where my father had fought with the French in the First World War: St. Mihiel, Soissons, Chateau-Thierry. It was a moving experience for him, and for us. He could identify tree lines and ridges and roads. He remembered a town and a restaurant where he had enjoyed a hot meal; it was still there. He was sure that they hadn't changed the checkered tablecloth in forty years.

After each new adventure they would rest up for a couple of weeks, then be off again. In this way they visited nearly all of France, as well as Belgium, Holland, Luxembourg, Italy, Spain, and parts of Germany, including Berlin. They spoke no foreign languages, but did very well with sign language and were treated kindly, because they themselves were gracious and patient. More than once tickets were found for them at "sold out" box offices.

All in all, they had a wonderful time, and I very much enjoyed having them. They stayed until May 1960.

In October 1959 Jacqueline and I took a two week trip to Italy. We enjoyed the charm of Venice, the cuisine of Tuscany, the art of Florence, and the beauty of Capri, and of course all of classical Rome. We were privileged to have seats overlooking the high altar at a Mass celebrated by Pope John XXIII, thanks to Father Louis Rogge, who was stationed in Rome at the time. Once again, no advance reservations were necessary anywhere.

For New Year's Eve that year, Jacqueline invited me to the home of her mother and stepfather in Bordeaux, to celebrate *Revillon*, the traditional feast to bring in the New Year.

Her parents were working class and of modest circumstances, but the spread her mother laid out that evening would exceed anything to be found at Maxim's or the Tour d'Argent. I wish I still had the list of twelve—count 'em 12—courses she prepared. We began at eight with an *aperitif*. Then the orgy began. There was a terrine of this and a galette of that and a quenelle of something else. There was homemade *potage* and a touch of *lapin* and a fish course and a meat course, each with exquisite sauces, followed by salad and a special gateau. There were white wines and red wines, all of the region, and at the end there was cognac and a cigar. It was a repast unmatched by anything I have had before or since, no offense intended to my gourmet chef wife. The conversation was in French, and I got more fluent as the evening progressed—or so it seemed to me.

It was almost 2 AM when I arose from the table, bid my grateful *adieux* and *Bonne Annee's* and staggered back to my hotel.

I discovered later that I had committed a terrible *faux pas*. I was supposed to take Jacqueline out dancing till dawn. Those French really know how to live.

During my sojourn in Europe I learned to ski. Up till then, I had never enjoyed winters. Ever since, I have always looked forward to the coming of snow. Of course it helps to live in a place where winter stays where it belongs, up in the mountains. The San Francisco Bay Area is one of the few places in the world where one can ski on one day and then come home and play golf or tennis the next.

In January 1960 my friend Doug Coleman suggested that we take two weeks and go to St. Anton, Austria, and really learn to ski. St. Anton, in the Tyrolean Alps, is where downhill skiing in Europe originated, and has the oldest continuing ski school. It took us a full two weeks of lessons, with our leather lace-up boots and long skis, compared to today's plastic boots, shorter skis, and vastly improved equipment when one can learn in just a few days. But at the end of two weeks we were able to get down any slope, however inexpertly.

Since then I have returned to St. Anton twice, more than forty years later, with our son Tim and our daughter Katy. St. Anton is even better now than it was then. There are 120 miles of trails and 70 lifts, including 10 gondolas. Over the past 45 years I have skied Vermont, Massachusetts, Pennsylvania, Aspen, Vail, Beaver Valley, Steamboat Springs, Sun Valley, Park City, Taos, and all the Lake Tahoe resorts, all of which are good and some sensational. But for my money you can't beat St. Anton.

At Lake Tahoe on Feb. 11, 2005, I achieved a long-planned goal: I skied deep powder and moguls on my 75th birthday. That evening, to impress my 22-month-old grandson Rowan, I stood on my head, from which position I dispensed the wisdom of the ages. He was not impressed. He did a somersault.

My son Tim has the best advice on getting ready for the ski season. Tim says forget about the treadmill and the stairmaster, the jogging and the deep knee bends. He says the way to get ready for the ski season is to find yourself a hill, go to the top, start running downhill, and practice falling down a lot.

By the summer of 1960 I began giving some thought to returning home. But first I wanted to see Ireland, as well as more of England and Wales. So in June I went to London and found a place that rented motor scooters. The proprietor asked, "Do you know how to operate it?" "Of course," I replied confidently, never having been on one in my life. I hopped on and gripped the handle, not realizing that the accelerator is in the handle, and shot out of the lot, across the street and into a brick wall. The kindly proprietor then gave me a few lessons and I was on my way.

After slogging in the rain for five straight days through the Cotswolds and Wales I was wet and cold, and twice upended the scooter going around curves ("Ay, them ruddy bends," commented one sympathetic farmer). The forecast for Ireland was more of the same, so I decided to call it quits. I scootered to Cardiff, put the thing on a train and headed back to London. It would be another fourteen years before I would finally get to Ireland, with my wife, and then I found it even more beautiful and friendly than I had expected.

There was something else I wanted to see: the Passion Play at Oberammergau, 1960 being in its ten-year cycle. One could only get tickets through a lottery, and I won two. I had become good friends with Ann Sebastian, who joined me. Ann was 23, a very attractive blonde with large expressive eyes and an All-American look. She was very bright and witty and thus great fun to be with. Ann was from Santa Fe and a recent graduate of The Colorado College in Colorado Springs who had made her way to Europe for fun, like the rest of us, and had taken a job as a secretary at the airbase.

The Passion Play was overlong (7 hours, in German) and somewhat dreary, done in the old melodramatic style. It rained a good part of the day, and although the stage is covered, the audience is not. But a trip through picturesque Bavaria is always worthwhile.

That final summer in Europe was rather frenetic. Knowing that before long I would have to return to the real world, I had to make the most of the time remaining. I had business trips to England and Paris, and pleasure trips back to Vienna and Venice. I awoke one morning and couldn't remember if I was in London or Vienna. It was then I knew that it was time to go home. I had covered all of France, and had visited Andorra, Monaco, and Liechtenstein, as well as 12 other countries, some of them more than once.

Chuck Getchell had returned to the states a couple of months earlier and had landed a job as an Assistant U.S. Attorney in San Francisco. (He and Ann Winthrop would be married the following year, in September 1961.) Chuck wrote that there might be another opening in his office and he would recommend me for the position. Things were looking up. Maybe I wouldn't have to go into a drudging private law practice in San Jose after all.

The timing was good because the Air Force in France was in a Reduction-in-Force mode, and by becoming one of those RIF'ed, I could get my transportation paid to my home of record, and could also apply for unemployment compensation. Ann Sebastian was ready to go too, as she had been accepted at San Francisco State in the graduate school of theater. Our departure date was August 15.

Some advance logistical planning was required. Ann and I were scheduled for a military hop to McGuire AFB in New Jersey, just outside of New York. My car was being shipped by freighter. And Jacques was booked on board the *S.S. France* out of LeHavre. Each was departing at a different time, and hopefully all would arrive in New York at about the same time.

Jacqueline and I met in Poitiers for poignant farewells, agreeing to stay in touch. [A couple of years later she married a Frenchman, and a few years after that, on a trip to the U.S., she and her husband visited my wife Susan and me in Washington. We had a delightful dinner and evening in our home.]

By some miracle dog, car, and people did arrive in New York on the same day. After spending a night with Ed Ellis (of *Le Mans* fame) Ann and I, along with Jacques, drove to Washington to visit Tim Murphy and other friends. Ann then flew to Denver, and Jacques and I drove across the country, stopping en route to visit friends and relatives.

In Denver I rejoined Ann and together we drove the rest of the way to San Francisco. My parents in Santa Clara were very happy to see me, and I them; I think my dad was equally happy to see Jacques, as the two had become great buddies in France. It was also wonderful to see Patricia and Frank and their kids again, and not long thereafter I drove down to Los Angeles to visit Mary Lu (now sister Thomas Patricia, after taking her vows).

*   *   *   *

The U. S. Attorney's office in San Francisco was located in the Federal Courthouse at 7th & Mission, now the home of the U.S. Court of Appeals for the 9th Circuit. Built in the early 20th century, it has some of the largest and most ornate courtrooms in the country, with high ceilings, mosaics, mahogany paneling—a majestic ambiance, as awe-inspiring as a cathedral. I walked into the courtroom of Chief Judge Goodman, and there was my friend Bill Cooney, representing the United States of America, conducting a jury trial. From that moment I knew this was the place for me.

I was interviewed by U.S. Attorney Larry Dayton, who said he would like to hire me, but there was a job freeze until after the November presidential election and possibly the inauguration in January. Although Mr. Dayton was a Republican appointee under Eisenhower, he never asked me my party affiliation, which I appreciated. Chuck Getchell told me it was a very congenial office, with about 15 Assistants. (I am told there are more than 70 today.)

I knew this was the one job I wanted, so it was just a matter of waiting. I moved back into my parents' home and began collecting unemployment compensation.

The election was approaching, and one day Ted Kennedy, then 31 years old, came to Democratic headquarters in San Jose to stir up interest in the campaign and recruit volunteers. I signed up as a precinct captain, which mostly involved distributing literature door-to-door (something at which I was experienced) and getting out the vote on election day. Later Ann and I heard John Kennedy at the Cow Palace, at which he announced his historic proposal for the creation of a Peace Corps. It became one of the most successful programs of his presidency, and for may years thereafter.

But all in all, this was a very difficult period for me. I had too much time on my hands, and was suffering withdrawal symptoms. It is said that everyone who returns from an extended period abroad goes through this. In some respects, living overseas gives one a greater appreciation of one's own country, with its freedoms, its openness and friendliness, and its unlimited opportunities. At the same time, in viewing the U.S. from afar, one can see its foibles and excesses. Why are two of our least desirable assets—fast food and pop music—our two major exports? Why do we waste our creative talents on packaging 43 different kinds of cookies, not to mention insipid sitcoms? Why are we so damn *loud*? In European restaurants conversation is kept at a moderate, almost hushed level; here all too often our enjoyment is shattered by the piercing cackles of women with too many drinks.

These were my thoughts as I moped around the house. I missed the fun and excitement of Europe. I also missed Jacqueline and I missed Ann, who had met another student, an actor, and by Christmas had become engaged. I was restless and lonely. I took to reading poetry, having concluded that great poetry is written only at the height of ecstasy or in the depths of despair. T.S. Eliot's *The Waste Land* stirred my soul, and I could identify with J. Alfred Prufrock:

> *I grow old…I grow old…*
>
> *I shall wear the bottoms of my trousers rolled.*
>
> *Shall I part my hair behind? Do I dare to eat a peach?*
>
> *I shall wear white I flannel trousers, and walk upon the beach.*

9.

ASSISTANT UNITED STATE ATTORNEY, SAN FRANCISCO, 1961-1962

It took me until January to snap out of the doldrums, when at last I became an Assistant United States Attorney. My dream had come true! John Kennedy had been elected, the hiring freeze was over, and I reported for work on January 15, 1961. I rented a studio apartment in North Beach, at 490 Lombard St., just below Telegraph Hill, in the neighborhood where Jack Kerouac and the beatniks had hung out just a few years earlier. I could ride the cable car to work. I was alive again!

Shortly after I arrived, President Kennedy appointed as the new United States Attorney Cecil Poole, the first African American in the country to be appointed to that position. Cecil was a highly regarded trial lawyer and had been active in the civil rights movement in the Bay Area. He was one of the best bosses I ever had. Universally respected and liked by both bar and bench, he was a "man's man"—straightforward and fair to all, with no airs or pretensions. He also had a wonderful self-deprecating sense of humor, and unlike many in similar positions, he was not a publicity-seeker. His door was open to defense counsel as well as to his own prosecutors, and he listened carefully to arguments on both sides of a proposed indictment. Once a difficult decision had been made, his staff could depend on his backing against any criticism, be it from a defense lawyer, a judge, or the press.

Nor did he hesitate to voice his displeasure with any directives coming out of the Justice Department in Washington hat he considered misguided or unrealistic. I often wonder how Cecil would have reacted these days to the directive from the current Justice Department that U.S. Attorneys "monitor" judges whose sentences are deemed too lenient by the Department.

My first assignment as an Assistant was to direct the Small Claims and Collections Office, a one-lawyer operation. Citizens find themselves in debt to Uncle Sam for all kinds of reasons: back taxes, defaulted VA loans or student loans, uncollected criminal fines, and for a host of other misadventures. If the agency to whom the debt is owed fails after numerous attempts to collect, it refers the matter to the U.S. Attorney nearest to the debtor. That office then tries to coax and cajole the debtor into some sort of payment arrangement, or if necessary, files suit. Usually the government obtains a default judgment, but it also gains the debtor's attention, and then the collection process begins in earnest.

The collection effort was important and necessary, and the total amounts collected were impressive, but I found the work tedious and not very challenging. Judges love to impose heavy fines on convicted felons, who seldom have steady incomes while behind bars and their reserves, if any, have been accounted for by their defense counsel. So we had people who, once they emerged from prison, were paying ten or twenty bucks a month on fines of fifty or a hundred thousand. The important thing was to get them to pay *something* on a regular basis. The same applied to civil debtors.

Then there were the sometimes unreasonable expectations from the agencies demanding payment. The worst example I encountered came from the Navy. In 1942, with the fall of the Philippines to the Japanese, a U.S. civilian government worker escaped into the jungle, where he somehow survived for nearly two years. Finally, with the help of guerillas, he was able to contact the U.S. Navy in Australia. A daring and successful rescue was made, and he was brought by submarine to

Australia. There he was placed on a navy shp and transported home to San Francisco.

The Navy was now, in 1961, attempting to collect from him the cost of transporting him from Australia to the United States! I thought there must surely be some mistake, and I called the Navy in Washington Their reply was, "What's he complaining about? We didn't charge him for the submarine ride."

That one somehow got lost behind my file cabinet.

This was not what I had in mind when I took the job. The title sounded great at cocktail parties, but I was eager for criminal trial work. I talked it over with Cecil Poole, and shortly thereafter he assigned me to the criminal division, where at last I could conduct grand jury investigations, write indictments, and try cases.

During about a year in the criminal division I prosecuted numerous jury trials in federal courts in San Francisco and in Sacramento. It was exhilarating, and the cases were varied enough to make every day interesting: drug dealers, illegal possession of firearms, bank robberies, interstate transportation of stolen property, and con artists and swindlers who used the mails and wires to defraud the public. I had a good rapport with and great respect for the federal investigative agents with whom I worked. Without their dedication and perseverance it would not have been possible to bring these cases to prosecution.

The federal prison at Alcatraz in San Francisco Bay was still in operation while I was in the U.S. Attorney's office. I discovered that the warden, Paul Madigan, was a fellow alumnus of St. Thomas, and so one day I called him. He invited me over for lunch, which we enjoyed in the dining room of his home on the island. Our waiter, who provided excellent service, was a convicted murderer. The cellblocks, however, were pretty grim.

The prison was closed a year later. The warden's house is now in ruins, having been burned down during the Native American incursion of the island in the 1970's. Little could I have known on the day of my visit that forty years later my daughter Katy would be in charge of the evening tour program at Alcatraz, now the most popular tourist site in San Francisco.

An Offer From Washington

One day in late March 1962 I received a call from Washington, from my friend Bill Ryan, a Marine lawyer with whom I had served at Camp Pendleton. I knew that Bill had left the Marine Corps a year or two earlier and had joined the Justice Department in Washington. Bill said that Attorney General Bob Kennedy was putting together a group of about fifteen lawyers to focus on Jimmy Hoffa and the Teamsters Union.

The Teamsters had been under an intensive and highly publicized investigation by the Senate Rackets Committee, chaired by Sen. John McClellan of Arkansas. Sen. John Kennedy had been a member of the committee before being elected president, and Robert Kennedy had been the committee's chief counsel.

The hearings had revealed to the American public that the International Brotherhood of Teamsters, the nation's largest union with 1.8 million members and with virtually unlimited power over nation-wide trucking, was controlled by leaders who were corrupt and closely allied with organized crime. James Riddle Hoffa, the union's autocratic and ruthless leader, had a long and shameful record of association with well known members of the Mafia.

After the McClellan Committee revelations, it was obvious that the Justice Department had to take action, and when Robert Kennedy became attorney general, he established as one of his top priorities the clean-up of the union, from Hoffa and his cronies down to the numerous corrupt locals.

Under the phlegmatic Eisenhower administration, a few over-worked Justice lawyers were looking into the Teamsters, without much interest on the part of either the attorney general or the FBI. In those days the big issue was internal security, thanks to the red-baiting rampage of Sen. Joe McCarthy and America's Cold War fear of communist infiltration of our government. J. Edgar Hoover was more interested in tracking down communist sympathizers than union racketeers or Mafia mobsters. In fact, he had denied the existence of the Mafia in the U.S. until the infamous Apalachin meeting in upstate New York in 1957, a gathering of all the top Mafia leaders in the country, as identified by Hoover's own agency.

Attorney General Kennedy knew what to do and he had the clout from the White House to do it, which included forcing Hoover to allocate the necessary investigative resources.

Bill Ryan told me that Kennedy was looking for lawyers with investigative and trial experience. They would work directly under Walter Sheridan, who had been the McClellan committee's chief investigator, and Sheridan would be responsible directly to Kennedy. Would I be interested in joining the team?

Like everyone else in the country I was aware of the Teamsters problem, and was flattered by the offer. But I told Bill I already had the best job in government, not to mention a bachelor pad in North Beach in the best city in the country. He said they'd pay my way to Washington for an interview, so why not consider it? I agreed. Who could turn down a free trip to Washington and a chance to see for oneself what the excitement of John Kennedy's New Frontier was all about?

I was not unfamiliar with Washington, having spent many weekends there during my days at Quantico in 1954-55. I remembered it as a beautiful city, and I enjoyed its monuments and museums, but in those Eisenhower Republican years it was quiet, conservative, and segregated. The government seemed to operate by rote and by mostly nameless, faceless, grey-haired men.

The election of young John Kennedy had changed everything. Almost immediately upon arrival I could sense the enthusiasm and vibrancy of the New Frontier. Kennedy's ringing inaugural exhortation, "Ask not what your country can do for you, but what you can do for your country," had attracted hundreds of bright young people, full of ambition and newly discovered pride in government service, eager to make their mark in public life.

An associate of mine at Justice, Ron Goldfarb, later wrote a book in which he poignantly captured the spirit of those days:

"John F. Kennedy's election brought glamour, new brain power and young professionals, extraordinary media attention, and an excitable optimistic generation of Democrats to the capital. Quickly, a newly energized bureaucracy seemed to become a place of can-do activism. The town itself began to come alive, socially and culturally, personified best by the elegant first lady, Jacqueline Kennedy, and the elan of White House parties peopled by artists, writers, musicians, and sport and entertainment figures. We younger recruits lived on the out-skirts of what later would be called Camelot, but not so far from its center that we couldn't feel the glow." [Goldfarb, Ronald. *Perfect Villains, Imperfect Heroes: Robert F. Kennedy's War Against Organized Crime*. New York: Random House, 1995, p. 22]

I found that many of my old friends from St. Thomas and the Marine Corps were already part of the New Frontier, in important positions that previously would have been denied those in their thirties. From St. Thomas, Phil Des Marais was a Deputy Assistant Secretary of Education. Gene Foley, also from St. Thomas, was head of the Small Business Administration and Lee Corcoran worked with him. Bob Treanor was a congressional aide to Rep. Eugene McCarthy, whom we had helped to elect in 1948, and who would later become Senator from Minnesota and a presidential candidate in 1968. Bob Lodge, a St. Thomas classmate and editor of the college newspaper, who also had a sonorous speaking voice, was broadcasting for ABC. From Marine Corps days, Mitch Rogovin was working for, and later became, the general counsel of the IRS. Tim Murphy was an Assistant U.S. Attorney for the District of Columbia, which office prosecuted all local as well as federal crimes. I had become good friends with Tim at Basic School and at the Naval Justice School. And my great friend Stu Land had joined the politically powerful Washington law firm of Arnold, Porter, & Fortas.

At Justice, Bill Ryan ushered me into Walter Sheridan's inconspicuous office on the second floor. Sheridan was 36, born on the same day as Robert Kennedy. (I was 32.) Walter was about my size, soft spoken and intense, but with the Irish sense of irony and humor. He spoke with fervor about the mission of the "Hoffa Squad," which was to bring Jimmy Hoffa to Justice and clean up what the Senate committee had termed "Hoffa's hoodlum empire." He was totally dedicated to Bob Kennedy, and their relationship was of the greatest mutual respect. He told me that the work would be difficult and challenging, that it would require creativity and innovative thinking, perseverance and long hours, considerable travel perhaps on short notice, and that we would be opposed by the ablest lawyers that the Teamster Union's unlimited funds could hire. We were to avoid publicity and keep a low profile, so as not to enhance the perception in some quarters that Bob Kennedy was pursuing a vendetta (*i.e.* unwarranted persecution) against Hoffa.

Sheridan introduced me to some of the other hand-picked lawyers in the group, who were not away on travel. They were of varying ages but mostly in their thirties, from all over the country. Some had come from other government agencies, some from other positions in Justice, and some from private practice. They were friendly and welcoming. They had a sense of camaraderie about them, having come to work for Walter Sheridan and Bob Kennedy because it was a great opportunity to do something challenging and exciting and perhaps make a little history. They were the sort of men I had always enjoyed being with. The lawyers were all men, but even the female secretaries were part of the team, and they were viewed by the lawyers as associates in a challenging venture.

I was hooked. Sheridan offered me a job at $10,000, and I accepted on the spot. I said I would report by the end of April. Frankly, I was thrilled.

Tim Murphy graciously invited me to live in the house he shared with two other lawyers, on 28th St. in Cleveland Park, just 15 minutes from downtown. The others were Peter Cella, a litigator in an insurance defense firm, and Ken Pye, who owned the house, and was a professor at Georgetown Law School. I had met Ken previously, and in fact he had once stayed for a night or two at our apartment in Paris. They even had a housekeeper. Perfect.

Back in San Francisco, there was an important matter to be resolved, a matter of the heart. In early January my friend Jack Merrill and I had gone to Sun Valley, Idaho, for a week of skiing. Not only is Sun Valley a terrific place to ski; the social life was also great. Every afternoon from about 5 to 7 there was live music and dancing at the Ram's Head, so there was a chance to meet new friends and later go out to dinner at one of the many restaurants in nearby Ketchum, and more dancing and carousing thereafter.

Jack and I enrolled in a ski class, which included several attractive young women. The day always ended with a long run down the back side of Mt. Baldy, at the bottom of which was a bridge over a creek and then a short trail to the lodge. One day near the end of the week, full of confidence and *machismo*, I decided to impress the women by taking the lead and schussing straight down that mountain. As I gained momentum I was also losing control and veering slightly to the right. Too late, I realized that I was going to miss that bridge. I careened straight into the creek and came up wet and freezing, much to the amusement of my would-be admirers.

One of those in the group was a lovely and vivacious young woman name Jeanine (Jean) Keckeisen. Jean was 27, from New Ulm, Minnesota, and was living and working in San Francisco. At the end of the week Jack and I gave Jean and her friend a ride back to San Francisco.

Once back in the city, Jean and I became fast friends. I think it is fair to say that we fell in love. Therefore when I decided less than three months later to move to Washington, we had to make a decision. Faced with the alternative of a permanent separation, we convinced ourselves that a permanent togetherness was far preferable, and decided to become engaged.

Jean would also move to Washington. My friend Mike Roseto, who owned a hotels-motels reservation business in San Francisco, also had an office in Washington, and he offered Jean a job there. In Washington, Stu Land had recently married, and he and his wife Gayla were renting a three bedroom home on Cathedral Avenue, just two blocks from where I would be living. They offered their third bedroom to Jean.

So, thanks to the generosity of my friends, everything fell into place. I would move to Washington in late April. Jean would remain in San Francisco until the Memorial Day weekend, at which time she would go to New Ulm. I would join her there from Washington to meet her parents and family. We would pick up the marriage license, and together we would then go on to Washington.

My parents were understandably crestfallen. They had been so happy to see me return to the Bay Area after an absence of six years, and now I was about to move 3000 miles away again. They were also wary about my becoming engaged to someone I had known for such a short time. Now that I am a parent, I can fully understand their concern and heartache. But as always, they wished and prayed only for my happiness, and they were genuinely pleased that I would be joining the New Frontier.

It was also difficult to leave Patricia and Frank and the children. I dearly loved all of them, and with the specter of cystic fibrosis, the future was uncertain for them. It also meant that I would see less of

Sister Thomas Patricia in southern California. After being almost inseparable as children, our times together were growing less frequent.

At the office, Cecil Poole expressed sincere disappointment at
my impending departure. But he liked and admired Bob Kennedy, who
on one occasion had come out to visit us, as he made a point of visiting
as many of the field offices as possible. At my farewell luncheon Cecil
said, "So I told them in Washington, 'at least you're getting a good trial
lawyer, which is something you people sorely need.'" Typical Cecil; I
loved him for it. Years later, after he had been appointed to the 9th
Circuit Court of Appeals and had to come to Washington for the annual
Judicial Conference, Cecil would often call me and we would have a
drink or lunch together.

10.

DEPARTMENT OF JUSTICE, WASHINGTON, D.C.

The Hoffa Squad

I arrived in Washington happy, excited, and eager to begin my new life. Washington shone in all its magnificent glory, as it does every spring. The azaleas were in full bloom everywhere—pinks and reds and purples and white. I had no idea Washington could be so lovely. I had always thought of it as a beautiful city, with its imposing embassies and monuments, but this was the first time I saw so many flowers. Goodby, fair San Francisco; I might not miss you so much after all.

On the morning of Monday, April 30, 1962, I walked through the doors of the United States Department of Justice, full of anticipation. I remember the date because it had been exactly four years earlier, on April 30, 1958, that I had started work at Chateauroux.

The Department of Justice encompasses a full block, from Pennsylvania to Constitution Avenues, between 9th and 10th Streets, but it has a huge center courtyard. Each of the five floors has a long center corridor, so that each office has a window overlooking either the street or the courtyard.

The second floor housed the Criminal Division. I made my way to Walter Sheridan's office, and after a brief welcome and introduction to the other attorneys, I was given my first assignment. I was to leave immediately for Newark, New Jersey, to assist in an ongoing criminal trial in federal court. I was to accompany Abe Poretz, a senior attorney whose long career as a prosecutor had begun on the staff of Thomas E. Dewey during Dewey's days as attorney general of New York. Dewey's "gang buster" reputation had propelled him to the governorship and eventually to the edge of the presidency, where he lost to Harry Truman in the historic election of 1948.

Abe and I hopped a plane to Newark. During the one hour flight Abe regaled me with stories of his days under Tom Dewey and later Tom Hogan, the legendary Manhattan district attorney, and then briefed me on our assignment.

Anthony Provenzano, head of the New Jersey teamsters, was on trial for shaking down employers; in legal parlance, extortion of monies by means of force or threats of force or violence in exchange for labor peace. Teamster leaders during Hoffa's reign were not interested in calling strikes for higher wages for their members. They were interested in *threatening* to strike, and then extracting large sums of money from employers in exchange for sweetheart contracts.

"Tony Pro" Provenzano was a powerful and notorious figure in New Jersey. A member of the Mafia and an international vice president of the International Brotherhood of Teamsters, he had the power of life and death over all trucking in New Jersey, and exercised it. It is Tony Provenzano who is believed to have masterminded the disappearance of Jimmy Hoffa from the Red Fox restaurant in Detroit in 1975, some thirteen years later, after Hoffa's release from prison and as he was attempting to regain control of the union.

The day before our arrival, and while the trial was in progress, a Teamster driver who was to testify for the government was shot dead on the way from his home to the courthouse.

Our assignment was to hold the hands of the government's other driver witnesses; to assure them that they were safe in the arms of their government, and that no harm could possibly come to *them*, and therefore they should not hesitate to testify. We did our best, but I doubt if they were any more convinced than we were.

One burly trucker, with biceps about the size of my waist, looked me straight in the eye and said, "Sir, my stomach is so upset that I think I'm losing my memory."

The next day Abe and I returned to Washington.

Tony Provenzano was convicted and sentenced to seven years in prison.

Labor Racketeering in the National Spotlight

In our society, public attention tends to focus on one or two major issues at a time, giving them names, such as the War on Poverty or the War on Crime. Social problems arise, and, aided by the media, we direct a great deal of attention to them and expect our leaders to find solutions. Daily news stories appear in the papers and on TV, columnists contribute their commentaries, and the issues are discussed at lively dinner parties. In the past fifty years, this phenomenon has been highlighted by televised Congressional hearings. In the early 1950's it was Senator Joe McCarthy's harangues against alleged communists in government. This was followed by Senator Estes Kefauver's sensational hearings on Organized Crime, as were the subsequent hearings in 1963. In that year the testimony of Mafia member Joe Valachi made the public aware for the first time of the power and influence of the Mafia in the United States, not only in the traditional rackets of illegal gambling, loansharking, and extortion, but its infiltration of labor unions, legitimate businesses, and even the corruption of local and state governments.

Most adults today recall other major issues that have captured the public interest from time to time: drugs, street crime, Watergate, the Enron scandal, and currently, the War on Terrorism.

I am not suggesting that these are not legitimate matters of public interest. All are of major concern, but since we seem capable of focusing on only one or two at a time, our priorities do shift from year to year.

In the early 1960's, when I arrived at the Justice Department, one of the major public concerns was labor racketeering. As I indicated earlier, the televised McClellan Committee hearings from 1957 to 1960 disclosed an appalling picture of violence, coercion, and corruption in a number of labor unions, including the Seafarers' International Union and the Laborers' International. But its main focus was on the International Brotherhood of Teamsters, headed by James Riddle Hoffa.

Hoffa was 5'5", built like a fireplug, with small hard eyes. A former warehouseman in Detroit, he had battled his way to the top of the Detroit teamsters local. Journalist and author Evan Thomas described Hoffa's younger days:

"Arrested and convicted of assault, conspiracy, and extortion, a veteran of many bloody labor battles, Hoffa always played rough. 'Guys that tried to break me up got broken up,' he bragged. He also flaunted his ties to gangsters. Union bosses who did not use underworld muscle, he scoffed, were 'fools.'" [Thomas, Evan. *Robert Kennedy: His Life*. Simon & Schuster, New York. 2000]

Ruling the Detroit local with an iron fist, he muscled his way up through the ranks to the top of the IBT, He succeeded Dave Beck as international president upon Beck's conviction in Seattle and sentence to fifteen years for racketeering. Some say that Hoffa, to feather his own nest, secretly provided the information that led to Beck's downfall.

In 1957 the AFL-CIO expelled the Teamsters Union on charges of corrupt leadership. This only emboldened Hoffa, who defiantly asserted that the AFL-CIO needed the Teamsters more than the Teamsters needed them. The Teamsters then began incursions into non-trucking industries: retail clerks, manufacturing workers, airline employees, hotel and restaurant workers, and others. They even challenged—with the connivance of the grape growers—Cesar Chavez and his United Farm

Workers' attempts to organize the vineyard workers in California. Wherever the Teamsters went there was violence, and when they won, it usually resulted in a sweetheart contract with the employers.

In short, the Teamsters Union was a disgrace to the trade union movement, corrupt from top to bottom, and in bed with the Mob. And standing at the pinnacle, feisty and defiant, was Hoffa, a hero to some, a menace to most.

What was the mutual benefit of a Teamsters-Mafia relationship? Let us consider some real life examples. Suppose you own a bar and restaurant in New Jersey, and you are resisting the Mafia's efforts to shake you down for protection money. But the trucks which deliver your beer are driven by Teamsters. Suddenly they fail to show up. Soon you learn that if you pay up, they will show up. Or maybe it's the linen supply trucks. Another example: Your restaurant, like nearly all businesses, depends upon regular trash collection. The local trash collection company is owned by the Mafia. If your trash doesn't get picked up you are in deep trouble. Meanwhile, the Teamsters are trying to organize your restaurant workers. You are vulnerable to demands from either the mobsters or the Teamsters. Thus the mob and the Teamsters worked hand in glove for their mutual benefit. These were real situations in many communities large and small, especially on the Eastern seaboard.

Some progress was being made against the local Teamster unions. Between 1961 and 1964 our group, under the direction of Walter Sheridan and working closely with the FBI and U.S. Attorneys throughout the country, obtained convictions of more than one hundred local and district officials of the Teamsters Union, for a whole spectrum of crimes.

But Hoffa himself was proving to be wily and elusive. He had been indicted in New York in 1957 but escaped with a hung jury—eleven to one for conviction. Retried in 1958, he was acquitted. Later in 1958 he was indicted in Washington for attempted bribery of a staff member of the McClellan committee, in an effort to spy on the committee. Halfway through the trial the eight black members of the jury received at their homes a copy of a local newspaper, the Afro-American, featuring a pro-Hoffa article. Then, near the end of the trial, on the day Hoffa took the witness stand, Joe Louis, the much-revered former heavyweight champion, walked into the courtroom and embraced Hoffa, in the presence of the jurors. Hoffa was acquitted. [The businessman who paid Joe Louis to do this thereafter got a large loan from the Teamsters pension fund.]

With each acquittal, Hoffa became more brazen and cocky. Sitting in his office in the white marble palace that is the Teamsters headquarters on Constitution Ave. directly across from the Capitol, Hoffa could literally thumb his nose at the U.S. government. He also became more bombastic, proclaiming to the world that he was the victim of a personal vendetta by that "spoiled millionaire brat, Bobby Kennedy."

Some in the media began to echo this sentiment. A Wall Street Journal headline spoke of an "Agonizing Reappraisal of Efforts to Topple Teamsters' Leader," predicting that "some voices will be raised in Congress denouncing the government's tactics," and that "even some influential Congressional friends of the Administration could take up the persecution chant."

Even some of my friends were saying things like "Good luck, but Hoffa will never be convicted; he's too clever and too powerful."

Power Grab on the Pension Fund

Robert Kennedy and Walter Sheridan were not to be deterred. Waiting and ripe for investigation was the manipulation of the Teamsters' Pension Fund.

Hoffa had created the Central States, Southeastern and Southwest Areas Pension Fund in 1955. It collected contributions from employers for retirement, disability and death benefits for more than 175,000 Teamsters in about 20 states. By 1962 the fund had grown to $180 million, and employers were contributing an additional $3.5 million per month. It was at that time the nation's largest single employee pension fund. That's a lot of cash which had to be invested somewhere, and the fund's managers were engaging in some very suspicious activities.

The pension fund was governed by eight employer trustees and eight union trustees, with Hoffa as chairman. Their responsibility was to preserve and invest the fund judiciously for the benefit of the rank and file members.

Instead, it was being invested in highly questionable real estate loans. While the Securities and Exchange Commission estimated that most trusts invest less than 3% of their funds in real estate undertakings, the comparable figure for the Teamsters fund was about 80%. Our investigation disclosed that large loans were made to finance such diverse ventures as motels, golf courses, a rubber products company in New Mexico, a laundry, and a cemetery. Significantly, large loans were also being granted for the construction of new casinos in Las Vegas, and many of the borrowers were connected with organized crime. Once again Jimmy Hoffa and the Mob had mutual business interests.

It became clear from a reading of the minutes of the meetings of the pension fund trustees that Hoffa was making all the decisions. As the employer trustees frankly stated in grand jury testimony, they didn't care how the money was invested, because it all belonged to the Teamsters anyway.

It also developed that these questionable loans would be approved only if submitted through a certain few "intermediaries," who happened to be friends of Hoffa. Further, these intermediaries were demanding and receiving compensation for their services, a portion of which, we suspected, was being kicked back to Hoffa.

Hoffa had his own personal motive behind this scheme, in addition to the satisfaction of wielding great power. He needed to bail himself out of a financial mess in Florida. He had committed $400,000 of his Detroit local's funds in a residential development purportedly for retired teamsters. Hoffa had promoted "Sun Valley Estates" as "the Teamster model city of tomorrow," but the land turned out to be mostly under water during the rainy season, and he was under indictment for fraud in connection with that scheme.

Sheridan appointed Charles Z. Smith to lead the group investigating the Pension fund. Charley, an AUSA in Seattle, had joined our group after successfully prosecuting Dave Beck. Other members of the team were Bill Ryan, Tom McTiernan, Jim Canavan, and myself. Hoffa became aware of the investigation and referred to us as the "Irish Mafia," ignoring the fact that Smith was an African American.

In June 1962 we began a grand jury investigation, which enabled us to subpoena records and witnesses. We rented offices and set up shop in Chicago, the home base of the pension fund. We commuted from Washington to Chicago every week, flying home most weekends. Along with several experienced and dedicated FBI agents, we began the long and painstaking effort that is required in every fraud investigation, known as following the paper trail, as well as the interrogation of grand jury witnesses, most of whom were hostile. The quote from Shakespeare, "O what a tangled web we weave, when first we practice to deceive," was certainly applicable here. Eventually we would uncover a blatant pattern of deception, misrepresentation, inflated valuations, false and misleading information, and diversion of proceeds, on loans dictated by Hoffa to be approved. But it would take a year to develop all the evidence necessary for an indictment for fraud on the pension fund.

Engagement on the Rocks

The weekly commute to Chicago had done nothing to enhance my engagement to Jeanine. We got together when I was home on weekends through the summer, but it was not much time to build on a pre-engagement foundation that was itself relatively brief. We had obtained a marriage license when I visited her family in Minnesota in May, but even then she was understandably reluctant to set a wedding date.

By early fall she told me that she was not ready for marriage and returned the ring. In retrospect, I'm certain she made the right decision, but it was emotionally wrenching for both of us. The following spring, after a stint as a live-in governess to the younger of Bob Kennedy's eight or nine children, which she found interesting but nerve-wracking and exhausting, she returned to San Francisco.

Teamsters Turmoil in Puerto Rico

In October of 1962 Walter Sheridan asked me to take leave of the pension fund investigation for awhile and initiate an investigation of the Teamsters local in Puerto Rico. Hoffa had sent one his favorite organizers, a 34-year-old swaggering tough named Frank Chavez from Texas, to head up Teamsters Local 901 in San Juan, and to take on the Seafarers International Union, as well as the Hotel and Restaurant Workers Union. The latter had been representing most of the employees of the resort hotels on the island. Applying the usual Teamster tactics, Chavez had caused so much violence and unrest on the island that it was affecting the tourist trade. The U.S. Attorney in San Juan was asking for help.

Sheridan asked me to look into the situation, and with that general briefing, I was on my way.

I arrived in San Juan, having no idea that for the next three years I would be spending about half of my time there and in the Virgin Islands. I would make many friends there, and some enemies. I would become aware that the main topic of conversation among Puerto Ricans was and still is the ultimate status of the island—commonwealth, statehood, or independence? I would become familiar with just about every hotel, restaurant, and bar in San Juan, and most in St. Thomas and St. Croix, V.I. I would experience exhilarating times and teeth-gnashing frustrations. Ultimately I would live there for a time with my wife and our first son.

The best things about Puerto Rico are its weather, its beaches, and its sunsets. The rum drinks are good too. My colleagues were envious, and each time I returned to Washington would inquire, "Where's your tan?" They were not sympathetic when I retorted that the sun shines only during working hours.

The worst thing about Puerto Rico was trying to conduct the government's business, as we shall see.

Upon arrival, I went to the federal courthouse in Old San Juan (now a museum, I'm told; there's no surer sign of aging than to learn that the place where you once worked is now a museum), and met with U.S. Attorney Francisco Gil. Mr. Gil, a member of the Puerto Rican aristocracy, was soft-spoken, gracious, and hospitable. He was also phlegmatic (though perhaps not by local standards), and resentful that the Teamsters were threatening to disturb his quiet life, and therefore was more than willing to give me full responsibility for the investigation, as long as he was the beneficiary of any favorable publicity that might ensue. He hoped to become a federal judge. He had two able assistants who were very helpful to me and with whom I became great friends.

Mr. Gil introduced me to the only federal judge in Puerto Rico, the Hon. Clemente Ruiz Nazario. Judge Ruiz, nearing retirement, was a feisty little man who was bilingual, which is to say that he was mostly unintelligible in both Spanish and English.

Next I met with the FBI staff, a great group of guys who were bored doing car theft investigations and eager to get into some labor racketeering. The local office of the U.S. Department of Labor was also welcoming. They had been looking for possible violations of the Taft-Hartley Act and the Landrum-Griffin Act by the Teamsters, but without much success. I became close friends with David Blum, one of their staff attorneys, and some years later, when Dave and I both left the government, we opened a law office together in Washington.

We began gathering information about the activities of Chavez and his cohorts. Local 901 had called a lot of strikes at numerous companies, but none ever seemed to be resolved. Pickets would show up for a few days or weeks and then their numbers would dwindle and finally they would disappear. The workers would either return to their jobs or would find employment elsewhere. In some instances the workers, after calling a strike, had later voted overwhelmingly to have Local 901 de-certified as their representative at the job site. All this seemed curious.

Then an examination of the Local's bank accounts showed large sums of money coming in from the International as strike benefits for those on the picket line, in some cases for far more workers than were actually employed at that particular plant, and in other cases long after the strikes had ended.

We began an investigation at six companies to determine 1) how many employees went on strike and for how long; and 2) how many received strike benefits and for how long. To tie it all together. we subpoe-naed the International's records to determine how much was paid to Local 901 and for how long as benefits for strikers at each of the companies. The grand jury was an essential part of this process.

A federal grand jury consists of 23 citizens chosen from the community at random. It has a term of 18 months and is called into ses-sion to hear witness testimony at such times as determined by the U.S. Attorney, and the latter issues subpoenas for documents and witnesses in the name of the grand jury. Neither the U.S. Attorney nor the FBI have subpoena power on their own. Failure to obey a subpoena can result in a conviction for contempt of court with a subsequent fine or imprisonment. Finally, no one an be indicted for a felony except by vote of at least 18 members of the grand jury.

Convening of the grand jury caused banner headlines in both the English and Spanish language newspapers in San Juan. In Spanish I was referred to as *El fiscal especial Kennelly*, and the Teamsters were *Tronquistas* or *Hoffistas*.

Upon issuing the subpoenas for records from the six companies I gave them six weeks to produce the documents. Imagine my surprise when on the appointed day not a single company showed up, nor had anyone bothered to call. Welcome to Puerto Rico! When I contacted them, all were friendly and cooperative but said they could not possibly produce the records in the short time allotted. But they would do their best. It was then that I realized this was going to be a longer process than anticipated.

At about the time we finally began to receive documents and the grand jury began hearing witnesses, in March 1963, Chavez himself one day showed up at my office, demanding to appear before the grand jury. I told him I knew he had a lawyer, and any such requests should be made through his lawyer.

The next day he appeared at the door of the grand jury room, handing to each juror an envelope containing nine pages of scurrilous materials personally attacking Robert Kennedy and "Mr. Kennelly, Bobby's right-hand hatchet man."

It is a federal misdemeanor for any person to contact a grand jury with intent to influence its action, and so I duly charged Chavez. Thus began my first experience in a Puerto Rican courtroom.

After a number of delays, the trial got underway seven months later. All federal jurors are required to understand English, since all proceedings are in English. This is not a real problem since most citizens are bilingual. However, many witnesses understandably prefer to testify in Spanish, in which case an interpreter is employed. Interpreters were of uneven quality, with the result that there was often a free-for-all in which the interpreter was corrected by the lawyers, by the judge, and sometimes by the witness, in a setting in which everybody but me understood both English and Spanish. A jolly good time was had by all.

I presented the testimony of the grand jurors who had received the materials from Chavez, and rested my case. Chavez' attorney, Cesar Andreu Rivas, a wily and colorful local character with a flowing white mane and histrionic demeanor, called me as the sole defense witness. It is not permissible under the federal rules to call an opposing counsel as a witness, but Judge Ruiz overruled my objection. In response to Rivas' questions, I testified that Chavez did indeed distribute the materials openly and in plain view of everyone and not secretly or in the dead of night.

In my summation I pointed out that secrecy is not an element of the offense, but the verdict was a hung jury, six in favor of conviction and six for acquittal. I could only conclude that half the jury believed me as the prosecutor, and the other half believed me as the only defense witness.

We did not bother to retry the case, as it was only a misdemeanor, and after that diversion we moved forward on the larger investigation.

I requested and received an assistant from Washington. Marvin Loewy came from the Criminal Fraud section at Justice. Marvin and I became kindred spirits at once. He had a good analytical mind and the ability to distinguish the important from the trivial. He also had the patience and perseverance to gather the necessary evidence and then relate it to the legal issues involved. In short, he had all the qualities of a good investigative lawyer. He would later prove to be a good trial lawyer as well. Most of all, his sense of humor helped both of us to deal with the daily foibles and frustrations of working in Puerto Rico. Moreover, he was a pleasant companion after hours, and anyone who travels on business a lot knows the importance of having associates who are not only pleasant to work with but agreeable dinner companions. Although we got a lot of publicity, Marvin never seemed to mind that the newspapers invariably misspelled his name, and Marvin Loewy appeared in print as Marvin Lowry, Melvin Loosely, and Merwin Lousy.

Eventually the evidence we gathered would show that Chavez and his cohorts had for three years operated a scam that had enriched themselves and the local union's treasury at the expense of their members and of the International Union. Their *modus operandi* was to call strikes, then submit strike benefit claims to the International, padding the claims to include non-existent persons, failing to pay strikers, and then continuing to submit claims long after the strikes ended. For example, at Gonzalez

Chemical, 38 workers went on strike, which lasted ten days. Yet the union submitted phony strike benefit claims and received payment for 126 workers for five months. Fewer than ten striking workers at Gonzales actually received any benefits, and then only for a week or two. The same pattern was followed at five other job sites.

Especially compelling was the plight of the female workers at Lee Manufacturing Co., a ladies ready-to-wear sweatshop at St. Thomas, V.I. The Virgin Islands, St. Thomas, St. Croix, and St. John are jewels in the Caribbean. The weather is perfect year round, the white sand beaches and emerald waters are wonderful for swimming and snorkeling, there are numerous charming hotels and guest houses, and the duty-free shopping is a bonanza for tourists and cruise ship passengers.

But for most of the locals life is hard. The thirty or so women at Lee Manufacturing worked long hours for low pay in a corrugated metal shed, sewing garments for an absentee owner. When Frank Chavez came to town and told them of the benefits of union organization they were eager listeners. He urged them to sign up with Teamsters and strike for higher pay. He promised them strike benefits equal to wages, emphasizing, however, that each employee must walk the picket line every day in order to obtain benefits. They all agreed and the strike began.

The women told the grand jury that they received about $20 in cash each week for the first three or four weeks, then were paid by check for a week or two, but the checks bounced and they never received any more money. Nevertheless, they continued to picket every day in the hot sun for another month or so, because Mr. Chavez told them to, notwithstanding that the plant had closed down a week or so after the strike began.

Meanwhile Chavez was submitting claims and receiving benefits from the International for 50 strikers (20 more than the total number of employees) for the next seven months, but paid nothing to the women. After seven months he sent a telegram to the International saying "Lee Manufacturing strike ended today." This was a complete fabrication.

All in all, Chavez obtained more than $500,000 in cash from the International, relating just to these six companies, of which more than $200,000 was obtained by fraud and never paid to striking workers.

But it took 18 months to gather all the necessary evidence, with the able assistance of the FBI, the Department of Labor, and the grand jury, not to mention the jailing of one union employee for refusing to testify. It was not until April 1964 that we would be ready to return an indictment against Chavez and three other union officials for use of the mails and wires in a scheme to defraud.

In the meantime, something wonderful happened to me back in Washington.

Lasting Love at Last

It was the evening of Sunday December 16, 1962, at a Christmas party given by an old friend from Camp Pendleton days. It was the third party of the day and fourth or fifth of the weekend, and I almost cancelled, but my social life had been spotty at best since the break-up with Jeanine a few months earlier, and I was still on the lookout for the woman of my dreams.

I wandered over to the popcorn bowl at the end of the bar, and there she was, a blue-eyed blonde, drop-dead gorgeous, with a knockout figure and the voice of an actress, well trained and sexy. I remember the dress, A-line, sleeveless, nubby wool and pink. A vision. And indeed she was an actress, having graduated three years earlier from the famed Drama Department of Catholic University under the renowned Father Gilbert Hartke. Her acting credits included the role of the Countess Olivia in *Twelfth Night* at the first Shakespearean Festival of Washington, performed at the Sylvan Theater on the Mall.

To my utter captivation, she was friendly, vivacious and witty. Later the drama critic of the Washington Post, Richard Coe, would describe her as "pert," defined by Webster as "trim and chic," an accurate but incomplete description.

The opening gambit was simple: we both loved popcorn. She was with a date somewhere in the crowd, but he was with the Tax Division at Justice, whereas I was with the *Criminal* Division, I hastened to point out. I do believe she found me more interesting. Every answer to my inquiries heightened my interest. Not only was she Catholic, she was Irish, with the enchanting name of Susy Powers, and she was a fellow Midwesterner, from Omaha. I could not believe such a beautiful and fascinating woman could possibly be obtainable, but I was determined to try, and had enough self confidence to feel I might have a chance.

My housemate Tim Murphy and I had been to separate parties that evening. The next morning at breakfast I could hardly contain my enthusiasm, and told Tim, "Last night I met the girl of my dreams. Her name is Susy Powers and I am going to marry her." Tim's reply was, "What a coincidence! Last night I met the girl of *my* dreams. Her name is Barbara Garrity, and I am going to marry *her.*"

And we both did, and each of us was best man in the other's wedding. Tim was a faster worker than I; he and Barbara were married less than a year later, on October 12, 1963. Susan and I were married on April 4, 1964.

Even with that confident prediction, I had no inkling of the delights that would be in store for me for the rest of my life. How could I have known that she would become a superb chef? That she loves to hike in the mountains? That when she reads aloud, be it stories to children or scripture from the pulpit, one always wants her to "go on, tell us what happened next!" That she would have unbounded energy, even when presented with three children in three years, and even more than forty years later. (Susan has often quipped that her dream was to marry an Irish Broadway producer, and she got a producer indeed.) How was I to know that her faith would be unwavering, that our values would always coincide and our preferences nearly always, and therefore making important decisions would be relatively easy for us? How could I have known that through her public relations work in our early years together the children and I would have the opportunity to know wonderful people like Pete Seeger, Joan Baez, Judy Collins, and the Clancy Brothers? And I surely could not then have imagined that her later travel business would take us on exciting adventures around the world for now more than twenty-five years. And how could I have predicted that after all these years she still makes me laugh?

But getting first and successive dates with her was not easy. She had not given me her phone number that first evening. She mentioned that she had been a reporter for the Washington Star, and although it had been a great job, she could no longer abide the 6 AM starting time for a morning paper, and was now working for an event-planning agency. I called her at the agency the next morning and asked for a date. No, she was booked up the rest of that week and then would be going home to Omaha for Christmas. She finally consented to a theater date on January 8th.

It was the longest three weeks of my life. After the first date I managed to pin her down to a couple more dates that month and then I was off to Puerto Rico again in early February for six weeks.

Absence apparently did indeed make the heart grow fonder, and upon my return she picked me up at the airport in her white Renault convertible (another pleasant surprise). From then on it was smooth sailing.

Susan was an only child. Her parents had married rather late in life. When she was born, her father, a practicing lawyer in Omaha, was 61, and her mother was 43. However, she was not the only child in the home. Her mother, an elementary school teacher for many years, and her father had reared, along with Susan, several children of two of her mother's brothers who had been widowed.

Susan's father had died in June 1962 at age 86, so I never had the pleasure of knowing him. I first met her mother in late June 1963 when she came to Washington for a visit. We got along fine, and Susan and I planned a trip with her to the Caribbean islands. My friend Jack Merrill from San Francisco (with whom I had skied at Sun Valley) also came to town at the same time and joined us.

Our first stop was Antigua, a gem in the Lesser Antilles where we stayed at the Admiral's Inn at Nelson's Dockyard, on the lovely bay from which Lord Nelson sailed to defeat the Spanish Armada at Trafalgar in 1805. We celebrated Susy's 26th birthday there, with a group of children singing in their calypso accent, "Hoppy borthday, Soosan." Later that evening on Shirley Heights, overlooking the bay and under a full moon, I proposed. She said she would think about it, and a few evenings later, at Magen's Bay on the island of St. Thomas, she accepted.

So the islands can be very romantic indeed, as long as you don't have to work there.

Later that summer I was doing my two weeks annual military duty at the Naval Justice School at Newport. Susy joined me there for a weekend. I told her I had discovered a new taste thrill, scotch and crack-erjacks. When she opened her crackerjack box to extract the "Toy Inside," she discovered a diamond ring. She has worn it ever since and to this day believes it is a real diamond.

Two Convictions and a Wedding

In November and December 1962 Hoffa was on trial in federal court in Nashville for accepting payments totaling more than $1 million over eleven years from a large trucking company in exchange for labor peace. The prosecutors were Jim Neal and Charles Schaffer from our group.

After two months, the trial ended in a hung jury, and once again the howls went up about the Kennedy vendetta against poor Hoffa.

Hoffa himself attacked Jim Neal as "one of the most vicious prosecutors who ever handled a criminal case for the Department of Justice." (Jim was flattered.) In Manchester, N.H., William Loeb, publisher of the Manchester Union Leader, wrote an editorial in which he likened Robert Kennedy to Caesar, attacking him for the trial of Hoffa in Nashville, alleging that "the only 'crime' Hoffa seems to be guilty of is that he will not knuckle under to the Kennedys." A few weeks earlier the Manchester Union Leader had received a $500,000 loan from the Teamsters pension fund.

But William Loeb did not know what we knew. During the Nashville trial Walter Sheridan had developed an informant from Hoffa's inner circle. Edward Grady Partin, head of the Teamsters in Baton Rouge, had been brought to Nashville by Hoffa to participate in a massive attempt by Hoffa's henchmen to fix the jury, with offers of $10,000 to $20,000 to vote for acquittal. (Hoffa also brought Frank Chavez from Puerto Rico.) Partin finally had his fill of doing dirty work for Hoffa, and secretly contacted Sheridan. Throughout the trial Partin kept Sheridan advised of this onslaught by the "improvers" to contact friends and associates of the jurors, and sometimes the jurors themselves, under the direct orders of Hoffa. Armed with this information, the FBI kept a close surveillance on these activities.

After the jury deadlocked and a mistrial was declared, the FBI and a new grand jury completed its investigation of the massive assault on the jury. Witnesses cooperated, and on May 9, 1963, Hoffa and five others were indicted for jury tampering. Hoffa was charged with "aiding, abetting, counseling, commanding, and inducing" the others to corrupt five jurors. The indictment made national headlines.

During this period I was dividing my time between Puerto Rico and the Teamsters pension fund investigation. In Chicago we were conducting extensive grand jury hearings, following up numerous leads concerning fraud and kickbacks on loans from the fund. We were able to identify seven intermediaries whose "expertise" was essential for a loan to be approved.

The intermediaries would beef up the applications with false information about the purpose of a loan, the financial credit of the borrower, the ability of a borrower to repay, and the assets, liabilities and net worth of the borrower. For example, one application estimated that a corporation had a net worth of $3.5 million when its actual net worth was less than $5,000. Another application stated that improvements on a hotel in Miami would cost over three million when in fact the work to be performed would cost only $700,00, thus enabling the balance to be diverted. It was common to highly inflate the amount of the loan requested, and the value of the mortgaged property, in order to divert the proceeds in the form of kickbacks to Hoffa and the others.

Hoffa's role in the conspiracy was to familiarize himself with the designated loan applications before they were presented to the other trustees. As the minutes of the meetings showed, he would then personally present the applications, making false representations and misleading statements and concealing material facts, and would then stiff-arm approval from his compliant fellow trustees.

By the end of May 1963 we had completed the writing of a 53-page indictment charging Hoffa and the seven others with using the mails and interstate telephone and telegraph services to obtain by fraud more than $20 million in 14 loans from the pension fund for themselves and others, and with diverting more than $1 million for their own use. The evidence would show that Hoffa himself had obtained funds belonging to Teamsters members for his own benefit, to the tune of more than $100,000.

The indictment was approved by Attorney General Kennedy and was returned by the grand jury on June 4, 1963. Once again it made banner headlines around the country. The Chicago Daily News, under the page one banner INDICT HOFFA HERE IN FRAUD stated that the indictment represented "the most massive legal attempt to date by Atty. Gen Kennedy to put the tough-talking Hoffa behind bars." The Wall Street Journal, while giving the story extensive coverage, also noted:

"This is the sixth time Mr. Hoffa has been indicted, but he hasn't been convicted in any of the cases."

Bill Mauldin, the famous World War II cartoonist, did a cartoon showing a truck bearing the name Hoffa & Co. with a ticket on the windshield with the words Mail Fraud Indictment. He labeled it "Big Ticket."

The Washington Evening Star, under the heading "Hoffa Indictment Caps Teamsters' Bad Week," noted that in addition to the pension fund indictment, heads of Teamsters locals in Philadelphia and New York had been convicted in federal courts that week, and that a total of 69 convictions of Teamsters and their associates had been obtained in federal courts since the beginning of the Kennedy administration.

The Nashville and Chicago indictments, coming less than a month apart, were at last to be the downfall of Jimmy Hoffa, but the trials would not take place until the middle of 1964. In the meantime, we were still hearing, "You'll never get him convicted and sent to prison."

It is worth noting historically that on the same day as the Chicago indictment, June 4, 1963, the world was mourning the death of Pope John XXIII, the beloved pontiff who in his five years of rule brought major changes to the Church by convening the Second Vatican Council.

Bob Kennedy was in contact weekly, and sometimes daily, with Walter Sheridan concerning our work. Every couple of months he would invite all of our group of fifteen to his office on the fifth floor of Justice for personal reports from each of us. We always addressed him as "General" in keeping with Justice tradition, but he called on each of us by our first names. He always worked in shirt sleeves and a with a loosened tie. When the meetings took place on Saturday mornings, he would usually bring Brumus, the family's giant Newfoundland dog, who sat placidly at his side. The atmosphere was informal, and Kennedy listened attentively to each presentation, making comments and asking questions. His interest in our work was intense, but his ready smile and Irish wit kept us all at ease.

On a couple of occasions he dropped unannounced into our suite of offices on the second floor, just to see how things were going, as if he didn't have a thousand other things on his mind, like the Cuban missile crisis and the civil rights battles in the South. Being part of the "Hoffa Squad" (though Justice never publicly admitted to such a group) was exhilarating, but the daily work of investigating and preparing a fraud case for trial is often drudging and wearisome. Bob Kennedy's visits were great morale and ego boosters. In my ten years at Justice I worked for five attorneys general, and no other AG ever came to my office, nor would I have expected him to.

I knew many people in Justice and other law enforcement agencies who, before meeting Bob Kennedy, expected to dislike him—this man who became attorney general at age 35—and who had been known as the "hatchet man" on the McClellan Committee and in his brother's presidential campaign. But I never knew anyone who, after having met him, did not instantly like him and have great admiration and respect for him.

The shocking news that President Kennedy had been shot in Dallas came just after noon on Friday, November 22, 1963. I was having crab cakes with friends at a restaurant near Justice. (For several years thereafter I was unable to eat crab cakes.) We rushed back to the office, by which time his death was confirmed. It was unthinkable. No president had been assassinated since McKinley in 1901. The national outpouring of grief and shock was overwhelming. The image of Camelot had come to a sudden and brutal end. Every adult alive on that day remembers exactly what he or she was doing at the moment the news came down.

On the following Sunday afternoon I invited Susan to join me on the balcony of the Justice Department as the cortege carrying the casket moved slowly down Pennsylvania Avenue from the White House to the

Capitol rotunda, where the president would lie in state overnight. The procession was led by the Marine Band, playing a dirge, with the traditional and symbolic presidential horse, Black Jack, carrying an empty saddle and empty boots facing to the rear. Though it was not planned, after the procession passed, people simply flowed into Pennsylvania Avenue and followed the casket up to the Capitol, ourselves included, and waited in line for hours to pay homage to a fallen hero.

On our way home, we heard the further shocking news that Lee Harvey Oswald, Kennedy's assassin, had been shot and killed by Jack Ruby.

Jimmy Hoffa's jury tampering trial began on January 20, 1964. It was held in Chattanooga because of the saturated publicity in Nashville during the previous trial. Hoffa arrived the day before the trial, proceeding from the airport in a forty-car caravan behind a police escort. That evening he gave a live television interview in which he talked about his wife, his family, and his innocense.

Bob Kennedy, recognizing a strong anti-federal and anti-Kennedy sentiment in the South, asked John Hooker, Sr., a highly regarded and eminently qualified veteran Chattanooga trial lawyer, to head the prosecution team, assisted by Jim Neal and the local U.S. Attorney. Hoffa, the other defendants, and eleven attorneys were grouped on the defense side.

Of necessity, the judge ordered the jury sequestered, housed in a local hotel for the duration of the trial under the watchful eyes of United States Marshals. Hopefully this would prevent further shenanigans by Hoffa and his cohorts who had once again swarmed into town, among them Frank Chavez.

Edward Partin's appearance as a witness for the government came as a complete surprise to the defense. His testimony about the massive and persistent attempts to get to the jury in Nashville was devastating. He quoted Hoffa as saying they "were going to get one juror or try to get a few scattered jurors and take their chances." Later, Partin testified,

Hoffa said, "I've got the male colored juror in my hip pocket. One of my business agents took care of it." Partin was viciously attacked during five days of cross examination, but his testimony was corroborated by overwhelming evidence, and Hoffa's desperate and agitated denials were not believed by the jury.

The defense fought tooth and nail for six weeks, but on March 3, 1964, Jimmy Hoffa was convicted on two felony counts of jury tampering. The other defendants were also convicted.

At the sentencing, Judge Frank W. Wilson stated to Hoffa:

"You stand here convicted of seeking to corrupt the administration of justice itself. You stand here convicted of having tampered, really, with the very soul of this nation. You stand here convicted of having struck at the very foundation upon which everything else in this nation depends, the very basis of civilization, and that is the administration of justice."

Judge Wilson sentenced Hoffa to eight years in prison. He remained free on bail pending appeal.

On the day of sentencing, Frank Chavez in Puerto Rico wrote a letter to Robert Kennedy:

Sir:

This is for your information. The undersigned is going to solicit from the membership of our union that each one donate whatever they can afford to maintain, clean, beautify and supply with flowers the grave of Lee Harvey Oswald. You can rest assured contributions will be unanimous.

Sincerely,

Frank Chavez Secretary-Treasurer Teamsters Local 901

Bob Kennedy had been understandably subdued since the death of his brother, but a few evenings after the Hoffa conviction, he and Ethel threw a party for all of us at Hickory Hill, their estate in the Virginia suburbs. Susy joined me. Kennedy's heartfelt remarks, as we sat around his living room after dessert, were not of a gloating nature, but an expression of his deepest gratitude for all those who had worked so long and diligently in the cause of justice. He tried not be distracted, during his comments, by the sight of Brumus slurping up all the dessert plates.

Less than a month later, Susan and I were married on April 4, 1964, at Holy Trinity, the Jesuit church in Georgetown. Susan had been one of Father Hartke's favored "kids" at Catholic University, and he graciously consented to preside and celebrate the Mass. The reception was held at the American Newswomen's club along Embassy Row.

Susan had accepted a position the previous fall as director of public relations at Arena Stage, Washington's professional regional theater. She was also on the board and company manager of the American Light Opera Company, which produced Broadway musicals in Washington, and was composed of highly qualified actors, singers, and dancers, many of whom went on to professional careers. So we had developed a rather wide circle of acquaintances, many of whom, in addition to our families from Omaha and California, our college friends, my Marine Corps associates now living in Washington, and my Justice colleagues, graced us with their presence at our wedding.

Because of Susy's schedule at Arena Stage, we took only a one-week honeymoon to St. Simon's Island, Ga., and Charleston, So. Car., vowing to do a longer honeymoon later in the summer.

We rented a three bedroom townhouse at 1811 37th St. N.W., in the Georgetown area. A month later Susy became pregnant with the first of our three children. In February 1966 we purchased and moved into an identical townhouse just four doors away at 1803 37th St. N.W.

Shortly after returning from our honeymoon, I had occasion to go to the Teamsters Building on Constitution Ave., armed with a subpoena for a large number of documents pertaining to Local 901 in Puerto Rico. I gave no advance notice, fearing that some of the documents might be destroyed. I presented myself to the house counsel and the two of us proceeded to the basement where, at my request, we commandeered all the photocopying machines.

After about an hour, down came Hoffa himself, demanding to know why the hell nobody could get anything copied. His attorney tried to explain the situation, but he turned on me with fury in his eyes, and snarled, "You dumb bunch of government wet-nurses, you never had to meet a payroll—you never could run a business." I couldn't resist replying, "Well, Hoffa, we were smart enough to convict you." Whereupon he flew into a rage, advancing menacingly toward me with fists clenched, and barked, "Okay, let's have it out right here." It was the schoolyard bully all over again. Fortunately for me, his lawyer intervened and sent him grumbling back to his office.

The Pension Fund trail of Hoffa and his seven co-defendants opened in Chicago on April 27, 1964. The lead prosecutor was Abe Poretz, assisted by Charley Smith. The eight defendants were represented by nine attorneys, including some of Chicago's most prestigious trial lawyers. The jury was sequestered at the Great Lakes Naval Training Station.

Shortly after the trial opened, Abe Poretz became ill and had to return to Washington. Named to replace him was Asst. U.S. Attorney William O. Bittman, from the Chicago office. Bill, an experienced trial lawyer in his thirties, quickly familiarized himself with the intricate details of the case, and conducted an aggressive and outstanding prosecution.

The jury heard colorful evidence of the fraud and deceit perpetrated upon the pension fund by Hoffa and his associates, which we had uncovered in our investigation. A loan of $650,000 went to a company in Miami at the behest of Sam Hyman, one of the defendants, for an apartment project. Not only was the work never done; there was no such company, and the money went to Hyman, which he distributed among the other defendants.

The Fontainebleau Hotel in New Orleans obtained a loan of $1.35 million in exchange for payment of $165,000 cash in small, old bills to Hoffa's co-defendants. A hospital in Florida owned by a defendant received a loan of $500,000. Hoffa told the trustees it was "to add a fourth floor." The floor was never added. The defendant's partner, called as prosecution witness and shown a picture of the three-story building, tried to explain that "the fourth floor of the building is also the ceiling of the third floor." He further complicated matters by adding, "It is not the roof in the usual sense but it is acting as a roof."

Another defendant's company obtained a loan of $3 million for the purchase of buildings in Los Angeles. The loan was made on the representation by Hoffa that the borrowing company had a net worth of $3,673,000. The evidence showed that its actual net worth was $634.17 and it was necessary to borrow $200 to open a bank account in which to deposit the loan proceeds. $40,00 of the money eventually made its way to Hoffa.

And so the pattern went, through 14 loans. As the climax of the government's case, FBI accountants traced the various loan proceeds and showed the complex pattern of widespread diversion, misrepresentation, and fraud.

In his final summation, Bill Bittman masterfully wove together all the threads of deceit, and condensed the 13 weeks of testimony and 15,000 documents into a coherent story of a mammoth scheme to loot the pension fund.

On July 26, 1964, the jury found Hoffa guilty on four counts and all of the other defendants guilty on from two to nine counts.

Once again, the results were reported in banner headlines around the country.

After the trial, Bittman transferred to Washington and continued his brilliant career as a government prosecutor. Later as a litigator in private practice he developed a reputation as one of Washington's greatest criminal defense lawyers.

On August 17, 1964, Judge Richard B. Austin sentenced Hoffa to serve five years in prison, to run consecutively to his eight-year jury tampering sentence. The other defendants also received prison sentences. As in the previous case, Hoffa remained free on bail pending appeal.

In addition to the convictions of Hoffa, from 1961 through 1964 there were 126 convictions of Teamster officials and their associates.

After the trial, Bob Kennedy gave a private party at one of Washington's downtown restaurants. It was to be the last social gathering of the "Hoffa Squad" and one of the last social events for Kennedy as attorney general. The loss of his brother had taken its toll, and he and Lyndon Johnson had never been on good terms, either before or after LBJ's presidency. He would soon resign from the Justice Department.

At the party, Kennedy recited from memory the St. Crispin's Day speech from Shakespeare's *Henry The Fifth*:

> Old men forget;
> yet all shall be forgot,
> But he'll remember with advantages
> What feats he did that day.
> Then shall our names,
> Familiar in his mouth as household words,
> Be in their flowing cups freshly remember'd.
> This story shall the good man teach his son;
> And Crispin Crispian shall ne'er go by.
> From this day to the ending of the world,

But we in it shall be remember'd.
We few, we happy few, we band of brothers....

At the end of the evening there were more than a few tears of joy, of relief, and of nostalgia.

On August 25, 1964, Kennedy resigned as attorney general and announced his intention to run for the U.S. Senate from New York. At Kennedy's request, Walter Sheridan resigned from Justice to join the campaign.

The press began to carry reports of the disbandment of our group. Clark Mollenhoff, writing from the Washington bureau of the Minneapolis Tribune, reported "The Justice Department is quietly folding the 'Hoffa unit' after more than 115 convictions and a dramatic success story that is comparable to the TV exploits of 'The Untouchables.'" He mentioned the names of several of the lawyers who had left the Department for jobs on the outside or private practice, and also noted that several others, including myself, had been shifted to other duties within the Department. (I had the trial of the Chavez case awaiting me.)

Hoffa's appeals were vigorous and protracted but were answered with equal vigor by the Department's appellate lawyers. The jury tampering case went to the Supreme Court, which denied the appeal, and the banner headline in the Washington Post read HOFFA PLEA FAILS, IT'S JAIL NOW. Actually there was another three months of maneuvering, but on March 7, 1967, Jimmy Hoffa entered the federal prison at Lewisburg, PA, to begin serving his eight-year sentence, still proclaiming that he was the victim of a government conspiracy to send him to jail. Eventually the Chicago convictions were also upheld.

The lead editorial in the Washington Star on March 8 summed up the Hoffa saga this way:

"It is sad that a man of 54, who fought his way to the top of the powerful Teamsters Union at $100,000 a year, and whose many talents are not subject to question, should wind up in this fashion. But it should not be forgotten, when all has been said, that Jimmy Hoffa was the architect of his own downfall."

In 1971, after four years in prison, Hoffa applied for parole. The U.S. Board of Parole asked Justice for any information concerning Hoffa's connections with organized crime. At that time I was deputy chief of the Oranized Crime & Racketeering section, and I appeared before the Board, outlining his numerous connections to organized crime, including the Mob's use of the Pension Fund as its own slush fund. The Board denied parole.

Later that same year, in December, President Nixon signed an executive grant of clemency to Hoffa, and he walked out of prison a free man. In 1972 the Teamsters Union endorsed Richard Nixon for reelection and contributed $400,000 to his campaign.

Shortly after his release, Hoffa announced his intention to regain the presidency of the Teamsters Union.

The corrupt and racketeer-influenced leadership of the union continued under Hoffa's successor, Frank Fitzsimmons. Moreover, there are strong indications that Fitzsimmons deeply resented and feared Hoffa's attempt to make his way back to the top.

In any event, Hoffa never made it. As is well known, he was last seen emerging frrm the Red Fox restaurant in a Detroit suburb on July 30, 1975. He was picked up in an automobile by unknown persons and has never been seen again. Rumors have persisted that he lies under the end zone of the Giants Stadium in East Rutherford, New Jersey, which was under construction at that time. Personally, I doubt that part of the story. I think it would have been too risky to transport either him or his body half way across the country in order to dispose of him.

Mob infiltration of the IBT and many of its locals, particularly in Chicago, New York, and Detroit, continued until well into the 1980's. Finally the Department of Justice filed an ant-racketeering suit against the union that charged Teamster leaders with having made a "devil's pact" with organized crime, siphoning off millions of dollars of union funds each year. One mob informer said that he collected $100,00 every *month* from Teamster locals in the New York area and turned the money over to John Gotti, the head of the Gambino family.

Out of that suit came a 1989 consent decree in which an independent review board was created to monitor the activities of the union. As a result of this intensive government supervision 90 Teamsters were expelled for being Mafia members or associates of Mafia figures.

Thanks to these persistent efforts, coupled with new leadership in the past few years, particularly (and surprisingly) that of James P. Hoffa, Jimmy's son, the Teamsters Union now is virtually free of racketeer influence, according to reliable reports.

To anyone interested in further study of the Hoffa saga, I recommend Walter Sheridan's book, *The Fall and Rise of Jimmy Hoffa* (Saturday Review Press, New York, 1972, 554 pp.); and Robert Kennedy's *The Enemy Within* (Harper & Brothers, 1960, 338 pp.).

Mississippi Contrasts

Before Bob Kennedy resigned as attorney general, he had one more assignment for our group, not related to the Teamsters. All hell was breaking loose in Mississippi in the civil rights struggle in the summer of 1964. The events of that summer were later portrayed in the 1988 film "Mississippi Burning." We were sent down to dampen the flames.

A year or so ago, in a writing course, I was asked to write about an experience in my life when things were not what they seemed to be. That summer in Mississippi came to mind. Here is what I wrote.

Mississippi is a beautiful state. Its gently rolling hills are covered with stately yellow pines that reach straight up to an azure sky. Country roads meander in and out of placid towns, each with a square whose centerpiece is a monument to the brave young men of the Confederacy.

In keeping with the serene nature of the land, the people are unfailingly polite and friendly. "Welcome y'all" and "Y'all come back" are as commonplace as grits'n'gravy.

That's the way it was in the summer of 1964. In the little town of Philadelphia that Sunday morning, Neshoba County Sheriff Lawrence Rainey and his deputy, Cecil Price, mustered up all the courtesy they were capable of when they picked up James Chaney, Michael Schwerner, and Andrew Goodman. This was no mean feat, considering that they were dealing with a black troublemaker from Meridian who was consorting with two white outside agitators from New York, and Jews at that.

Although the young men were held in custody all day, they were not mistreated. After dark, they were released, and the sheriff and his deputy and a few of the local men were kind enough to escort them to the edge of town and show them the road back to Meridian. A few minutes later they were ambushed. Schwerner and Goodman were shot in the chest and Chaney was beaten to death. Their bodies were placed in trash bags and buried in an earthen dam.

We arrived in Mississippi a couple of weeks later. The motel clerks were polite and courteous, and the smiles did not leave their faces even when they discovered we were attorneys from the Department of Justice, Criminal Division, Washington, D.C.

There were eight of us, designated as special assistants to the Attorney General. That spring, Congress had at last enacted powerful civil rights legislation, and thousands of college student volunteers from throughout the nation had flocked to Mississippi to help African Americans register to vote. They called it the Summer of Freedom, and the situation was combustible, to say the least.

Our assignment from Bob Kennedy was to go out to towns like Laurel and McComb and Magee, where no blacks had ever been registered to vote. We met with mayors and chiefs of police and sheriffs, many of whom were members of the White Knights of the Ku Klux Klan, to let them know or our presence and to assist them in seeing that there would be no trouble in enforcing the new laws. Out subliminal message was clear: We were there to keep an eye on them.

Without exception, they were outwardly friendly, gracious and hospitable, and assured us that they had happy folks (meaning blacks) in their town and "there won't be no trouble." One chief recalled, "It looked like there was gonna be trouble a while back. One o' them teachers [using the N word] began talkin' uppity stuff to his class, but a few of our boys paid him a call one night. The next day he left town and we ain't had no trouble since." Satisfied smiles all around. We were speaking different languages, but they understood ours.

In each town we also looked in on the Summer of Freedom volunteers. They were young, brave, frightened, and angry. They were getting people registered, but they thought the Department of Justice should be protecting them. They wanted a U.S. Marshal on every street corner. They were too tired and too scared to listen to reason.

And so it went. Each day we were charmed by the bad guys and berated by the good guys. It was unreal.

But that's the way it was, among the gentle hills and placid towns of Mississippi, that summer of 1964.

The day after Bob Kennedy resigned, we were recalled to Washington.

Gradually, the voting rights legislation took effect. In Mississippi in 1964, 7% of blacks voted, but by 1968 nearly 60% voted. These changes occurred throughout the south, and by the 1970's African

Americans began to be elected to statewide offices and to federal positions in the southern states.

No state or county charges were brought against Sheriff Rainey, Deputy Price, or the others. But they were charged in federal court with violating the civil rights of the victims. Rainey was acquitted but Price and six others were convicted. Price got a six-year term and served four and a half years.

Forty years later an enlightened district attorney in Neshoba County reopened the case and brought murder charges against the still surviving ringleader of the lynch mob, Edgar Ray Killen, now age 81. On June 21, 2005 he was convicted and sentenced to 60 years in prison. Many young people thought the punishment too harsh. It is impossible for them to fully understand the depth of the hatred and fear that permeated rural areas in the south during that era.

Second Honeymoon: Surfing to the Dentist's Chair

In late August 1964 Susan and I seized the opportunity for a second honeymoon. We headed for Hawaii, stopping off in Santa Clara where my parents held a party to introduce their daughter-in-law to friends and neighbors. We spent several leisurely and delightful days on each of the islands of Maui, Kauai, the Big Island, and Oahu.

Our last two days were on Waikiki Beach. After a day of watching the surfers glide over the waves I decided I had to give it a try. It looked so easy. Some trepidation set in after I rented and lifted the 7-foot wooden surfboard which seemed to weight about 75 lbs.

"You need any lessons?" asked the bronzed and muscular young attendant.

"Nah," I replied in my most assured manner, and tucking the board nonchalantly under my arm, I staggered off down the beach.

Paddling out just beyond the breakers, I was amazed to discover that it's almost impossible to get up on the damn things—the board keeps slipping out from under foot. How come it *looks* so easy? I developed an immediate reverence for those surfer dudes you see in the movies. After about twenty tries, I finally got to my feet, shakily. An instant later I slipped off the back, causing the board to shoot straight up and then straight down, striking me square in thne mouth and bending back one of my front teeth. Thus I spent the last afternoon of our honeymoon in the dentist's chair, where he forced the tooth more or less back in position. That was my first and last attempt at surfing.

There is a sequel to this story. Thirty-five years later that same front tooth went bad and had to be extracted. Replacing the tooth required a bridge, and as anyone who has had this kind of dental work can verify, the adjoining teeth need to be carved and sharpened in such a manner as to create a decidedly snaggle-tooth look before the bridge is inserted. Dr. Sam, my Napa dentist, put in a temporary bridge, saying "This will do you for about two weeks while we're having the permanent bridge made."

The next day Susan and I left on a 15-day trip to China. On the 14th day, in Beijing, our group of about 70 was enjoying the traditional Peking Duck dinner. Just as I was savoring the last of my duck, the temporary bridge fell into my plate. Exactly one second later I heard the voice of our group leader: "Ladies and gentlemen, tonight we are pleased to announce that two members of our group are celebrating their 35th wedding anniversary. Let's all turn and applaud Tom and Susan Kennelly!"

There I was, trying to retrieve my bridge from the duck. We were obliged to stand and accept a bouquet of flowers, Susy smiling broadly and me with one hand in the plate and the other over my mouth. The absurdity of the situation and the exquisite timing caused me to start giggling, so much so that it brought tears to my eyes. And then I heard a female voice say, "Oh look, Tom is so overcome with emotion he's crying. Isn't that sweet!"

The next day was spent in the dentist's chair in Beijing. But that's another story.

11.

BACK TO PUERTO RICO

I had spent the week before our wedding putting together a prosecutive memorandum for Jack Miller, head of the Criminal Division, to support the proposed indictment of Frank Chavez and three other Local 901 officials for submitting false strike benefit claims in violation of the federal mail and wire fraud statutes. Included with the memorandum was a proposed 21-count indictment.

Upon my return from the honeymoon the indictment was approved, and on April 29, 1964, the grand jury returned the indictment in the District of Columbia. Given the choice of venue in Puerto Rico, where the defendants lived, or D.C., where the "victim," the International Union, was headquartered, I chose the latter. I figured I would have a better shot at an impartial jury, and one that would not be tampered with by Chavez.

The defendants, Chavez and three other union officials, Amador, Trias, and Pagan, were charged with obtaining more than $200,000 in phony strike benefits from the International.

The case, heavily publicized in Puerto Rico, initiated a series of defense maneuvers and delaying tactics which, coupled with a few bizarre events (perhaps not so bizarre for Puerto Rico), occupied the next eighteen months leading up to the trial.

First the defendants, with Teamster lawyers from the U.S., moved for a change of venue to Puerto Rico, claiming that 385 defense witnesses would be called. The judge in Washington granted the motion and transferred the case to San Juan, where Judge Ruiz Nazario set the trial for November 9. On November 4, the defendants claimed they still had to interview 350 witnesses, and the judge set a new hearing date for February 9, 1965.

While waiting for the February 9 hearing Susan and I were also awaiting the arrival of our first child. Since the due date was around the third week in January, we had made no plans for the Inaugural Ball for Lyndon Johnson on January 20. But as Inauguration Day approached and our little bundle from heaven was not showing any signs of being inaugurated, Susy was feeling very large and not a little depressed. Missing a big party is not something she takes lightly. So on the evening before the inauguration we decided to try our luck at crashing some of the State Society parties being held in various hotels. We made it into the Nebraska party, and then met an old friend, Jack Bradshaw from Indianapolis, who got us into the Indiana party. Later than evening we met an acquaintance of Susy's, the drama critic for one of the papers, who offered us a ticket for one person to the Inaugural Ball the next evening at the Mayflower hotel.

That's all Susy needed. The next morning she began going through her wardrobe, tugging at this and stretching that, until she came up with an amazingly attractive ball gown. Then off we went, I in my tux and she looking ravishing in her gown, and by some legerdemain she got us both in. We danced the night away, including the Charleston, attracting a few gasps from some of the more staid attendees. The next day she resumed her matronly vigil, now happy and contented. It would be another three weeks before the baby made his appearance.

At the February 9 hearing in San Juan, counsel for the defendants requested an additional postponement of four months, now claiming they expected to call 500-600 witnesses, of whom only 155 had yet been located. They also claimed that presentation of defense witnesses alone would consume four months of trial. All of this was a complete fabrication, but it was enough to scare off Judge Ruiz, who took the case off the calendar for at least five months, pending appointment of a visiting judge.

Marvin Loewy and Mr. Gil handled the February 9 hearing, because on the previous day, February 8, 1965, Susan gave birth to our first child, Patrick Joseph, at Holy Cross Hospital. Her mother was also present, and it was the second happiest day of my life, after our our wedding day.

This being our first experience with a baby, we hired a practical nurse, a robust lady named Mildred Robinson, to be with us for the first two weeks. Mildred knew everything about tiny babies, and also cooked the meals. One evening during the first week I came home in the midst of a snow storm. In preparing dinner Mildred, while attempting to extract something from the freezer with a meat fork, managed to puncture one of the coils, whereupon Mother Powers exclaimed that the escaping Freon would surely kill us all, and we should run for our lives into the raging blizzard.

At this moment Boffo, the family cat, sensing that something was wrong and that poor Mildred was the cause of it all, dashed over and peed on Mildred's leg.

Shortly thereafter, suffering from post-partum depression, I went off for a few days of quiet skiing at Stowe, Vt.

It was the custom in Puerto Rico to invite visiting federal judges from the states to come down to help with the caseload, and there was never a shortage of eager volunteers, especially in the winter months. So our first visitor on the Chavez case was Chief Judge Alfred P. Murrah from Oklahoma. Several years later, after his death, a new federal building in Oklahoma City was named in his honor, and that is the building that the terrorist Timothy McVeigh blew up on April 19, 1995, causing the deaths of 168 innocent people.

On April 12, Judge Murrah set a trial date for July 12, 1965, now fifteen months past the indictment date. Shortly thereafter, defendant Amador was killed in a barroom brawl.

On May 6, Judge Murrah announced that he would not be trying the case, and he returned to Oklahoma. On June 16, Judge Ruiz set a new trial date for July 19.

Anticipating that I would be spending he rest of the summer in San Juan, we decided that Susy and Patrick, now four months old, would join me. We sub-leased our house for the rest of the summer, and rented an apartment in San Juan near the beach. All in all, it was a delightful time. The Puerto Rican women fawned over our beautiful little fair-skinned, blue-eyed, red-haired boy. We had no trouble finding baby sitters, and so we went out with friends for dinner and dancing frequently. We also found time for the three of us to visit other parts of the island, as well as the Virgin Islands, between pre-trial bouts in the courtroom. Marvin Loewy also brought his wife and three small children down from Washington.

Our next visiting judge was William Mathes from Los Angeles, a no-nonsense veteran of 20 years on the bench, who had written the book of jury instructions which was used in every federal court in the country. Judge Mathes came prepared to start the trial on July 19. But the crafty Teamster lawyers were just getting warmed up. Jacques Schiffer from Chicago, representing Trias, moved for a further continuance and for an order directing all parties to go to Cuba to take the deposition of a "vital defense witness," who happened to be in Castro's army. This witness formerly worked for Local 901 and was the only person who could exonerate his client. Trias was not in the courtroom. Judge Mathes ordered that he be brought to court. When Trias arrived he asked the judge to appoint a new lawyer for him because he had not heard from Schiffer in five months. At this point Judge Mathes said, "Mr. Schiffer, I've had enough of your chasing dust on the trail," and dismissed him from the case.

Trias then got another lawyer and a few days later pleaded guilty. Judge Mathes set August 16 as the new trial date.

Then came a flurry of new motions. They moved to strike the entire jury panel on the ground that it excludes persons who do not speak English. They claimed that the granting of commonwealth status to Puerto Rico in effect made it independent, and therefore no federal court had any jurisdiction on the island. They claimed that a 1917 statute provided that visiting judges could only be judges of the Supreme Court of Puerto Rico. They again renewed their motion to require all counsel to go to Cuba.

All of these silly delaying tactics required our written responses, and all were eventually denied.

Then they moved to transfer the case back to the District of Columbia and that one was granted! Apparently Judge Mathes had had his fill of these people.

So, after 16 months, 18 court hearings, and four aborted trial dates, we were right back where we started.

This sudden change of events presented a slight problem. Anticipating a long trial, Susan and I had subleased our house until the middle of September, and this was August 20! So we decided to take some vacation time to visit our families in California and Omaha and show off our new baby. After a few final days of sailing and deep sea fishing and enjoying farewell dinners with our many friends in San Juan, we flew to San Francisco first and then to Omaha.

We had a great time in both places, and family members were duly congratulatory on the wondrous six-month-old son we had produced. We were particularly fortunate to be in Santa Clara at the same time as my sister Mary Lu, now Sister Thomas Patricia, home on leave from her high school teaching assignment in San Diego.

Susan and I spent a couple of days alone in San Francisco where, among other things, we managed to conceive our second son, to be named Timothy Francis.

12.

THE CHAVEZ TRIAL

After a few more dilatory defense motions, the Chavez trial began in Washington on October 25, 1965. The remaining defendants were Frank Chavez and Luis Pagan. The judge was Luther W. Youngdahl, former Republican governor of Minnesota, who had been appointed to the federal bench by Harry Truman so that he would not be the Republican candidate for the Senate in 1954 against Hubert Humphrey, who was running for his second term. Youngdahl had a reputation among the prosecutors in Washington as a judge who feared being overruled on appeal and therefore, when in doubt, always ruled in favor of the defense. They were overjoyed to learn that Marvin Loewy and I would be keeping him out of their hair for several weeks.

It was necessary to hire interpreters to translate all the proceedings for Pagan, who claimed to speak no English, although it was he, through his attorney, who had moved to transfer the case back to Washington.

The trial lasted six weeks.

Marvin and I called as our first witnesses two officers of the International. John F. English, general secretary-treasurer, and William Mollenholz, the union's comptroller, were longtime and honest employees of the union, long before Hoffa came upon the scene. Both testified that all strike benefit claims submitted by Local 901 were paid on the assumption that the strike data was accurate.

We then called employees of all the companies in question, who testified that they never received the benefits submitted in their names nor signed the claim sheets. Others testified that the strike ended long before the dates represented by Local 901. In all, we called 50 witnesses to prove our case.

We thought the women from the Virgin Islands sweat shop would particularly impress the jury, being poor, unsophisticated, and having picketed in the hot sun for weeks without ever getting their strike benefits. To our surprise, they all showed up in fancy new outfits—hats, gloves, the works—and looking like fashion models out of Ebony magazine. They had persuaded the U.S. Marshals in the Virgin Islands that it would be cold in Washington and therefore they would all need new wardrobes. The sympathetic Marshals obligingly fitted them out to the nines, using federal funds.

The defense called twenty witnesses, including Chavez. (Note that part of their original delay was the alleged need to interview 500-600 witnesses.) Their defense was multi-faceted and fanciful. They alleged a conspiracy between business leaders and the Puerto Rican government to drive the Teamsters off the island. They asserted that the strike benefit claims were prepared by inexperienced and overworked employees who made honest mistakes. They also claimed that they imported outsiders to strengthen the picket lines and paid them off the books and in amounts several times more than the amounts shown on the strike benefit claims, None of this was corroborated.

The climax of their case came with the testimony of Harold Gibbons, a vice-president of the International and member of its board of directors. He testified that Chavez was sent to Puerto Rico with a free hand to spend as much money as necessary to organize the island. He said there was no need to submit phony strike benefit claims; if Chavez had asked for the money legitimately he would have received it anyway.

The trial ended on December 1, 1965. After a day and a half of deliberation, the jury returned a verdict of not guilty on all 21 counts as to both defendants.

I can attest that the essence of "humbling" for a prosecutor is hearing the words "not guilty" pronounced 42 times.

We interviewed the forelady of the jury afterwards. She said the jurors discussed all the issues pro and con and made their decision on the basis that since we hadn't proved the defendants got any personal gain, and since the International wasn't complaining, the jury couldn't convict even though they felt the defendants had not acted properly. It is a matter on which reasonable people can differ, and since they decided it on the issues it did not shake my faith in the jury system.

A weakness in our case was that we were never able to place the union's ill-gotten gains in Chavez' pockets. Nor did it appear that he lived a particularly lavish life style, other than a few mistresses, which was certainly not unusual in Puerto Rico. Legally it was not necessary to prove that the defendants were personally enriched; only that they fraudulently obtained monies from their "victim," the International Union. In this case the victim was neither aggrieved nor an object of sympathy. I subsequently learned from experience that if you are going to prosecute someone for fraud, you had better have either an aggrieved victim or an enriched defendant, and preferably both. Here we had neither.

Of some consolation was a call from the Assistant Attorney General to say he was proud of the way we had worked and prepared the case, and we should have no regrets. And Judge Youngdahl told us he had seldom seen a case so well presented.

In retrospect, my approach to the case was too legalistic. I think I would have had a better chance for a conviction if I had narrowed the case just to the women at the garment factory, naming them as the victims—preferably in rags. But at the time I felt that since the Department of Justice, including the FBI, had spent so much time and money uncovering the length and breadth of Chavez' criminal activities, I had to include the whole scheme.

All the files pertaining to this case have been placed in the archives of the John F. Kennedy Presidential Library in Boston.

EPILOGUE: Two years later Frank Chavez was killed, shot to death in his own office in a fight with his own bodyguard.

In 1965 Susan renewed her freelance public relations business which had been interrupted by her sojourn at Arena Stage and then the birth of Patrick in February. Her main client was Stanley-Williams Presentations, a concert management agency founded by her friends Bob Stanley and Harding Williams. S-W promoted musical and dance troupes from around the world, and with the upswing in popularity of folk singers in the sixties, they brought to Washington most of the big names. Even before we were married, Susy gave a memorable post-per-formance party at her Georgetown, home, which was covered by the Washington Post, for Joan Baez (then about 23) and Pete Seeger (about 45), who were appearing jointly at the Washington Colosseum. It was Baez' first appearance in Washington, and Pete's first since his blacklist-ing by the House Unamerican Activities Committee in the dark days of anti-communist hysteria in the 50's.

The Clancy Brothers and Tommy Makem also made their first appearance in Washington in 1963 (and annually thereafter for the next twenty years or so) under the auspices of Stanley-Williams with Susy doing the publicity. So also did Judy Collins, Simon & Garfunkel, Tom Paxton, Arlo Guthrie, and many others, including the fabled French singer, Jacques Brel.

During this time she was also a board member of the American Light Opera Company, which was invited to sing at the White House during the lighting of the National Christmas Tree and in honor of the visit of Chancellor Erhard of West Germany. As a favor to her, she and I were permitted to join the group but only to *mouth* the words, but it resulted in a picture that appeared in Time Magazine (12/31/65. P.14).

13.

CON MEN, SWINDLERS, AND BANK PRESIDENTS

When the Hoffa Squad was disbanded, I moved over to the Fraud Section of the Criminal Division. It consisted of about 20 lawyers, headed by Nathaniel B. "Tully" Kossack, a career Justice lawyer in his fifties with a great booming voice and a warm heart.

The Department depends on career professionals like Tully Kossack. Attorneys General and Assistant Attorneys General come and go with changes in the White House. They establish general policies and set priorities; and if they are wise, they seek the guidance and listen to the advice of experienced old hands like Tully and the other section chiefs. In my era they included people like Henry Petersen, chief of the Organized Crime & Racketeering Section (of whom we shall hear more later), and Bea Rosenberg, chief of the Appellate Section. Bea, a brilliant lawyer in her late sixties, had argued more cases before the Supreme Court than any other person in history.

These people were totally dedicated to the cause of justice. They were not obsessed prosecutors or ideologues. Their experience enabled them to view both sides of an issue and to make disinterested judgments concerning vital issues. They were well aware of political implications but were not controlled by them. These men and women took pride in their loyal service to both Democratic and Republican administrations while retraining the ability to "call 'em as they see 'em." And they inspired their staffs to retain the same professional detachment.

Generally, in my ten years at Justice, the political appointees heeded the judgment of the career professionals. I deeply hope that is still true.

Some may call these career government lawyers bureaucrats, but I never thought of them as such. To me bureaucrats were pencil-pushers over in Commerce or Agriculture. These lawyers were my professional colleagues, and they were some of the finest people with whom I have ever been associated.

The U.S. Postal Service, through its Chief Inspector, has the responsibility for bringing to justice those who use the mails to cheat the public. When such schemes are brought to their attention, the postal inspectors conduct a thorough investigation, gathering hundreds of documents—letters, literature, victim interviews, narrative reports, etc.—and then present these materials to the office of the U.S. Attorney nearest to where the culprits are operating. If that office determines that prosecution is warranted, an indictment is returned by the grand jury.

The Postal Service had conducted two lengthy nationwide investigations in which the culprits were headquartered in Washington, D.C., but the U.S. Attorney's office was so overloaded handling street crimes that no one was available to take over these cases. I gladly accepted Tully's request to take them on, as I had found I enjoyed putting together the legal equivalent of jigsaw puzzles.

I was given a large room on the third floor of the federal courthouse, quiet, windowless, and containing a dozen or so file cabinets filled with documents. I determined that prosecution was warranted in both cases, and then prepared them for indictment and trial. I was ably assisted by the experienced postal inspector who had supervised both investigations from the beginning. I reviewed both simultaneously, but present them here in the order in which they went to trial.

The New Mexico Oil and Gas Lease Exchange

Clyde Bowles, age 51, was a quiet-living longtime Washingtonian. His father had been a smalltime hood for the mob in New York. Clyde himself had served some time, but somewhere along the line he decided that it was possible to become rich without being violent. For the past ten years he had been the creator and sole owner and operator of the New Mexico Oil and Gas Lease Exchange. It had the prestigious address of 1215 Connecticut Ave., N.W., just a few blocks from the White House, but was a one-room operation.

Clyde had discovered that the State of New Mexico sold oil and gas leases on state-owned desert land in southern New Mexico. Some parts of the state did have oil, but this land had little or no oil or gas possibilities, and was known in the industry as "goat pasture." However, anyone who wanted to take a flyer that some day Standard Oil or Texaco might want to start drilling on the land, could buy up these leases at auction for a dollar or less an acre. Clyde bought thousands of these leases for an average of 82 cents an acre.

He then printed up a batch of fancy literature suggesting that this land was near other parts of New Mexico where there *is* oil, and through his salesmen all over the country he sold the worthless leases at $800-$1000 per 40-acre tract, inducing purchasers to believe they had a great chance to strike it rich.

Clyde selected as his salesmen only the very finest and most experienced snake-oil rogues, and armed with Clyde's alluring literature, they swindled farmers and lawyers and doctors and housewives from coast to coast. Clyde allowed them to charge whatever the traffic would bear, and he in turn faithfully paid them their commissions. Clyde found it necessary to be in his office only in the mornings, leaving plenty of time for the racetrack in the afternoons.

The Postal Service estimated that during the course of its operations, the Exchange had filched in excess of $5,000,000 from the public, and nobody had struck oil.

The grand jury indicted Bowles and twelve salesmen. In its press release the Postal Service described the salesmen as "the greatest collection of swindlers ever gathered together under one indictment." All twelve eventually pleaded guilty and agreed to testify at Bowles' trial. They were an indeed a colorful and entertaining lot, and in their interviews I got some wonderful stories from them. I asked one fellow to tell me the secret of his success, and he replied, "We depend entirely on the *cupidity* and the *stupidity* of the public."

Clyde Bowles went to trial in mid-January, 1966, six weeks after I had finished the Chavez case. As always, trial preparation and the trial itself were arduous. In a letter to my parents on January 30, I apologized for my tardiness in writing, explaining that I had worked the past 26 days in a row. In addition to conducting each day's trial session, one must make sure that the next day's witnesses have arrived, prepare them one last time for their testimony, line up the necessary documents to be introduced in evidence, discuss that day's successes and failures, and also handle any mid-trial defense motions to be researched and responded to, as well as prepare jury instructions and a closing argument.

Young potential trial lawyers should be aware that trial work does involve a lot of stress. As a colleague of mine said, "To be a good litigator you have to enjoy the stress. You have to be quick on your feet and be ready to make decisions pretty much off the top of your head." It's true that there is a lot of pressure, but I can't think of a more enjoyable occupation.

To my great benefit, a young lawyer from the Fraud Section named John Risher was assigned to assist me at trial. Although John had no previous trial experience, he was a very bright lawyer who quickly adapted to the courtroom and was a great help to me. Later in his career,

John became the first African American partner in the major Washington law firm of Arent, Fox, Plotkin, and Kintner.

The Bowles case was actually more interesting than the Chavez case because this time we had lots of aggrieved victims who had been bilked out of their life savings. Among the 14 who testified at trial were an Arkansas farmer, a New Jersey school teacher, a California clergyman, and a Missouri chiropractor. All had been told and shown maps that oil had been found "nearby," and that it was only a matter of time before one of the big oil companies would come knocking to buy up their leases at huge profits to them.

I had found in Roswell, N.M. an expert petroleum geologist who could explain to the jury in simple terms *why* there was no chance of finding oil in the area where Bowles peddled his leases. A real showman, he graphically demonstrated how oil can be found in some places but not in others. He explained that oil comes from fossils in ancient seas, far underground. "If you are a couple of hundred yards back from the high tide line on a beach," he said, "you can say you are near the ocean, but you will never get your feet wet." In other words, if there are no fossils, there will be no oil. Or again, "If you are on a cement walkway through a tulip bed, you may be surrounded by tulips, but they ain't never gonna come up through that cement walk."

For this reason, he testified, the leases sold by Bowles had no oil or gas potential, and in fact were not even close to the "high tide line" or the "cement walk." The jury loved it.

Bowles' lawyer, Myron Ehrlich, a well known and shrewd Washington advocate, put Bowles on the stand on direct examination for five days, proceeding slowly and attempting to show the jury that his client was a very nice, mild-mannered fellow (true) who could not possibly have intended to mislead anyone (not true). His defense was that he acted in good faith ("You never know where oil might me found") and that he was not responsible for the misrepresentations made by his salesmen, whom he preferred to call "independent brokers."

One of the most effective ways of discrediting a witness is through his prior inconsistent statements: getting the witness to admit that he had previously said or written something directly contrary to his testimony on the stand.

I was loaded with Bowles' prior inconsistent statements. He had written reassuring letters to customers, letters full of misleading promises; there was literature he himself had prepared containing numerous false and deceptive statements; and there were instructions he had sent to his salesmen on what to tell customers to make the sale. Bowles was forced to admit all of these.

On the second day of cross-examination, he threw in the towel. His lawyer called a recess and Bowles entered a plea of guilty. After 15 days, the trial was over. Afterwards, some of the jurors said they hated to see it end, they were enjoying it so much. For me it was a real morale booster after the Chavez trial.

Bowles received a sentence of five years in prison and a heavy fine. The salesmen received lighter sentences, and a couple of them got probation. It would have been nice if the judge could have also ordered Bowles to pay restitution to the victims, but at that time there was no provision in the law for doing so. The sentencing laws have since been changed.

After the trial I received a letter from the Commissioner of Lands in New Mexico which concluded: "On behalf of the people of New Mexico, I am sending our thanks." One can only wonder why the great state of New Mexico sold these worthless leases in the first place.

The McHale Brothers: Debt Consolidators Par Excellence

Someone once described a debt consolidator as one who, for a fee, combines all your little debts into one big back-breaking load. The McHale brothers—Joseph, Martin, and Robert—all with checkered backgrounds and mind sets just below the level of used car salesmen, found great financial satisfaction in coming to the assistance of people who were overwhelmed with debt and hounded by creditors. They set up shop in the District of Columbia and nine other eastern cities. They operated under various corporate names, and before they went defunct they had attracted more than 10,000 gullible customers in four years.

Debt consolidators are not illegal as such, but there is a great temptation to step over the line and mislead customers as to the nature and value of their actual services. The McHales eagerly bounded over the line. Through ads, mailings, and phone calls, the brothers and their associates promised to consolidate all of their customers' existing bills, set up a system of regular payments and enable them to get out of debt in one year or less with payments they could afford.

The McHales were not interested in the truly poor. They preferred to attract relatively unsophisticated people who earned regular paychecks with a genuine desire to pay their bills but were hopelessly mired in consumer debt. Their "debt counselors," with alluring promises such as "We'll take care of all your bills," and "Within four weeks all your creditors will be paid and you'll be on easy street," left the impression that the consolidator would pay all their bills now and the customers would make reimbursement in easy stages. In reality, payments to creditors would come exclusively from the weekly amounts sent in by the debtors, less an "installation charge" to open the account and a service fee on each and every payment to a creditor.

The customers were promised that the "counselors" would prepare a budget for the clients, and that the installation fee would be deducted over a period of time.

All of this, though expensive and of questionable value, would not have been illegal, and should have been sufficient to provide a good living for all the McHales and their associates. But they got greedy. They never prepared a budget for their clients, and simply set as high an amount as they could for the customer to pay in each week. They pocketed the entire installation charge up front, causing further delays in payment to creditors and more dunning notices to the debtors. (They were told to ignore these.) Then they raised the installation fees retroactively and increased the service fees without ever informing their customers. Finally, as their avarice increased beyond their revenues—big cars and charter flights between offices, for example—they simply stopped paying the creditors and pocketed all the money. They went out of business after four years, leaving all their bank accounts overdrawn. In addition, Robert McHale stole $20,000 that was owed to the IRS for his employees' withholding taxes.

I organized the voluminous records gathered by the diligent postal inspectors and prepared the case for prosecution.

The grand jury indicted the McHales and five of their accomplices. One of them, Peter Firra, was a fugitive, and "Wanted" flyers went up in all the post offices around the country. As far as I know, he was never found. The Postal Service was quite proud of the fact that this was the first federal prosecution of this type.

The trial began in mid-May 1966 in Washington before Judge Howard Corcoran, who was an excellent and congenial jurist and treated both sides with cordiality and fairness.

My parents came to Washington during the trial and had an opportunity to see their son in court. It's a good thing they did, because they were needed in the midst of the trial. May 30 was Memorial Day and the court was not in session, but I was in my office preparing the next day's witnesses. I got a call from my mother that Susan was about to deliver our second child and my dad had rushed her to Georgetown Hospital. For years afterward, he told the story that when they arrived, he was asked if he was the father. "I've been accused of a lot of things," he replied, "but on this one I claim innocense." I arrived at the hospital just as Susan was being wheeled out of the delivery room with little Timothy Francis, and one could not have asked for a sweeter and more loveable child. The next day in court I handed out cigars (the custom of the time) to the judge, all the lawyers, and the defendants.

The trial, like the previous one, featured a variety of aggrieved victims. The jury was visibly shocked to learn, for example, that of 5,059 customers in Washington, only 49 had all of their bills paid in full.

There were also some memorable moments. An effective defense tactic in a fraud case is to present witnesses who were *not* cheated by the defendants. In fact, if I ever decided to be a con man, I would take care to cheat only half of my customers; then for every victim presented by the prosecution I could offer a satisfied customer, claiming that there must have been some misunderstanding or that the government's witnesses were at worst dissatisfied cranks.

Defendant Michael Callahan's attorney tried this tactic by presenting a witness who testified that all her bills had been paid, and moreover she had received a "Christmas bonus" from Callahan of $75. We then able to show that not only was the "bonus" her own money but that Callahan owed her an additional $70 which she never received.

Harry Taylor, the attorney for Robert McHale, tried to show that the whole case was cooked up, not by debtors, but by an overzealous postal inspector, in cahoots with Kennelly. His cross-examination of a former customer, a prosecution witness, went as follows:

"And after you terminated your contract with National Budget Services, you didn't hear any more about it until the postal inspector contacted you, isn't that right?"

"Well, yes I did."

"What did you hear?"

"Do you really want me to tell you?"

"Yes, yes. We're all anxious to hear."

And the witness replied, "I heard they stole all the money and skipped town!"

The judge, the jury, and even the other defense attorneys broke up. Mr. Taylor had no more questions and sat down, having violated the first rule of cross-examination: Never ask a question to which you do not already know the answer.

Joseph McHale took the stand and tried to convince the jury that he was a brilliant businessman and inventor who would never stoop so low as to try to cheat a customer. He had invented what he called a Vibro-Pedic mattress and also some sort of Lazy Susan for executives, both of which he described in glowing detail. He also pointed with pride to the fact that the records showed that he had never once raised a customer's installation charge.

His attorney made much of this in his summation to the jury, and in my rebuttal I alluded to it. Later, while the jury was in deliberation, the defense attorneys presented me with a small loving cup inscribed "To Prosecutor Tom Kennelly From All the Defense Counsel in U.S. vs. Joe McHale, Jun 27, 1966." In the cup was a certificate signed by all the attorneys which read:

> Presented to Tom Kennelly, U.S. Prosecutor, in recognition of his rebuttal in the mail fraud trial of the U.S. vs. Joe McHale wherein he said, "Joe McHale didn't have to raise the installation charges. All he had to do was sit down on his Vibro-Pedic mattress, lean over his Lazy Susan and write himself a bonus check."

It was one of the most delightful and touching moments in my legal career, and I still have the trophy and certificate.

All the defendants were found guilty. It was one of my most satisfying trials as a prosecutor.

However, I was dismayed by the light sentences awarded by Judge Corcoran: three to six months in jail for some defendants, and straight probation for others. On the same day, street criminals were sentenced to up to six years for assault with a dangerous weapon. I wrote to my parents: "I guess you can steal as much as you want as long as you don't hit 'em on the head when you're doing it."

The Brighton National Bank Goes Belly Up

The arrival of little Timmy blessed us with two babies under seventeen months, and Susan was incredibly busy. In addition to caring for the children, her public relations business was continuing apace. It was time to get her some help. So we persuaded cousin Bill and Kay Kennelly's oldest daughter Kathleen, 17, who is also my godchild, to come out from Chicago to spend the summer with us. It would also be an opportunity for her to explore Washington. She was wonderful with the children, a delightful and enthusiastic addition to our household, and Patrick adored her.

However, within two weeks of her arrival, we all packed up and spent most of the summer in Denver. Immediately after the McHale case, which ended on July 1, I was asked to assist in the criminal trial of one James Egan, president of the defunct Brighton National Bank, near Denver. The trial was to begin on July 18.

Brighton National Bank started up in the heyday of the early 1960's when the chartering of new national banks was being encouraged by the Comptroller of the Currency, who regulates national banks, and charters were being granted with relaxed rules concerning capitalization and regulation. As might have been anticipated, this ultimately resulted in a number of national scandals, both in banks and savings and loan institutions. These occurred particularly in small communities, where outside adventurers, using naive or avaricious local bankers as front men, seized the opportunity to obtain large sums of cash from depositors and then use the funds to further their own roguish purposes. One such example was the Brighton bank.

Located in a trailer in the little town of Brighton, 18 miles from Denver, it opened in April 1963. The principals were James Egan, a former insurance salesman from Miami; Richard Horton, a former Hollywood television producer who had served time in San Quentin for fraud; and Hugh Best, a local Brighton banker. The capitalized the bank with half a million dollars, $488,000 of which came from a 90-day loan from a Denver bank. They lured depositors with higher-than-market interest rates. When the bank folded just 21 months later, it owed its depositors and creditors nearly $2 million.

The scheme was simple enough, but laying out the criminal case was difficult and complex. There was a maze of transactions, some real and some sham, involving other small banks in Colorado and Missouri; loans and payoffs involving real and fictitious entities and individuals; and forged stock certificates masquerading as collateral. There were dozens of such dealings, all for the purpose of deceiving the federal bank examiners and keeping the sham alive.

The U.S. Attorney in Denver was a good man but a lightweight, and the case had been developed over many months by the Fraud Section at Justice by two of its most experienced prosecutors, Frank Cunningham and Joe Cella. I joined the team for the final preparation and the trial itself. Best and Horton had plea bargained to one count, but Egan, the principal stockholder, insisted on going to trial on all nine counts of fraud, claiming he had been duped by the others.

It was short notice for me, but a chance to take the family along, and Susy jumped at the opportunity to escape the heat and humidity of the Washington summer and to return to Colorado. She and her parents had spent their summer vacations at Rocky Mountain National Park at Estes Park, north of Denver, from the time she was 9. Susy enjoys nothing more than hiking in the mountains, and we promised ourselves we would spend a few days there after the trial.

By sheer serendipity we found a 3-bedroom furnished apartment available for the summer in the lovely Cherrydale section of Denver. It was ideal, and Susy's Mom came from Omaha to be with us.

Presiding over the trial was Chief Judge Alfred A. Arraj, one of the most tyrannical and unpleasant jurists I have ever encountered. Canines with distemper are put down, but federal judges have lifetime tenure. In addition, he was a "homer;" he made frequent snide remarks to the jury that he didn't see the need to bring lawyers all the way from Washington when there were perfectly capable prosecutors right there in Denver (as though it was any of his business.) We laugh about it now, but one day Susy's mother attended the trial. At the end of the day she said the judge had no right to be disrespectful to her son-in-law and his colleagues and was all for marching right into his chambers to tell him so.

We completed our presentation in about ten days, and then Egan took the stand in his own behalf. Although only 49, he had a history of heart trouble, and midway through cross-examination by Joe Cella, he fainted dead away. Judge Arraz called a recess and summoned a cardiologist.

"He's had a mild heart attack, your honor," said the doctor, "but I don't think it's life threatening."

"Then prop him up and let's go," replied kindly Judge Arraz.

Needless to say, Joe's further cross-examination was extremely brief.

At the conclusion of the trial the jury returned verdicts of guilty on three counts. Prior to sentencing, the judge ordered a complete cardiological examination by a panel of experts. They concluded that Egan had a life expectancy of two to five years, whereupon kindly Judge Arraj awarded him three years in prison.

The trial got a great amount of coverage in the Denver press. A final wrap-up of the history of the case by the Denver Post ended as follows: "Government prosecutor Thomas Kennelly of Washington put it this way: 'The Brighton National Bank was a sham in the beginning, and a shambles at the end.'"

After the trial, Susy's mother and Kathleen cared for the boys while she and I spent five glorious days at Estes Park. The park is as awesome as she had described. The mountains are spectacular, the hiking trails exhilarating, and the views breathtaking. It was the first of our many visits there, together and with all the children. In 1978 I climbed Long's Peak, the highest peak in the park at 14,255 ft., and Patrick, at 13, made it almost to the summit. Then in 1984 Susy, Patrick, Katy, and I made it to the top. It is probably the most difficult climb we have ever done. We started at 4 AM and returned at 9 PM—a tough 7.5 mile climb, but a wonderful experience. Our most recent visit to the park was in 2002, to celebrate Susan's 65th birthday.

There is an epilogue to the Brighton trial: One year later, on the very day that the Court of Appeals affirmed his conviction, James Egan died of heart failure.

Olive Bitter and George Kennelly just prior to their marriage, 1924

George and Olive with grandsons Patrick and Tim, 1967

Tom, 4, with father's truck, 1934

Tom, 7, First Communion, 1937

Tom, 12, at Whitefish Lake, with "Moby Dick," 1942

Tom at Marine Officer Candidate School, Quantico, 1954

Tom (r) with buddy at Basic School, Quantico, 1955

Tom and Susan in Santa Clara, 1964

Susan with Tim, Katy and Patrick, Easter 1968

Tom and Susan with Mother Theresa, Washington D.C., 1982

25th Wedding Anniversary with Katy, Tim and Patrick, 1989

14.

WE TAKE ON THE MAFIA

Henry Petersen was frustrated. A career prosecutor, he had recently been elevated to Chief of the Organized Crime & Racketeering Section at Justice, but the government's efforts against organized crime seemed to be going nowhere. For the past 45 years this country had been plagued by the Mafia. Particularly in large urban areas like New York, Philadelphia, New Jersey, Chicago, and Detroit these syndicates had been in control of the traditional rackets like illegal gambling, loan sharking, hijacking, fencing stolen property, and drugs. By the late 1950's organized crime had begun to infiltrate and corrupt organized labor. Further, through its enormous wealth, it was increasing its holdings and corrosive influence in legitimate businesses, including banks, insurance, and real estate. And in order to maximize its profits and minimize its risks, the mob relied heavily on corruption of public officials at the local, state, and even federal levels.

The American public has been allured by the mystique of the Mafia since the days of Al Capone and the Roaring Twenties. The Mafia originated in Sicily after the collapse of the Napoleonic regime. Since there was no effective local government, wealthy landowners hired thugs to protect their property and keep order. Legend has it that these men were called "Mahvias," the local word for the caves in which they had dwelled along the shores of southern Sicily. Gradually they strong-armed their way to supremacy in their regions. When Mussolini came to power in 1922 he viewed them as a threat to his dominance and began to liquidate them. Hundreds fled to the United States. Their arrival coincided precisely with the onset of Prohibition in this country, a situation made to order for their organizational skills in providing illegal goods to a thirsty public.

Here they encountered competing gangs—Irish, German, and Jewish. Most of the gang warfare in the Roaring Twenties consisted of turf battles among these ethnic groups. Gradually the Sicilian gangs achieved dominance, and by 1931 Charles "Lucky" Luciano had pulled them together into a cohesive group, climaxed by the infamous "night of the mustachios," September 10, 1931, in which 41 rival mob chiefs were whacked in a single night.

Luciano regulated external relationships among the 24 Mafia groups, called families, giving each control over all criminal enterprises in its designated geographic area. The most populous areas had more than one family; for example, New York City had five and Chicago three.

Luciano also established discipline and clear lines of authority within each family. At the top was the boss (*capo*), followed by the underboss, various captains and lieutenants, and at the lowest level, the button men or soldiers. The highest ruling body was the Commission, composed of representatives from only seven families, and headed by a *capo di tutti capi*. In each family the code of silence, the *omerta*, was strictly enforced. This fear and intimidation was a major factor in the Mafia's continuing success. The police could never expect a witness to come forward.

Each family operates more or less autonomously, with the Commission stepping in only when necessary to settle disputes. Another distinguishing feature is its continuity. Unlike the James gang, which ended with the death of Jesse, the eventual deportation of Lucky Luciano only meant that Vito Genovese stepped in and took his place.

Elliott Ness and the "Untouchables" had made some inroads during Prohibition, and Al Capone had been sent to Alcatraz for tax evasion at age 29, but in general the criminal syndicates had operated with little hindrance from law enforcement since the 1930's.

At least the public was becoming more aware. The threat of organized crime had been graphically documented in hearings by Sen. Estes Kefauver in 1950, the first Congressional hearings ever televised to the nation. In 1957, the FBI came upon a meeting of the Commission, attended by 58 Mafiosi, in a small village in upstate New York, and the "Apalachin Meeting" caused a national sensation. The McClellan Senate Rackets Committee spent four days probing the attendees, their connections with legitimate businesses and labor unions, and their relationships with the whole structure of organized crime throughout the country.

The Apalachin Meeting also managed to bestir the attention of J. Edgar Hoover. Hoover had never shown much interest in organized crime. He much preferred tracking down suspected communists and leftist pinkos. He also preferred having his agents solve bank robberies and recover stolen vehicles, because these activities were cost effective. He toted up the value of the recovered monies and vehicles, and each year he could tell Congress that the FBI recovered more value than he was asking for in operating funds. But organized crime investigations were not cost effective; they were time consuming and difficult and resulted in few arrests or convictions relative to man hours expended.

So what Hoover did was place surreptitious wiretaps and bugs on the phones and at the meeting places of suspected Mafia members and associates. This resulted in a lot of good intelligence, which made him appear as authoritative, but he was not making any cases because the bugs and taps were illegal and the evidence could not be used in court. Hoover was talking the talk but not walking the walk.

The sensational Valachi hearings in the Senate in the fall of 1963 added to the public's awareness of the Mafia and the pervasiveness of its criminal operations. Joe Valachi, a member of the Genovese family in New York and serving a life sentence, learned that he was marked for murder by Vito Genovese. He then turned informer.

Valachi's colorful testimony was the first public confirmation of the huge, tightly knit organizational structure of this criminal subculture. He disclosed the identities and the criminal activities of the various families. He described the initiation ceremony, and told of beatings and murders. Valachi also revealed that, although on the outside the organization was called the Mafia, the Outfit, the Mob, or the Syndicate, on the inside they referred to themselves as La Cosa Nostra (Our Cause).

My parents were visiting Washington at this time to meet Susan, and I arranged for us to attend the hearings and Valachi's testimony, which they found fascinating.

Henry Petersen was frustrated because organized crime was on the rise while law enforcement, at all levels of government, seemed to be treading water, if not drowning. Further, the mob was moving into new areas of opportunity, including the theft of credit cards and the forging and theft of corporate securities. Perhaps most ominous of all, they were beginning to target the Las Vegas casinos. By controlling the casinos they could skim off the profits, providing untraceable cash to finance any number of corrupt enterprises.

To make matters worse, even reliable intelligence was drying up. By 1966 there had been numerous disclosures about the extensive use of illegal wiretaps and bugs by the federal government. In fact, both the FBI and the IRS, without the other's knowledge, had placed bugs and taps in several Las Vegas casinos. When these disclosures came to light, Lyndon Johnson was embarrassed and incensed, and forbade any such further use.

Law enforcement seemed stymied for several reasons. The code of silence was a major obstacle. Even if a smalltime hood was caught, he knew that if he talked it would mean sudden death to him and/or his family. For the same reason, informants were hard to come by, and because the families were so close-knit, it was extremely difficult and dangerous to insert an undercover agent.

At the local level, most police departments were overwhelmed handling street crimes, and had neither the personnel nor the expertise to conduct sophisticated organized crime investigations. Organized crime work is different from regular police work. When a crime is reported, police officers and detectives are trained to find the perpetrator. Organized crime is just the opposite. You know who the criminals are; you have to find the crimes they are committing. You have to find the loan shark victim or the illegal gambling operation or the corrupted labor union or public official. Nobody is going to report these crimes to you.

Also at the local level, law enforcement tends to be fragmented. In any large metropolitan area there may be a half dozen local communities, each with its own police department. Add a layer of county sheriffs' offices. Then there are state and federal agents in the same metropolis. Traditionally, none of these agencies are eager to cooperate with any others, out of fear of having their intelligence compromised, or of losing jurisdiction over an important case, or simply out of jealousy, pride, or suspicion. In law enforcement, turf battles are the name of the game.

I used to say that if I ever decided to rob a bank, I would live in DC, plot the crime in County A in Maryland, recruit my accomplices in County B, commit the crime in County C in Virginia, mail the loot to a post office box in County D, and then move to West Virginia. Even if everybody knew I committed the crime, there would be a 50-50 chance that I would never be brought to trial, because of jurisdictional battles.

At the federal level, at least seven different federal agencies had ongoing organized crime investigations, but there was little or no sharing of information, evidence, leads, or strategy. Ever since the Organized Crime Section was formed at Justice in 1958, there had been proposals to get all the agencies working together. Bob Kennedy had made visits to all the federal districts and got the agencies to meet together, but when he left town they gradually drifted apart again.

The Buffalo Project

The time was ripe for a new approach. Petersen, with the assistance of Bob Peloquin, formerly of the Hoffa squad, put together a proposal for a pilot project, in which experienced investigators from various agencies, working together with five attorneys from the organized crime section, would be located in one suite of offices in one city and would set their sights on organized crime in that area. The investigators would be top-level supervisors whose job it would be to direct (force, coax, cajole) their own agents toward a common objective in the target region. They would operate quietly, without publicity, and would also seek the cooperation of state and local law enforcement where feasible, *i.e.* not corrupt.

It would be a six-month project and if successful, would be a model for other such groups.

The proposal was accepted by Attorney General Ramsey Clark, and received the enthusiastic endorsement of the heads of the following:

The Internal Revenue Service, which would designate agents from both the Intelligence and Audit Divisions;

The Secret Service, which had jurisdiction over the theft of and forgery of government securities;

The Bureau of Narcotics and Dangerous Drugs (later changed to the Drug Enforcement Agency);

The Alcohol and Tobacco Tax Bureau (later Alcohol, Tobacco and Firearms);

The Department of Labor;

The Customs Bureau.

J. Edgar Hoover declined to participate, still not trusting any agency than his own, but promised to provide "liaison" to our group.

Buffalo, New York, was selected as the target city, for a number of reasons. It was controlled by the Magaddino Family, which was relatively small, about 150 known members, but powerful. It controlled the rackets all across upstate New York, including Rochester, Syracuse, Utica, and Albany. Moreover, its capo, Stefano Magaddino, was the head of the Commission, the *capo di tutti capi.* His cover was the Magaddino funeral parlor in Niagara Falls.

The Magaddino Family's influence also extended into Ontario and Quebec, including Toronto, Ottawa, and Montreal. Thus the Royal Canadian Mounted police, the federal police force for Canada, enthusiastically accepted an invitation to join the Buffalo Project. It is believed to be the first such joint effort between the two countries.

Buffalo was also selected because the enforcement record against the Magaddinos was so dismal that any improvement would look terrific. In the previous 12 years there had been only three prosecutions, of which one was for a misdemeanor, and another resulted in an acquittal.

But it was a vicious gang. Magaddino himself was quite elderly and not in good health, so the operation was run by the underboss, Freddie "the Wolf" Randaccio, ably assisted by Pasquale "Icepick Patsy" Natarelli. A year or so earlier, the FBI had picked up a conversation between the two in which they gleefully discussed how they had treated a suspected informant, one Albert Agueci, by slicing off chunks of his flesh, and then burning him alive. His badly burned body was found a few days later. His arms and legs had been broken, his jaw shattered, and half of his teeth knocked out. Natarelli, by the way, had earned his nickname by his deft application of an icepick to the eardrums of loan shark borrowers who had gotten behind in their payments.

Peloquin was to be in charge of the group, and asked me to be his assistant. He had also selected three very enthusiastic young attorneys from the section, Mike Blommer, Gary Gardner, and Don Campbell. I had very much enjoyed working with Bob on the Hoffa squad. He was a year older and a born leader with a winning personality.

The Buffalo Project presented a fascinating challenge. I wrote to Sister Thomas Patricia, "The only real justification for staying in government is to do something exciting and worthwhile and to serve where help is needed most. It's the same sort of foolishness that make soldiers want to go to Vietnam, I guess."

With two babies under two, Susan was not happy at the prospect of my shuffling off to Buffalo for six months, but as usual she was understanding and supportive. After all, we told ourselves, I'll be home on weekends and it will be for only six months. It's just as well we didn't know that it would be for two and a half years, and that before long there would be three babies under three.

In frozen and snowbound Buffalo, we set up shop in January 1967 in the offices of U.S. Attorney John Curtin, who was delighted to have us. Our supervisory agents were among the best in government service. They included Don Bowler and Mark De Louis from the IRS, Andy Berger from the Secret Service, Phil Smith from BNDD, Bill Behan from ATTB, Ed Mullin from Labor, and Fenelon Richards from Customs. They came from as far away as Los Angeles, and all had families at home, some with six, seven, and nine children. Our young attorneys were excited and rarin' to go.

It was a little disillusioning to discover that our Canadian Mounties did not wear scarlet uniforms, as in the old Nelson Eddy—Jeanette MacDonald movies. In fact the Mounties had got rid of all horses, except for parades. But Calvin Hill and his partner Murray Swift regaled us with tales of mushing through the frozen Yukon with dog sleds and surviving on dried beans.

We opened investigations in all directions: drugs, gambling, hijacking, smuggling, income tax, labor unions, and others. It was impressive to see what could be done when experienced agents sat down and planned things together.

Our first job was to smooth ruffled feathers. Here we were, barging into Buffalo, cutting across bureaucratic lines, trampling fences. So first we had to explain to everybody in law enforcement that we were not some sort of internal spy group planning to give their previous efforts bad marks. Bob Peloquin was persuasive, projecting a perfect balance of authority, urgency, and comradeship, and the federal agents on site could see that top-level people from their own agencies were part of the team. It took a while, but we finally convinced most of the local and federal people that our only mission was to make cases. We needed their cooperation and they would share in the successes, if any. We repeated this process in Rochester, Syracuse, and Albany.

North of the border, we considered ourselves fortunate to know and work with the Canadians, who were extremely competent and cooperative in every respect. Bob Peloquin and I were invited to speak at a gathering in Ottawa of the attorneys general from all the provinces in Canada. There we made the acquaintance of Pierre Trudeau, then attorney general of Canada. Later he would become one of Canada's most distinguished prime ministers, but even then he clearly had star quality. Later I was invited to speak to a convention of the RCMP in Montreal and I again received a warm reception, especially when I gave a short introduction in French.

The Beverly Hilton Scores

Our first big break came in the person of Detective Sgt. Sam Giambrone from the Buffalo Police Department. Sam had grown up on the Italian west side of Buffalo, where every boy grew up to be either a cop, a crook, or a priest—just like in the old James Cagney—Pat O'Brien movies. Sam told us about Paddy Calabrese, whom he had known since childhood. Calabese, 28, after serving in the Marine Corps, had returned to Buffalo and joined the mob. He was highly regarded for his specialty, which was robbery. In fact, he had pulled off a daylight heist at City Hall on tax collection day, making off with a canvas bag containing $300,000 that was sitting on the cashier's counter waiting for the Brink's truck.

Later Calabrese was identified and indicted, and an arrest warrant was issued. Calabrese was in Los Angeles at the time, planning another score for his bosses. Freddie Randaccio ordered him to return and surrender, promising that the fix would be in and he'd get off. He was convicted. Freddie then promised that he'd get a very light sentence. He got ten to thirty years, which he didn't think was so light. The next thing he heard was that some of the boys were fooling around with his wife Rochelle. Paddy was very unhappy.

A couple of FBI agents heard of his unhappiness and went to visit him in the state prison. He indicated that he might be willing to tell some things about his old boss Randaccio, but only under certain conditions: a) he would have to get paroled; and b) he and his family would need to be taken care of because he knew there would be an immediate contract on all their lives.

The FBI agents said they were sorry, but the government had no means for fulfilling those conditions, and they left.

Sam Giambrone also heard about Paddy's unhappiness, and he also went to visit Paddy. They talked about old times in the neighborhood. After awhile, Sam told Paddy about this new group he was working with, and maybe they could come up with some suggestions. Sam said, "Let me go talk to my people."

Sam told us about Calabrese, and Bob Peloquin said, "Find out what he's got on Randaccio, and if we can corroborate it, maybe something can be worked out."

Calabrese then told Sam the following story. He had been sent to Los Angeles by Randaccio and Natarelli to case two possible scores at the Beverly Hilton hotel. The tip had come from Charley Caci, a former Buffalo boy now trying to make his way as a Hollywood night club singer under the name of Bobby Milano. Caci had been contacted by Lou Sorgi, another former west side denizen who just happened to be head of security at the Beverly Hilton. Sorgi had described how it would be possible to rob the armored truck on its Monday morning pick-up from the hotel. Sorgi said the Monday bag would be loaded with checks and never less than a hundred grand in cash. Further, Sorgi had the personal trust of a wealthy widow from Phoenix who every year stayed at the hotel while racing her horses at Santa Anita. She lived in a suite on the 8th floor and carried around nearly half a million in jewelry. Sorgi would provide a master key and would know the combination to her room safe.

Calabrese, the master robber, was to pull off the scores with Steve Cino, another Buffalo gangster, and then, after fencing the jewels through Cino's uncle in San Francisco, they were to return to Buffalo with the proceeds. All participants would be handsomely rewarded.

Calabrese said that on his way to L.A. he had stopped in Pittsburgh and registered at a motel under an assumed name. The next day at poolside he had met a woman who had given him a book which she autographed.

Arriving in Los Angeles, he had stayed with Bobby Milano whose address he remembered, and had met with Sorgi. Sorgi had explained the armored car routine and had shown him the suite where the widow would be staying, as well as the date of her arrival. It was at this point that he was summoned back to Buffalo.

Bob Peloquin dispatched our team of agents to see if Calabrese's story could be verified. He sent Phil Smith from Customs, Ed Mullin from Labor, Bill Behan from Alcohol & Tobacco Tax, and Andy Berger from the Secret Service. This was unprecedented. It they had been back with their agencies, they would have been permitted to conduct investigations only for violations within their agency's jurisdiction.

The story checked out. The motel in Pittsburgh and the woman were located, and she identified a photo of Calabrese, the book and her autograph. In Los Angeles, Sorgi was indeed in charge of security at the Beverly Hilton, Bobby Milano's address was verified, and the armored car routine and the account of the Phoenix widow were exactly as Calabrese had described. It was terrific investigative work. This was information Calabrese could not possibly have obtained on his own, and that made the story credible, including the involvement of Randaccio and Natarelli. It was a conspiracy that a jury could accept beyond a reasonable doubt.

But was it a federal crime? Robbery is ordinarily a local crime, not to mention that the robberies never occurred. However, Congress had enacted the Hobbs Act, which provides that anyone who "obstructs, delays, or affects commerce by robbery or extortion, or *conspires* to do so" commits a federal crime. The armored car would have carried checks. Checks are part of commerce, and a robbery would have affected their movement. Also, the jewels or their proceeds would have been brought back to Buffalo, and it is a federal crime to transport or conspire to transport stolen goods across state lines. Therefore we believed we could nail the mob leaders even though they never left Buffalo and no one was robbed.

The next major problem was how to keep Calabrese, his wife and three children ages 7,6, and 4, alive. We called Attorney General Ramsey Clark, and he got the Pentagon, most reluctantly, to agree to hide the family on an Air Force base in Maine.

Shortly thereafter, in June 1967, Paddy Calabrese was removed from state prison to a specially prepared cell in the U.S. Marshal's office in Buffalo. Simultaneously, the Marshals picked up Rochelle and the children in unmarked black cars and drove them to Loring Air Force Base near Presque Isle, Maine. Rochelle was given an alias and she and the children were placed in married officers' quarters. She was to tell the neighbors that her husband was a Marine pilot on a secret mission overseas.

A few days later the grand jury returned indictments against Frederico Randaccio, Pasquale Natarelli, Steven Cino, Charles Caci, and Louis Sorgi. It was sensational news in upstate New York.

As we anticipated, a contract immediately went out on Calabrese and his family. Rumors had the offering price at $100,000.

Later that summer Bob Peloquin, with a wife and six children at home in Washington, left the government to join a Washington law firm. I was placed in command of the Buffalo Project.

Susan and I had decided that she and the boys would come up to Buffalo for the summer. She was expecting our third child in November. Through a friend of John Curtin, the U.S. Attorney, we were offered the use of a "summer house" on an estate at Derby-on-the-Lake, a few miles outside of Buffalo. The house was a 13-room mini-mansion with Georgian columns and a circular driveway, and with a huge yard fronting on Lake Erie. It was the ideal set-up. Kathleen Kennelly rejoined us for a few weeks, along with her younger sister Pat. Both my parents and Susy's mom also visited us. We had many parties that summer, and we always invited Harold and Rosemary Esty, the owners, who were wonderful people. Harold, who had a prosperous but somewhat humdrum career, was thrilled to be named an honorary member of the Buffalo Project.

I resisted the temptation to try the Randaccio case because of my other responsibilities. Besides, it would be better to have a Buffalo prosecutor, and John Curtin assigned his most experienced assistant, Andy Phelan, a great trial lawyer highly regarded by Chief Judge John Henderson, who would preside over the trial. Judge Henderson was an imposing man in his sixties, a brusque and impatient but fair judge, whose rulings bespoke not a trace of doubt or hesitation.

The trial lasted three weeks. Calabrese held up under withering cross-examination, notwithstanding the defense's portrayal of him as a "convicted felon, a thief and a person whose word is worthless." (The standard answer is that you don't find many bishops among a pack of thieves.) The corroborating evidence was effective, and the jury returned verdicts of guilty against all five defendants on November 21, 1967. Judge Henderson revoked bail, and for the first time, Freddy Randaccio and Patsy Natarelli were in jail.

Judge Henderson imposed the maximum sentence of 20 years on Randaccio, Natarelli and Cino. Caci/Milano and Sorgi each got ten years. Later the U.S. Court of Appeals affirmed the convictions, the first time the Hobbs Act had been upheld on appeal when the accused plotters never left the state and the robberies never occurred.

Meanwhile, I was at home, holding Susan's hand and awaiting the arrival of our third child, sort of. On Friday, November 17, the Clancy Brothers appeared in Washington under the auspices of Stanley-Williams, with Susy doing the publicity. The baby was overdue, as usual, and the doctor had told her that if necessary he would induce labor the next day. After the concert, we all adjourned to Matt Kane's, at that time the only Irish pub in Washington. At about midnight Tom Clancy climbed onto a table and proclaimed to all assembled, "Here's to the little baby that's to be born tomorrow." There were cheers all 'round.

And sure enough, at about 6 PM the next day, November 18, 1967, we were blessed with little Katherine Theresa. It would be impossible to describe our delight at the arrival of this beautiful blue-eyed blonde, and Katy has been a joy to us since that very first day.

Birth of the Witness Protection Program

With the convictions of Randaccio *et al*, we were now faced with the problem of how to take care of Calabrese and his family. This had never been done before in a federal criminal case, and there were no institutional guidelines on how to proceed. Nor was there any funding for this purpose. We were literally charting a new course.

Our first priority was to get Calabrese paroled from the state penal system. We had kept Ralph Oswald, the chairman of the New York Parole Board, advised of our purposes at the time we got Calabrese transferred to federal custody. Thus Oswald had paved the way for my appearance before the full Board after the convictions. They were impressed by the importance of Calabrese's testimony and our plan to relocate him and his family with new identities, and he was granted unconditional parole.

Meanwhile our agents were working on a plan. The family selected alias names. Ed Mullin of Labor was a former CIA agent, and he knew how to get new birth certificates for the whole family. Someone obtained social security cards. Sam Giambrone got baptismal certificates from a sympathetic priest. Someone else was a friend of a school superintendent in another state who agreed to provide records for the two children of school age. Phil Smith of Customs had a brother who was an executive in a manufacturing plant in the Midwest, and he agreed to hire Paddy, under an assumed name, as a fork lift truck driver. He also found a rental house for them. We got the Justice Department to pay their way to the new location and to provide the first three months' rent.

Finally, they needed transportation. One of the agents got driver's permits from Alabama. All of our agents and attorneys chipped in and we bought them a used Chevy for $800.

Paddy was relieved to be out of custody and he and Rochelle were happy to be reunited. But they were not exactly ecstatic. They thought they would be under the full time protection of U.S. Marshals, but it was explained that this would only draw attention to their situation. So they were on their own. The rest was up to them. For the first time in his life, Paddy would have to carry a lunch pail and work a 40-hour week.

That was about it. It was haphazard and seat-of-the-pants, but it was the beginning of the federal witness security program, and it was effective. It was an antidote to the code of silence. A witness, caught in a bind, could be induced to cooperate if he could see an alternative to sudden and violent death.

The witness security program later became institutionalized by Congressional legislation, and has become the subject of many books and movies, as we shall discuss later.

Dead Eye and Willie

In some ways the Buffalo mob, for all its brutality, was akin to the gang in Jimmy Breslin's hilarious *The Gang That Couldn't Shoot Straight*. Take the case of Dead Eye and Willie.

This was another score disclosed by Paddy Calabrese. An armored car messenger in Buffalo named Joe Erhart, looking to augment his salary, had tipped off the mob to an easy score. His truck arrived at certain bank at a certain time each day to pick up the day's cash receipts. He had noticed that an efficient bank clerk always placed the bag on the counter in advance, awaiting his arrival. If the timing was perfect, someone could dash in, grab the bag and make a quick getaway.

Paddy Calabrese was the obvious choice for the job, but had to turn it down because he was otherwise occupied. Danny Domino and Tommy Carella, Magaddino lieutenants, decided to hire strangers from out of town so as to reduce the chances of identification. They contacted Al Magrini, a Buffalo associate now doing well as a bookie in Wierton, West Virginia. Magrini had just the pair for the job, a couple of roustabouts named Dead Eye and Willie. The only way you could tell them apart is that *Willie* had only one eye. Dead Eye had earned his moniker as a pool hustler. Magrini figured they could use the money to pay off their gambling debts to him.

Dead Eye and Willie came to Buffalo, and on the appointed day and at the precise time, they approached the bank, Dead Eye at the wheel, and pulled up at the curb across the street. Willie placed a pistol in his belt and hopped out. As he was crossing the street, the pistol fell to the ground. At that very moment, Dead Eye noticed a police officer approaching from the rear. Panicking, he gunned the motor and took off down the street, with Willie in hot pursuit, shouting and waiving the pistol. The ever-alert arresting officer testified that he had intended only to notify them that they had parked in a red zone.

So once again there was no actual robbery, but there was a conspiracy to rob, and Domino, Carella, and Erhart went on trial, with Andy Phelan prosecuting. Calabrese testified, and Magrini, Dead Eye and Willie were granted immunity for their testimony. Magrini accepted an offer to be relocated, but Dead Eye and Willie allowed as how they could fade into the shadows without any help from the government.

Al Magrini was an odd looking fellow, whose hair stood straight up, whether from fright or otherwise I cannot be sure. Someone described him as looking as though he had been executed and hadn't died yet. But he was a pretty good witness. One of the defense lawyers attempted to show that the government had bought his testimony by giving him a new identity, paying to move him and his family across the country and finding new employment for him:

Q. And the government paid your way, isn't that right?

A. Yes sir.

Q. And they found you a job, too, didn't they?

A. Yes sir.

Q. You were a bookie back in Wierton, isn't that right?

A. I was.

Q. How much were you making as a bookie?

A. About two thousand a month.

Q. What kind of job did the government find for you?

A. I'm a watch repairman.

Q. And how much does that pay?

A. $82.50 a week.

End of cross-examination.

All defendants were duly convicted.

The Generosity of Sam Pieri

Sam Pieri, ranked third in the Magaddino family, went on trial in federal court for fencing stolen jewelry. The case was not going well for the government; the evidence was circumstantial and the witnesses were weak.

Sam was apparently not aware of this, for one day as the court broke for lunch, Sam approached a woman juror in the lobby of the courthouse and handed her a one hundred dollar bill. By sheer happenstance this small gesture of magnanimity was witnessed by five FBI agents who were at the time engaged in other tasks, such as making a phone call, buying a newspaper, or heading out for lunch.

Sam was arrested on the spot. The fencing charge was dismissed and Sam was indicted and convicted of jury tampering, for which he was awarded five years of free board and room. It was also the most help we had received from the FBI thus far.

The kicker on the story is that when the beneficiary of Sam's largesse returned to the jury room and related the incident to one of her fellow jurors, that lady's reaction was, "Wow! Do you think he'd give me a hundred bucks too?" Wonderful town, Buffalo.

Strike Forces

By the end of our first year, 1967, we had indicted 21 Mafiosi, and Attorney General Ramsey Clark publicly disclosed for the first time the existence of our group, and of its success. He called us a "strike force", which resonated with the media. The *Los Angeles Times* ran a story entitled "U.S. 'Strike Force' Wins First Convictions." The attorney general also announced that additional strike forces would be formed in Chicago, Detroit, Manhattan, and Boston.

In reporting on the attorney general's announcement, both Washington newspapers noted that "FBI Not on Crime Team." The FBI is part of the Justice Department, and the attorney general could have ordered the FBI to participate. But that was not the way things worked in Washington. J. Edgar Hoover was appointed director of the FBI by Calvin Coolidge in 1924 for ten years and was reappointed by every president for the next 48 years until his death in 1972. The Bureau's reputation for professional competence and discipline was unsurpassed, but it operated under Mr. Hoover's sole direction. And he simply was not willing to work with or share the Bureau's intelligence with any other agency. The nearly unanimous view among state and local law enforcement people was that working with the FBI was a one-way street.

No one, even at the highest levels, dared cross Mr. Hoover, because of both admiration and fear. The Congress admired him because he could always show that the Bureau recovered more funds than it expended. He was feared because of the general perception that in his files he had something on everybody. He had a particular dislike for the Kennedys and Lyndon Johnson, each of whom had more than one opportunity to fire him for public insubordination, but passed. There is an inside story that LBJ summed it up best to his advisors: "Ah'd sooner have him inside the tent pissin' out than outside pissin' in."

No one in our group was unhappy about the FBI's lack of participation. We were doing just fine, and state and local people were more willing to work with us without the Bureau. Besides, as far as we could tell, the only thing the Bureau was getting was intelligence from useless or illegal sources—nothing that could be used in court.

On the home front, Susan was very busy with three little ones. Patrick, the oldest, was not yet three, and I could help only on weekends when I blew in from Buffalo. Here is an excerpt from a letter to my parents in January 1968: "Boy, we are realizing the amount of work involved with three little helpless ones, but at least they are healthy.... Incidents like last Saturday morning make it all worthwhile. Susy had fed Katy her bottle about 7 AM and then left her in her infant seat on the couch while Susy crawled back into bed. Shortly thereafter Patrick came in, and thinking we were asleep, sat down next to Katy for a brotherly chat. 'Katy, I haven't had a chance to talk to you. Would you like me to sing to you?' He then sang through 'Jingle Bells' and 'Merrily we row our boat gently down the street.' At this point she apparently fell asleep and he was heard to say, 'Open your eyes, pretty girl.'"

15.

ACTING UNITED STATES ATTORNEY

Most of December 1967 and early January 1968 was spent traveling to Detroit, Chicago, New York, and Boston with Henry Petersen and his assistant, Bill Lynch, to help set up the new strike forces in those cities. Each was staffed by excellent and dedicated lawyers and federal agents.

In January 1968 John Curtin, the U.S. Attorney, was appointed to the federal bench, thus creating an opening for his position. New U.S. Attorneys must be appointed by the president and approved by the senate. Normally the president appoints whoever is recommended by both senators from the state. But Jacob Javits, the Republican, and Robert Kennedy, elected to the senate from New York in 1964, could not agree on a nominee.

Chief Judge Henderson, who in case of a deadlock was authorized to make an interim appointment, declined to get involved. That left it up to Ramsey Clark, the attorney general, who on January 12, on the recommendation of John Curtin and Henry Petersen, appointed me as Acting United States Attorney, in addition to heading up the strike force. I think the appointment came primarily because I was neutral and was already there.

It was the best job I ever had, and it lasted for ten months. The Western Judicial District of New York consists of that part of the state running east from the Ohio border to Syracuse and south from Lake Ontario to the Pennsylvania border. It comprises a population of about four million, and its main cities are Buffalo and Rochester. At that time there were six Assistant U.S. Attorneys in Buffalo and two in Rochester.

The U.S. Attorney is not only the chief federal prosecutor in his district; he represents the Department of Justice in all other areas in which the federal government has an interest, such as civil litigation, environmental issues, and anti-trust actions. This gave me an opportunity to expand beyond the criminal field for the first time in my career, and I found it fascinating. I had always thought of myself as a social activist, and here was a once-in-a-lifetime opportunity to use the instruments of authority to promote the common good (as best I saw it); to try to make an impact, however slight and for however short a time. And it was a perfect situation. As an outsider, I was completely independent of local political, business, or other pressures. I had no axes to grind or fences to mend. At the same time the strike force was humming along nicely with our excellent staff, augmented by John Lally, a veteran from the organized crime section in Washington, so I could devote some time to being the United States Attorney.

I appointed as First Assistant Andy Phelan, 36, who had so brilliantly prosecuted our criminal cases. Andy, a local boy with political ambitions, deserved the recognition.

The Pennsylvania Railroad Co. had pleaded guilty the previous June to charges initiated by the Justice Department for dumping oil into the Buffalo River, and it was coming up for sentencing just after I took office. There would be a fine, all the law permitted, but small by corporate standards. The company was under an order by the state to construct a device which would prevent future pollution, but had failed to comply. Working with the state, we got Judge Henderson to agree to postpone sentencing until the preventive mechanisms were completed, and to monitor the progress. This was accomplished, a small but satisfying victory.

I then issued a public warning to all industries in the area that negligent or deliberate dumping of wastes in Western New York lakes and streams would no longer be tolerated. "The old way of doing business is coming to an end," I said. "Lake Erie and our rivers belong to the people, not to the industrial polluters."

Working with the Civil Rights Division at Justice, we brought suit against Bethlehem Steel, a major Buffalo employer, for egregious racial discrimination in employment. Studies showed that African American employees were assigned primarily to hot, dirty work such as the blast furnaces; that some departments refused to accept any African Americans; and that pay scales were significantly lower than for whites. In addition, African Americans were denied training programs available to whites, and promotion opportunities were all but non-existent. It was a disgraceful situation. As result of our suit, Bethlehem finally agreed to sweeping reforms in all these areas, including an affirmative action program headed by a recruitment specialist who himself was African American.

I discovered that among the thorniest problems facing U.S. Attorneys were the allegations of civil rights violations through police brutality. Typically in Buffalo it involved a hippie passing out leaflets (usually innocuous enough) in the midst of a racially tense situation. The police, understandably enough, would feel that he was throwing gasoline on troubled waters and they would whisk him off to jail, sometimes with some resistance on his part. The police would also usually claim he was waving a gun or something and resisted arrest. He would always claim he was just exercising his right of free speech, had no gun, and the police beat him viciously. The truth was usually somewhere in between, but always difficult to find.

One of the highlights of my tenure was the annual conference of all 92 United States Attorneys in Washington in May. For a week I was able to mingle with and establish lasting friendships with some outstanding federal prosecutors like Tom Foran of Chicago, Matt Byrne of Los Angles, Paul Markham of Boston, Sid Lezak of Portland, and Stan Pitkin of Seattle. Also, the U.S. Attorney for Minnesota was Pat Foley, a good friend who had graduated a year behind me from St. Thomas. Best of all was re-connecting with my old boss, Cecil Poole from San

Francisco. The culmination of the conference was a visit to the White House and an individual photo with President Johnson.

One of the least enjoyable situations I faced as U.S. Attorney was dealing with military draft resisters. Opposition to the war in Vietnam had reached a fever pitch by 1968, especially among young people. Lyndon Johnson had committed 500,000 troops to South Vietnam, who seemed to be making no progress. We were definitely not winning the "hearts and minds of the people" and seemed to be mainly propping up a corrupt, inept, and unpopular South Vietnamese government. Our military's trumpeting of daily enemy "body counts" did not mask the fact that our own casualties were mounting hideously, and by the end of the war would total 50,000 dead.

Resistance to the war began primarily on college campuses, with the Students for a Democratic Society being the most vociferous national group. Gradually more and more Americans saw the war as a futile and costly effort, and opposition was voiced by some of our most respected political leaders, including Eugene McCarthy and Robert Kennedy, both of whom announced for the presidency in 1968. Lyndon Johnson, sensing the magnitude of opposition to his war policies, declined to run for re-election. That left the door open for Vice President Hubert Humphrey to become the third Democratic contender.

In retrospect, I cannot think of a year in my lifetime when there have been three such outstanding presidential candidates as Hubert Humphrey, Robert Kennedy, and Eugene McCarthy. It was a time when we could look up to candidates who possessed great intelligence, wisdom, and nobility, coupled with extensive experience in the art of politics in the true Aristotelian meaning of the term. Sadly, today we seem to look for candidates who are just like ourselves, somebody we could go out and enjoy a beer with. I liked it better when our candidates seemed to have more smarts and leadership qualities than the rest of us.

Given the times, it was natural that there would be great resistance to the military draft among young people throughout the country.

At the same time, military conscription was the law, and the U.S. Attorney's job was to enforce the law.

In Buffalo I was faced with a situation which generated a lot of controversy. Two young men, age 20, showed up at the induction center under orders from the Selective Service System, accompanied by a large group of sympathizers, and announced that they would not report for induction. They then fled to a nearby church, which by previous arrangement had offered them sanctuary.

Charges were filed and the U. S. Marshall delivered summonses to them at the church on a Wednesday afternoon. In a public demonstration, they burned the summonses on the church steps before a crowd of about 125 supporters, as reported by the media.

Upon our request, Judge Henderson then issued bench warrants for their arrest. For the next five days we attempted to negotiate their peaceful surrender, without success. Finally I authorized the marshals to forcefully enter the church and bring them out. They were met by a group of demonstrators standing shoulder-to-shoulder, blocking the entrance and chanting "Hell no, we won't go!" A melee ensued, lasting about 20 minutes, and in the course of bringing them out, three marshals incurred injuries requiring hospital treatment.

My sister in the convent (Sister Thomas Patricia), learning about this, asked the following in a letter: "Since a U.S. Attorney has some discretion in cases he wants to push, why are you concentrating on draft evaders? Is it just for law enforcement, or do you have strong moral feelings about it?" A thoughtful question. I replied as follows:

"It is primarily a matter of authority. I think it is important to demonstrate that the law must be enforced, particularly where there is widespread and highly publicized resistance to it. As I write that statement, it sounds very repressive in tone. Not so intended. But these boys who refuse to submit expect to be prosecuted—actually they show a lot of moral courage—and I can't believe their respect for law and order is increased if nothing happens. The public meanwhile loses all respect for law and order when these guys get a big splash at the induction center and then nothing further is ever heard. Morally and politically I'm a dove on Vietnam; but one does have to consider also that the burden does fall greater on those who do serve." I think my response today would be pretty much the same, with the same ambivalent feelings.

The Assassination of Martin Luther King

I was home on the weekend of April 4, 1968, and we went out to dinner to celebrate our 4th anniversary. On the way home we heard the terrible news of the assassination of the Rev. Martin Luther King, Jr. in Memphis. That night all hell broke loose in the inner city areas of Washington, and the rioting, burning, and looting lasted for three days. Ultimately the National Guard had to be called in to restore a semblance of order. It was similar to the terrible riots in the Watts area of Los Angeles in August 1965, and in Detroit and Newark in July 1967. It has been estimated that during the mid-1960's more than 200 persons died in over 100 city riots, with more than 4000 wounded. The Kerner Commission found that the basic cause was social deprivation—unemployment, bad housing, racial discrimination—and in each case the upheaval was set off by some triggering incident: a traffic violation, a raid on an after-hours bar, a rumor of a black man beaten by a white cop. For the people in inner city Washington it was the murder of the black man's symbol of hope.

Thus in Buffalo I found myself in the middle of a major effort by officials at all levels, together with concerned citizens of all races and faiths to foresee and forestall similar occurrences in the community during the hot summer. The coordinated effort was impressive and generally successful. Of course none of the root problems were solved that summer, but I think there was at least a greater community awareness of the need for solutions.

Susan and I moved to Buffalo for the summer again, and we rented a grand old Victorian at 105 Lancaster St., owned by a local lawyer whose family moved to their beach house on the Canadian side of Lake Erie. We were just ten minutes from my office, and the neighborhood had lots of children for our kids to play with. In Washington Susan had hired Dora, a woman from El Salvador to help with the children during the week, and she agreed to spend the first month with us. Susan's mother also joined us from Omaha for most of the summer.

This gave Susan some free time, and she volunteered to do publicity for the Mayor's Council on Youth Opportunity, one of the programs developed to improve life in the inner city. She was provided with an office in city hall and did her usual outstanding job in getting the residents involved in the various programs offered to young people, including participation in arts programs, jazz concerts, and other entertainment and learning opportunities. Getting to know all kinds of people in Buffalo was also an enjoyable experience for her. We had some pleasant times that summer, renewing acquaintance with the Esty's, as well as the Kevin Maloney family whom I had known from Camp Pendleton days, and making new friends. Among our most enjoyable outings were visits to the Shaw Festival at Niagara-on-the-Lake, just over the border in Ontario, where we had excellent dinners and saw some wonderful theater.

The Death of Robert Kennedy

In Buffalo, my colleagues and I went to bed on the night of Tuesday, June 4, 1968, elated by the news of Robert Kennedy's victory in the California primary, a huge step on the way to the Democratic nomination to the presidency.

We awoke the next morning to the horrific news that he had been shot in the head just after giving his victory speech at the Ambassador Hotel in Los Angeles, and died within hours. The assailant was a lone malcontent named Sirhan Sirhan, who harbored a grudge about his immigration status. There was no evidence of a conspiracy.

The nation was in shock once again. Coming so soon after the death of his brother the president, and only two months after the assassination of Martin Luther King, it seemed to many that this was further proof of the general disintegration of law and order in America. As U.S. Attorney, I issued a statement urging those caught in a wave of despair about the kind of society we had become to remember the words of Robert Kennedy at the time of the death of Dr. King: "The sniper's bullet is only the voice of madness, not the voice of the people." I concluded: "I am confident that we will retain our national pride, our belief in our nation and ourselves. We will not permit small men who attack great men to destroy what those great men have struggled to create."

Judge Curtin and I flew down to New York from Buffalo Friday afternoon and Susy met us at the airport. Bob Peloquin joined us and we went at once to St. Patrick's Cathedral. We were able to get in immediately, which made Susy and me feel a little guilty after seeing the people lined up for a mile of blocks on the sultry streets of Manhattan. We were ushered into the family pews in the front. While we were there Jacqueline Kennedy, Caroline, and young John came in, and many others. We stayed about two hours.

It was my great privilege to stand with the honor guard at the casket from 5:30 to 5:45 PM. Never will I forget that moment. The people came and came and came, just people, many weeping, some crippled, some very old, some with babies in arms. Blacks and Puerto Ricans and businessmen from Wall Street. Sargent Shriver was in the group I stood with, and I was replaced by Pierre Salinger.

The coffin lay in state at the head of the central aisle at St. Patrick's Cathedral for a full day and night. The New York Times reported that nearly 200,000 people waited for hours "in a serpentine queue that wound more than a mile among the glass and steel office towers and the stately old apartment buildings of midtown Manhattan" to pay their respects.

That evening the old Sheridan group began to find each other. It was incredible, in that huge city. There were absolutely no pre-arrangements or even any central meeting place. A few would meet in a hotel lobby by chance, and the word would be spread, and eventually we all got together at Toots Shor's. They were nearly all there, and they came from Detroit, Phoenix, Boston, and Atlanta, in addition to Washington. The finest group of people I have ever worked with, and all separated since 1964. We laughed and cried together and talked about great times and challenges met, and we all got a little drunk. The unspoken common thought was, why couldn't we have been meeting at the Inauguration? More than anything, I think, it was a tribute to Walter Sheridan, who had devoted himself completely to a man and his principles for eleven years, only to have it all snuffed out. To most of us, Walter Sheridan *was* Bob Kennedy.

It was impossible to get tickets for the Mass, and so we watched it on television and then went out to watch the cortege proceed down Fifth Avenue. The Mass was celebrated by Cardinal Cooke, and Senator Ted Kennedy, in a moving and emotional eulogy, asked the nation to remember the words of his brother: "Some men see things as they are, and say why. I dream things that never were, and say why not?"

After the service, the coffin was placed aboard a 21-car funeral train which made its way slowly to Washington, with hundreds of thousands paying their respects along the way.

After the Mass, Susy and I flew back to Washington. At 4 o'clock a memorial service was held at the Justice Department. About five hundred of Bob Kennedy's former associates were there. Ramsey Clark summed it all up when he said, "He brought out the best in each of us, and he gave us all a feeling of belonging."

Bob Kennedy, like his brother, saw life as an adventure. Susan and I are proud to have shared a small part in a very great adventure.

The Democratic convention in Chicago that August was a tumultuous mess. War protesters, led by the Weathermen, the violent faction of Students for a Democratic Society, staged nightly riots, smashing store windows and setting cars on fire, and were brutally put down by Mayor Daley's storm troopers. Hubert Humphrey received the nomination, but the party was in more than its usual disarray. Humphrey, as vice president, was saddled with LBJ's war policies, even though he had privately counseled the president against those policies, and had publicly disavowed them a month before the election. Richard Nixon, who claimed to have a "plan" to end the war, won the election in one of the closest races ever.

It is believed by many, myself included, that Humphrey could have won if he had received the enthusiastic support of his fellow Minnesotan, Eugene McCarthy, who retained a large following, especially among young people. But McCarthy, who had been one of the first public officials to challenge an incumbent president on the morality of war, withheld that endorsement until a week before the election, much too late. Whether out of pride, a strong moral conviction, or just plain stubbornness, Gene McCarthy could not bring himself to come to the aid of his old colleague.

We were to mourn the death of another good man that month: my father, George Kennelly. He suffered a heart attack on Saturday, November 2, and I immediately flew out to Santa Clara. He lived to vote for Hubert Humphrey, whom he greatly admired. He suffered a stroke the day after the election and died peacefully the following Sunday, November 10, 1968, at the age of 75. Susan flew out to join the rest of the family for the funeral, bringing our little Katy, who never had the opportunity to know her grandfather. During the visit we celebrated Katy's first birthday, and she took her first steps.

My dad had not been in good health for the last 25 years of his life, but this did not keep him from enjoying life. During the years following his second hospitalization for tuberculosis, when he was no longer able to work and my mother was still working as a secretary at Willow Glen High School in San Jose, he managed the household and prepared the evening meal. He also augmented their modest income by avidly and shrewdly following the stock market.

He often said that his so-called "golden years" were among his most enjoyable. He and my mother led full and active lives with their friends and neighbors. And he dearly enjoyed being with his children and grandchildren. Whenever I would come home to Santa Clara (or they would come to Washington), the two of us would talk late into the night about his favorite subject and mine, politics and current events. He was possessed with an uncommon amount of common sense, and his keen insights into human nature came from the perspective of the working man. He never could understand how a working man could vote Republican, the party of the rich and powerful. And he had nothing but disdain for the farmer, who he said "voted Democratic until he got the wrinkles out of his belly," and then went back to voting Republican.

Among the last things my father said to me was, "I am proud of my children, and as far as I know, they are proud of me. What more can a man ask of life?" I like that a lot.

16.

JUDGE HENDERSON HAS A CHANGE OF HEART

As United States Attorney, I was in a unique position with regard to the FBI. All applications for search or arrest warrants had to be approved by me before they could be presented to a federal judge for issuance. In each instance the agents would describe to me the nature of the case and the evidence supporting the required "probable cause" for a search or an arrest, and I would routinely approve the application.

But in November 1968 a strange thing occurred. The agents asked me to approve arrest warrants for Stefano Magaddino—the *capo di tutti capi*, the prime target of the strike force—and nine others on gambling conspiracy charges. Their agents had never discussed any ongoing investigation of this type with any of our people. I was suspicious and asked them to disclose the source of their information. I suspected an illegal wiretap or bug, probably not their own because the president had forbidden the use of such devices, but more likely from the Niagara Falls police department. The agents refused to disclose their sources, but assured me that the information was valid, and they stressed what a great coup this would be, and what wonderful publicity we would all get from the arrest of the Big Cheese. Andy Phelan strongly supported the plan, but I was adamant. No disclosure, no warrant, I said. Then the Special Agent in Charge, Neil Welch, came on the scene. Welch had been giving us problems since the day we arrived in Buffalo, sending regular reports to Hoover telling how bumbling and incompetent the strike force was. Bill Behan, one of our agents who came from the Carolina hills, had the perfect description of Welch. "If you ordered a carload of assholes," said Bill, "and only Neil Welch showed up, you wouldn't be disappointed."

Welch stormed in and said, "We're not answering any more questions." When I persisted, the discussion grew heated, and at one point Welch offered to take me out in the alley and "punch you into orbit." This makes me one of the few people, I suspect, who has been threatened by both Jimmy Hoffa and a chief of the FBI. In any event, I stood firm.

A couple of days later I received a call from Judge Henderson, telling me that he had decided to appoint Andy Phelan as the interim United States Attorney. Under the circumstances it was not too surprising, even though he had called me a couple of months earlier to tell me that I was doing a "helluva job," and expressed the hope that I would stay on permanently.

A few days after Phelan took over, the FBI obtained its warrant and the Buffalo papers front-paged the arrest of Stefano Magaddino and the other nine on gambling conspiracy charges. An editorial in the Buffalo Courier-Express waxed euphoric: "What has unfolded with the FBI arrests on the Niagara Frontier in the last 10 days is the second stage in what probably is the most sustained federal campaign against organized crime anywhere in America since the second World War, perhaps since the prohibition era."

Doctors testified that Magaddino was too ill to come to court to be arraigned, so Judge Henderson took the court to Magaddino's home and arraigned him there. More front page stories and pictures.

Then the defense filed a motion to quash, which required the FBI to disclose the source of its evidence. The FBI refused, and the whole case was dismissed.

Several years later, when I was in private practice, I did some consulting work for the National Wiretap Commission. I was assigned to interview local police departments in upstate New York to determine the extent of their use of electronic surveillance during the 1960's. The police department in Niagara Falls, where Magaddino lived, told me they were the source of the illegal tap (or bug) in question, and they had indeed given it to Welch.

By the end of 1968, the strike force concept was well established. Attorney General Ramsey Clark, in his final annual report on crime, announced that strike forces in eight cities had secured 189 indictments during the year, including several Mafia leaders, most notably the notorious Raymond Patriarca, longtime Mafia boss in New England. The strike force leader in New England was my friend Ted Harrington, formerly of the Hoffa squad and my partner during the Mississippi days of interviewing local sheriffs and mayors. Ted eventually became a federal judge in Boston.

In addition, a *New York Times* editorial noted as "an encouraging turn of events" that a House Republican Task Force on Crime had submitted to President-elect Nixon a report recommending that the strike forces be retained and expanded.

As 1968 drew to a close, my weekends at home were spent trying to accomplish a few household chores. Patrick was three, Tim two, and Katy had just had her first birthday. A letter to my mother related: "I did get a little house painting done last weekend. Naturally I had two eager helpers. I spread out papers on the grass, gave them each a little bucket, brush, and some boards, and carefully explained that they were to paint nothing else. They were very good. However, I then went in to lunch and when I returned Patrick had painted most of the cement porch, steps, aluminum door, and some of the stone front of the house—all in yellow. I must say he's a lot faster than I. Also he did a nice job on Timmy's hair. Fortunately it was water-based paint but it took Susy and me an hour with hose and wire brushes to clean it off. I was just furious but he looked up with those big blue eyes and said 'Dad, I thought I'd do the porch and door so you wouldn't have to.'

17.

TONY FALANGE AND THE ELIZABETHTOWN CAPER

In early 1969, having been freed from my assignment as U.S. Attorney, I was able to take care of some strike force business in Utica. If ever there was a contest for armpit of the world, Utica, New York would undoubtedly be in the finals. In 1969 it was decrepit, rundown, and filthy—the quintessential rust belt town that had literally stopped living. Thirty-five years later, The New Yorker, in its October 1, 2004 edition, described Utica as "a small, depressed, formerly industrial city about fifty miles east of Syracuse...full of vacant lots, boarded-up buildings, and closed-down pizza parlors." Obviously not much has changed. Utica's only saving grace is that it makes Syracuse look good, just as Syracuse makes Buffalo look good.

Why any self-respecting gangster would choose to live in Utica is beyond me. But sure enough, the mob boss in Utica was Joseph Falcone, and he was ably assisted by Anthony Falange. Falcone and Falange were beholden only to Stefano Magaddino in Buffalo. They controlled all the rackets in Utica, perhaps the city's liveliest industry. Anyone aspiring to a career of nefarious activities had to pay homage to and take orders from the bosses. Falange's specialties, among his other talents, were loan-sharking and fencing stolen goods, operating under the cover of Tony's Swap Shop in downtown Utica.

Utica was also known as one of the most corrupt cities in America. It was a common saying in town that its public officials were so crooked that when they died they were not buried but were screwed into the ground.

George Elias and John Zarnoch, both in their late twenties, were not members of the Mafia, and were not even Italians, but they were a pair of pretty good burglars, and they worked for Tony Falange. They had pulled off burglaries all over upstate New York and as far away as Colorado and California. They were proud of their work, and proud of the fact that they worked quietly and with stealth, and never hurt anybody like robbers do. Robbers, on the other hand, look down on burglars as wimps and sneaks, afraid of confrontation. Robbers and burglars have a mutual contempt similar to that of cowboys and sheep herders in the old west.

In 1968 Elias and Zarnoch were serving terms in separate state prisons in New York for, not surprisingly, burglary. Elias, the more alert of the two, heard about the strike forces and the witness protection program, and decided to try to help himself. He contacted the New York state police, who after interviewing him, contacted our strike force. He told the following story.

Tony Falange had heard about a possible score in Elizabethtown, North Carolina, which could bring in over $100,000 in rare coins. Falange, like his counterparts in Buffalo and elsewhere, liked to hear of opportunities in faraway places that he could send his boys to pull off quickly, and then return home, thus reducing the chances of getting caught. [I would make a point of this out whenever I gave speeches about organized crime in places like Minnesota or Nebraska, where the Mafia was thought not to exist.] The coin collection was owned by a wealthy businessman named Baddour who, according to Falange's information, kept the collection in a secret compartment in a closet in the hallway of his home. Falange sent Elias and Zarnoch to Elizabethtown to check it out. They found the house and learned that the Baddours went to church every Sunday at 10 AM. They returned to Utica and reported back to Falange. He authorized the job and Elias, Zarnoch, and three others were sent down to pull it off.

On Sunday morning, while the Baddours were at church, the gang broke into the house and found the secret compartment. However, it contained only a few coins and about $900 in cash. They returned to Utica to incur the wrath and disappointment of Tony Falange.

We met with Elias at Attica state prison. He had not been in contact with Zarnoch since they were both sent to prison. We then contacted Zarnoch, who agreed to cooperate, and corroborated Elias. Our agents then set about to see if their stories could be corroborated by independent evidence. Mr. Baddour said he had indeed kept over $100,000 in rare coins in the place described, but had moved them to a safe in the basement about two months before the burglary.

Our agents found a motel clerk where our witnesses said they had stayed en route, who was able to identify two members of the group; one Joe Tebsherany, who had registered under the name of "John Romano of Buffalo", and the other, Del Dyman, whom the clerk had engaged in conversation for about an hour. The agents were also able to identify Tebsherany's fingerprint on the motel registration card.

We now had enough evidence to make the case, but the indictment, arrests, and transfer of Elias and Zarnoch to safekeeping required careful planning. All the planning was done in Syracuse because no one in Utica could be trusted.

On day 1 Elias and Zarnoch, because they would not be safe after the arrests, were removed from their state prisons to federal custody in separate locations, so they could not be accused of comparing stories.

On day 2 the arrests of the four defendants were carried out by four teams composed of federal agents, state police, and the Chief and two officers from the Utica police department. For political reasons it was necessary to include the Utica police, but they were not informed of the nature of the operation until they arrived at the command post.

Grand Jury testimony began in Syracuse on day 3 and on day 4 the indictment was returned, charging the four with conspiracy to transport stolen property in excess of $5,000 across state lines.

In addition to Falange, Tebsherany, and Dyman, the fourth defendant was one Rocco Taurisano. Rocco had spent 35 of his 62 years in prison. His most recent term had been for second degree murder. Rocco was a hired killer, but his eyesight wasn't what it used to be, so he had drawn a circle with an X in the middle on the sidewalk in front of his target's home. Rocco then hid in the bushes across the street. When his victim emerged from his house and reached the circle, Rocco let him have it between the eyes. In Utica, this was *second degree* murder.

I prosecuted the Elizabethtown case, with the help of Don Campbell of our Buffalo strike force, for two weeks in February 1969. It snowed every day in Utica, which at least had the beneficial effect of covering up the grime.

The judge and defense counsel were a colorful lot. Presiding over the case was a visiting federal judge up from New York City, the Hon. Lloyd McMahon. Judge McMahon's reputation in New York for being a dyspeptic and mean spirited old crank was not diminished in Utica, and in fact was probably enhanced by his being exiled there for two weeks.

Rocco Taurisano's lawyer, one Moses Goldbas, was a feisty little fellow in his sixties. He was a former professional bantamweight boxer. His cross-examinations, while harmless, were pugnacious and entertaining, as he bobbed around the courtroom on the balls of his feet.

Tebsherany was represented by Charles L. Smith, who had a drinking problem. On the night before final arguments he fell off a bar stool and broke his leg. He showed up in court the next morning with his leg in a cast, and asked the judge for permission to address the jury from a wheelchair. True to form, Judge McMahon denied his request, and poor Mr. Smith had to give his (brief) summation balanced on one leg.

In his summation, Moses Goldbas opened with the following statement: "Ladies and gentlemen of the jury, we have been privileged to have had this trial presided over by the honorable Lloyd McMahon from New York, who for the past two weeks has showered his wrath and irascibility equally on both sides." This brought down the house, and even the judge permitted himself a small self-satisfied smile.

All four were duly convicted. Falange and Dyman received the maximum five years, and Taurisano and Tebsherany each received three years.

Then there was the problem of relocating and providing new identities for Elias and Zarnoch. Once again I appeared before the New York State Parole Board, and both were granted parole. Re-inventing Zarnoch was relatively easy, as he was unmarried, not overly bright, and amenable to any alternative to prison life. After he chose a new name we were able to procure the necessary documents (birth certificate, driver's permit, etc.). We found him a job on the assembly line of an automobile factory in the Midwest. I saw him again about a year later and he was happy as a bug. He told me that his job was tightening the nuts on car engines. He said he had been offered a promotion to carburetors, but turned it down.

George Elias was a more difficult problem. He was very bright and articulate, but without much formal education, and he had a wife and child. He was a cheerful fellow but he overestimated his own abilities, professing to be an expert in computers. After some effort, I found him a job, through a friend, as a computer programer trainee at a high-tech company in the San Francisco Bay area. I brought him with me to stay at my mother's house in Santa Clara for a couple of nights until we could find lodgings for him and his family. (My mother commented that it was the first time she had had a burglar in her house for a whole night.)

After a couple of months it became clear that Elias did not have the aptitude for the computer job. He then expressed an interest in becoming a locksmith, something for which he had a proven aptitude. We were actually able to obtain a Small Business Administration loan of $15,000 for him to set up his own business. He was successful for a couple of years, but ultimately could not resist the temptation to revisit some of his customers' houses, one of which he was in the process of burglarizing when apprehended. The last I heard was that he was in a California state prison.

One evening while I was working late in my Washington office on the relocation of Elias and Zarnoch, Gerald Shur, a young career professional who had founded the intelligence unit of the organized crime section, dropped into my office and asked if he could help. This led to Shur's taking charge of all future witness security and relocation matters, much to my relief and gratitude.

Eventually the Witness Security Program became institutionalized in the Omnibus Crime Bill, enacted by Congress in 1970. For the next thirty-four years, until his retirement, Gerry Shur directed the Witness Security Program with the assistance of the United States Marshals Service, handling not only mobsters and racketeers but also spies, Colombian drug dealers and international terrorists, including their wives, children, and lovers. For a fascinating account of his experiences, see *Witsec: Inside the Federal Witness Protection Program*, by Pete Earley and Gerald Shur. Bantam Books, New York. (2002).

18.

DEPUTY CHIEF
ORGANIZED CRIME & RACKETEERING SECTION

The inauguration of the Nixon administration on January 20, 1969, brought changes in the Justice Department. John Mitchell, who had been Nixon's campaign manager, replaced Ramsey Clark as Attorney General. The new Assistant AG in charge of the Criminal Division was Will Wilson, who had been Attorney General of Texas. He had fought hard against the illegal gambling rackets in Texas and therefore came to Justice with a special affinity for the organized crime and racketeering section. Henry Petersen was promoted from Chief of the organized crime section to deputy to Mr. Wilson, and Bill Lynch became chief of the section. This created an opening for a deputy chief, and I was appointed to the position. Finally, in May 1969, after two and a half years, I could return to Washington. Since we now had 70 lawyers to supervise, including eight strike forces, a second deputy position was created, and Ed Joyce, a longtime member of the section, was appointed.

In addition, Congress in 1969 enacted legislation authorizing limited court-authorized electronic surveillance (phone taps and bugs) in organized crime investigations, under strictly controlled conditions. Thus we created a unit called "Title III" (referring to that section of the law), whose attorneys initiated the paper work. Each court application for electronic surveillance had to be reviewed for sufficiency at three levels and then personally signed by the attorney general. Notwithstanding the effort involved, the technique proved extremely effective and resulted in important indictments and convictions.

We also created a labor racketeering unit, and to lead it we hired a young attorney named Charles F. C. Ruff. Chuck Ruff and his assistant, Tom Henderson, successfully prosecuted—in a sensational trial—Tony Boyle, longtime head of the United Mine Workers, for orchestrating the murders of his opponent, Joseph Yablonski, and Yablonski's entire family, as they slept in their beds. Chuck Ruff, who was wheelchair-bound, was one of the most brilliant, and most congenial, lawyers I have ever known. He was at the beginning of a spectacular career both in and out of government. After leaving Justice he became a partner at Covington & Burling, Washington's oldest and most prestigious law firm. From there he took periodic leaves of absence to become, respectively, the final Watergate Special Prosecutor, the United States Attorney for the District of Columbia, the DC Corporation Counsel (equivalent of City Attorney), and finally White House Counsel under President Bill Clinton. Everyone who watched Clinton's impeachment trial in the Senate on television remembers Ruff's brilliantly organized and successful defense of the president. Sadly, Chuck died of a sudden heart attack within a year thereafter, in his early sixties.

Tom Henderson, after leaving Justice, became executive director of the prestigious and powerful American Trial Lawyers Association, and served in that capacity longer than any in its history, until his retirement in 2005. I consider it a distinct privilege to have had a part in hiring and supervising these two outstanding lawyers early in their careers.

At about this time, J. Edgar Hoover ended his two-year holdout and decided to join the strike forces. Hoover had never liked Ramsey Clark, who he considered soft on criminals and pinko leftists, but had a great admiration for the Nixon Administration, especially after Nixon, as one of his first official acts, extended Hoover's term beyond the normal retirement age of 70.

With regard to Hoover's change of heart, the *Washington Post* reported that "insiders give most of the credit to Administration officials who made clear that the strike force method was producing concrete results—indictments and convictions—and that the FBI would be expected to help deliver."

In his presidential campaign, Richard Nixon had pledged to escalate drastically the federal war on organized crime. To fulfill that promise, the White House in the summer of 1969 asked us to submit a budget for strike forces, current and future. Will Wilson replied that we had eight strike forces in operation, and were planning to expand to twelve. Somehow the word got garbled; the White House added eight and twelve and announced plans for *twenty* strike forces; and Congress appropriated an extra $25 million for the purpose.

We were then faced with the task of doubling our staff from 70 lawyers to 140, and of finding twelve more cities in which to install strike forces. By the end of 1970 we had teams in Buffalo, Boston, Manhattan, Brooklyn, Newark, Detroit, Philadelphia, Pittsburgh, Cleveland, Chicago, Miami, New Orleans, St. Louis, Kansas City, Dallas, Los Angeles, and San Francisco—a total of 17. We then created one more, called Strike Force 18, located at Justice, a kind of on-call Swat Team, and called it quits. There simply was not sufficient justification for putting one in any other city. (It may be noted that there was none in the District of Columbia. We did not consider Washington to have an organized crime problem. Some said it was because the Mafia knew when it was outclassed. I always maintained that there was no public corruption in the District of Columbia because the local government was so inefficient that even if you bribed someone, you still couldn't get the job done.)

We also added a third deputy chief. All of us, along with Bill Lynch, the chief, spent a tremendous amount of time interviewing applicants for the seventy new attorney positions. Our preference was for people with some trial experience, who were eager for some exciting adventures, had good judgment but were not overzealous, and were willing to move to any city to which we might assign them. There was no shortage of applicants. At my urging, we drew heavily on men with military JAG experience. We also took some recent law school graduates and found that the University of Texas Law School, as suggested by Will Wilson, produced some top-of-the line recruits.

Incredible as it may sound today, the criminal division had no women lawyers, except for the legendary Bea Rosenberg. We hired two, Jill Wine Volner and Mary Lou Dowd(?). But we kept them in Washington billets and would not let them go out to strike forces, because we considered it too dangerous for women. By today's standards, this would be discriminatory. Jill, after leaving the Department, gained fame as the member of the Watergate Special Prosecutor's team who cross-examined Rosemary Woods, Nixon's secretary, about the missing eighteen minutes of tapes and had her tied up in knots. Mary Lou's later career led her to become General Counsel of Playboy Enterprises. All in all, we assembled an outstanding cadre of lawyers.

Each of the three deputies assumed responsibility for creating, staffing, and supervising strike forces in five or six cities. Mine were Philadelphia, Miami, New Orleans, St. Louis, and Kansas City. We offered advice, helped solve problems, and reviewed all prosecutive memoranda, which they were required to submit to support any proposed indictment. We also accompanied Will Wilson, who loved to visit each strike at least once a year, providing a morale boost for the troops in the field. Thus we were on the road quite a lot, but it was still better than being in Buffalo five days a week.

On Bureaucratic Nomenclature

In recent times, following the catastrophic events of September 11, 2001,—"9/11"—it was felt that efforts to combat international terrorism must be elevated to the Cabinet level, and the Department of Homeland Security was created. This offers an interesting example of how bureaucracies work.

It is in the nature of bureaucracies to expand. This is not necessarily bad. As times change, and needs change, Congress passes new laws and it is the responsibility of the executive branch to carry them out. Thus new departments, divisions, sections, agencies, and bureaus are created.

Each new entity must be given a name. Logic dictates that the name relate to the function, no matter the problem for the telephone receptionist. Thus among Homeland Security's 22 segments we find the "Critical Infrastructure Assurance Office" and the "National Infrastructure Simulation and Analysis Center."

Back in simpler times, namely about 1969, the Criminal Division at Justice decided to create a new section, to cover selective service (the military draft), election fraud, and pornography. A memo was sent around to all supervisors to recommend a name for the new section. Following the logical format, I suggested it be called the Selection, Election, and Erection Section.

As might be expected, grayer heads prevailed. After a thorough review by committee, it was designated the Government Operations Section.

A Call for Help from a Father

One day in the summer of 1969 I received a call from a lawyer in Buffalo who identified himself as Sal Martoche, representing Tom Leonhard, who wanted to see his children. What children, I asked? "His children by his former wife, Rochelle, now married to Paddy Calabrese. He had visitation rights, and he visited them every Sunday until you all spirited them away two years ago, and he demands his right to see them."

It seems that when we moved Rochelle and the children to safety in June 1967 she had neglected to tell us, and we had failed to inquire, or if she did we had failed to give it any thought in our eagerness to get them all to safety, that the three children were hers by a former marriage, and that the father had visitation rights. Now, after two years, he was demanding to see them.

At first I was skeptical. Why has this man waited two years? Was this a legitimate call, or a ruse by the mob to try to find Paddy and his family? I told Martoche that I was sorry but I had given my word that I would not disclose their whereabouts to anyone, for their safety. But I agreed to forward a letter from Leonhard to his ex-wife.

The letter from Leonhard outraged Rochelle and Paddy. They called and angrily reminded me that I was sworn to secrecy. And no, they were not interested in bringing the children to meet their father in a neutral place. In fact, they said, they would "disappear off the face of the earth" if I did anything to help Leonhard find them. I relayed their messsage to Martoche, but Leonhard wrote two more letters to Rochelle. Finally she replied, through me, that there was no way she would ever allow him to see the children.

I was later to learn that Leonhard was a decent, hard-working guy, not connected to the mob, who dearly loved his children, and after they disappeared, did not know where to turn. He had approached two other lawyers, but both said they couldn't help, before Martoche agreed to take the case. Sal Martoche was an honest lawyer who in later years became the United States Attorney in Buffalo. Even had I known all this, I would not have been willing to disclose the whereabouts of the children. It was a terrible situation. As a father, I could sympathize with Leonhard, but I could not break my pledge to the Calabreses; not only for their protection, but because I felt the entire Witness Security program could be jeopardized if a witness could not rely on the government's promises.

Martoche then went into the local court in Buffalo and obtained an order granting custody of the children to Leonhard. Armed with the custody order, he then sued the Attorney General and myself in federal court, demanding that the government disclose the whereabouts of the children. (At that point I was the only one who knew where they were, as they had moved from their original location.) I filed an affidavit stating in part: "It is my professional and personal judgment that to divulge the whereabouts of the aforesaid children to anyone in Buffalo would seriously jeopardize their personal safety." I also stated that the Calabreses had told me that if I was ordered to disclose their location, they would immediately move to another location and tell no one where they were.

In a 28-page opinion, Judge Henderson expressed sympathy for the father, but held that Kennelly had not abused his power in promising anonymity in a situation in which protection of certain witnesses and their families is necessary; and further, that since the government was no longer responsible for the whereabouts of the children, the court had no authority to order it to comply with Mr. Leonhard's request.

Martoche then appealed the judge's decision to the U.S. Court of Appeals. All of this took a number of years. On February 8, 1973, a three-judge panel of the Second Circuit Court of Appeals reluctantly but unanimously denied the appeal. The court ruled that resolving the competing interest of Leonhard's claim and the children's safety would take the "wisdom of Solomon," but that Kennelly had acted in good faith to protect the children's lives, and so had committed no wrong that a federal court could right. Four months later the U.S. Supreme Court declined to review the case.

The case generated a considerable amount of publicity. "Informer Shield Upheld Over Rights of Father" (New York Times, 6/19/73). "High Court Rebuffs Man's Bid to Locate Children" (Washington Post, 6/19/73). "The Children Chase" (Time, 4/9/73).

A Hollywood producer named Frank Cooper picked up on the story and commissioned author Leslie Waller (*Dog Day Afternoon*, among others) to write a book, entitled "Hide in Plain Sight" (Delacorte Press, New York, 1976). Waller interviewed all the parties, with my assistance, and the book is about 90% accurate.

Cooper then produced a movie of the same name, directed by and starring James Caan. It is "based" on this case—Cooper called it "nonfiction fiction"—and is about 30% true to the real story. At a special premier screening of the film in Washington, I met Sal Martoche and Tom Leonhard for the first time. It was a cordial but uneasy meeting.

The ironic twist to the whole sad story is this: While Waller was writing the book, and wondering how on earth he was going to end it, Rochelle Calabrese placed a phone call to Sal Martoche. She announced that she and Paddy had had a big fight, that Paddy had left town and they were getting a divorce. Tom Leonhard could come and visit the children.

Leonhard and his new wife did so. But it was now eight years since the father and children had been together. After several visits, the children elected to remain with their mother. It is now my understanding that in order to prevent this situation from happening again, new rules were adopted requiring the government to notify non-custodial parents when their children entered the Witness Security program, so they would have the opportunity to visit their children in a safe place arranged by the U.S. Marshals.

The Undertaker Outpoints the Senator

Our parish church was Holy Trinity in Georgetown, the oldest Catholic church in the District of Columbia, founded in 1787. It was attended by John Kennedy when he lived in Georgetown as a senator, and it is the church in which Susan and I were married. It is known for the spirituality of its liturgies and the excellence of it homilies by its Jesuit priests, and for its community outreach programs. Catholics come from all over the District, as well as from Maryland and northern Virginia, to attend Mass at Holy Trinity.

Vatican II had recommended the creation of parish councils of lay persons to assist pastors in the administration of the church. In 1969,

Father Tom Gavigan, the pastor of Holy Trinity, asked me to chair a committee to organize a parishwide election. We put announcements in the Sunday bulletin, asking parishioners to submit their names in nomination for the fifteen positions.

When election time came, we had 102 candidates. Among them were Georgetown University professors, sub-cabinet officials, administrative assistants to three U.S. Senators, CPA's, doctors, lawyers, and a lot of just plain good men and women. Also included was Senator Ted Kennedy, who came to Holy Trinity regularly from northern Virginia with his wife Joan and their young children. The ballot ran five pages.

When the votes were counted, the top vote-getter was Donald DeVol, president of DeVol Funeral Home. Senator Kennedy was second. The story made both Washington papers. I was fifth. Ted Kennedy regularly attended the meetings and was an active participant.

Elbowed Aside by J. Edgar Hoover

As I have noted earlier, our political leaders seem to have a proclivity for addressing every national social and economic problem as a "war." We have had the war on poverty, the war on drugs, and the war on crime, among others. In each instance it is our declared objective to eliminate forever the evil we are combating. Perhaps some day we'll have a war on war.

Once these rhetorical wars are declared, the president almost inevitably creates a National Council or a National Commission to devise a strategy for winning the war. Thus it was that in 1970 President Nixon created by executive order a National Council on Organized Crime, whose mission was to "formulate a national strategy for the elimination of organized crime." It was headed by the Attorney General, and included the Secretaries of the Treasury and Labor, the Postmaster General, the heads of the FBI, the Secret Service, the INS, Customs, the chairman of the SEC, and a few other notables who might contribute something to the great battle.

Part of the ritual is the signing of the executive order creating the national body, which provides a photo opportunity for all these people, along with the chairpersons of the pertinent Congressional committees, to have their pictures taken with the president. I was invited to the ceremony at the White House, along with Will Wilson, Henry Petersen and Bill Lynch.

There were seventeen of us who gathered in the cabinet room, adjacent to the oval office, on June 4, 1970, shaking hands and making small talk while awaiting the president's entry. I had been advised that on these occasions it was important to position oneself in advance directly behind the president's chair for the picture taking, and so I did. However, I underestimated my more experienced competition. When the door opened, it was as if somebody had yelled "hut!," the blitz was on, and I was the quarterback. In a flash, I was shoved aside by the mighty shoulder of old J. Edgar himself, who in the official photo is seen directly behind Mr. Nixon, with me peeking over his left shoulder. At least I got a signed copy of the order and one of the pens used by the president, all of which, along with a photo, I have handsomely framed and stored in my garage.

In accordance with the standard ritual, all the heads met at the first meeting of the Council, and at subsequent meetings sent substitutes, usually lower level underlings, including myself on a few occasions. I cannot honestly remember if we ever developed a national strategy, and I know very well that we did not eliminate organized crime.

On the other hand, I am proud of the fact that we in the criminal division at Justice, working with the Congress, were able to develop some significant legislation during this period. The Omnibus Crime Act of 1970 not only institutionalized the Witness Security program; it created the Racketeer Influenced and Corrupt Organizations act, the famous (or infamous) RICO statute. For the first time, it prohibited any person from conducting an enterprise through a "pattern of racketeering activity" (as defined in the statute). Further, it prohibited the investment of any funds derived from a pattern of racketeering activity into any enterprise engaged in interstate commerce. This meant that prosecutors could now describe defendants as members of organized crime and could prosecute them for conducting any business, such as trash collection, in which they employed racketeering methods. Also, if they used the profits from the trash collection business to buy another business, let's say a night club, the assets of *both* businesses could be seized by the government and sold, even though the night club may have been run legitimately. This has happened on numerous occasions since enactment of the statute.

RICO was the brainchild of G. Robert Blakey, who had been in the organized crime section but by 1970 had joined the staff of Senator John McClellan. We were able to work with Bob and the McClellan Committee in creating the language of the statute which made its way through Congress and was signed by the president. Later Bob became a longtime distinguished professor at Notre Dame law school.

However, none of us could have envisioned the extent to which the RICO statute has since been applied in diverse situations; for example, against an organized group of pro-lifers picketing abortion clinics. And even as I write this, the New York Times reports an ongoing trial in Washington in which "the government charges under the Racketeer Influenced and Corrupt Organizations Act, cigarette companies have engaged in fraud and deceit for half a century to sell their products." (11/19/04).

On the Road Again

Mario Puzo's 1969 potboiler, "The Godfather," was an immediate national bestseller and has continued to be an enduring success. It also enlarged our national vocabulary, giving us such phrases as "an offer he can't refuse" and "sleeping with the fishes." The book and subsequent films created a near-frenzy for information about organized crime and the Mafia in the U.S. and what the government was doing about it. At Justice, we began receiving requests from state and local law enforcement agencies, civic and business organizations, and universities, to provide speakers and panelists. There were also a few requests from my own friends from around the country. Fortunately for me, not many of my fellow supervisors were eager to go out and make public speeches, so I jumped at the chance, and sort of became the designated speaker for the organized crime section.

From the Marine Airbase at Cherry Point, N.C., came a call from Paul St. Amour, my fellow lawyer from Camp Pendleton days, as a result of which I appeared before the Cherry Point/Camp Lejeune Bar Association as their Law Day speaker. At the National Council of Trial Judges, an adjunct of the American Bar Association convention in St. Louis, I appeared on a panel with Ralph Salerno and George Higgins. Ralph was a detective from the New York police department who had spent his career chasing the Mafia and who after retirement had become a consultant with the National Council on Crime and Delinquency. George Higgins was an assistant U.S. Attorney in Boston who handled organized crime cases. He later became a prolific and best-selling author of novels about the Boston underworld (*The Friends of Eddie Coyle, The Digger's Game* etc.), and he was a genius at recreating the dialogue and dialect of his characters. Both Ralph and George were dynamic speakers and great fun to socialize with. The same was true of Charles Rogovin, director of the Pennsylvania Crime Commission. I was on several panels with all three over the years, and we had some great times together. Ralph Salerno used as a visual aid a depiction of organized crime as a giant octopus, with its tentacles reaching out into all sectors of our society. It was very effective, and he helped me create a similar one for my own purposes.

I was invited to St. Thomas College, my *alma mater,* and was the speaker at a dinner hosted by its president, Father Terrence Murphy.

The next day I spoke at a Ramsey County Bar Association luncheon in St. Paul, arranged by my college friends and fellow lawyers Bob Donlon and Mike Galvin, and later that evening did a television show.

I made two visits to Dallas, to speak at Southern Methodist University, and later to the Texas Sheriff's Association (better known as the Texas Rangers). I had to stretch a bit to show the reach of organized crime into Texas (tough competition with the politicians) but my appearance led to two lead editorials in the *Dallas Times-Herald*, one the next day and another four months later, warning the public about the dangers of organized crime in their midst, and urging the legislature and law enforcement to take effective action.

In Dallas, the sheriff proudly took me on a tour of the county jail, where Lee Harvey Oswald had been confined. The jail was appallingly primitive and overcrowded. I was also taken to a private audience with H.L. Hunt, one of the original Texas oil wildcatters who became one of the richest men in the world and one of the most feared men in Texas. He was also a legendary curmudgeon and skinflint. Having the opportunity to meet him was supposedly a great honor for me. The old gentleman was pleasant enough to me, but he unmercifully berated one of his toadying sons in my presence. He also gave me an autographed copy of his biography, in paperback.

Then there were speeches at Mankato State College in Minnesota, Wisconsin State College at Eau Claire, and at Notre Dame, the latter arranged by Susan's cousin Dennis Donovan from Omaha, a student there at the time. Cousin Bill Kennelly and his family came down from Chicago for that appearance, and it was great to see them again.

Even Idaho was interested in the Mafia, and I conducted a two-day seminar for the Idaho Organized Crime Commission at Idaho Falls.

I enjoyed speaking to the Brookings Institute in Washington, and I joined Will Wilson and Postmaster General Winton Blount on a panel at the conference of U.S. Postal Inspectors in Washington.

One of my most enjoyable trips was to a magnificent resort on Whidby Island in Puget Sound, where I spoke to a gathering of Washington state district attorneys. U. S. Attorney Stan Pitkin, a wonderful host, delivered my colleague Tim Oliphant and me there in his private plane from Seattle, and we had time for some tennis afterwards. Tim covered the Northwest for the organized crime section. He was also a free spirit, unusual for a government lawyer, and a stimulating and fun person to be with. Later when he set up a private law practice in Steamboat Springs, Colorado, I went out there to ski with him a couple of times.

Martha Mitchell, the charming and outspoken wife of the Attorney General, who subsequently gained considerable notoriety during the Watergate days, was also interested in the world of organized crime, and I made a presentation at a meeting she arranged with some women friends in her husband's conference room. Later that same day she sent me a very cordial personal note of thanks.

Somewhere along the line I met and became friends with an affable fellow named Wayne Hopkins, who was director of public relations at the U.S. Chamber of Commerce, and who was eager to learn more about organized crime and legitimate business. There was a great deal of interest in the business community about the encroachment of mobsters into the world of commerce. The good members of the Chamber did not like the idea of their competition engaging in bribery, corruption, or predatory practices, something they themselves would of course never think of doing. So Wayne and I put together a dog-and-pony show, in which I discussed the methods of the mob, and Wayne told our listeners how to detect and report such activities in their communities. We took it on the road and were a great success in places like Richmond and Fort Lauderdale, among others.

Through the auspices of Judge Patrick Lynch in Omaha, a cousin of Susan, I was asked to go to Columbus, Nebraska, to make a presentation about the evils of organized crime at a conference of all the justices of the Supreme Court of Nebraska. I recruited as cohorts George

Higgins and Joel Pflaum, then with the office of the attorney general of Illinois, who later became a judge on the U.S. Court of Appeals for the 7th Circuit.

The conference was held at the Columbus Golf and Country Club. We were hard pressed to connect our boiler plate presentation to anything relevant to the cornfields of Nebraska, so we decided to emphasize the mob's control over nationwide illegal gambling, and to warn that even in seemingly safe areas like Nebraska, illegal gambling "feeds the coffers of the evil empire." The good justices listened politely, applauded, and thanked us. It wasn't until we were on our way out that we discovered that the room immediately adjacent to our conference room contained a large number of green felt tables, all set up for craps and blackjack, not to mention a row of slot machines.

That evening as the three of us sat watching a local softball game, the only visible recreation in the town, we wondered how the noble justices were disporting themselves.

There were other events in our lives during this period, some small, some large, and some cosmic.

On July 20, 1969, a hot midsummer evening in Washington, we watched along with some 600 million people around the world as astronaut Neil Armstrong stepped onto the surface of the moon, the first human ever to do so, and pronounced the memorable words, "That's one small step for man and one giant leap for mankind." It occurred around midnight our time, but we got Patrick, then just four, out of bed to witness the historic moment. We were also joined by my godson Pat Deluhery, who was at that time, as I recall, on the staff of Senator Hughes of Iowa.

My sister Mary Lu (Sister Thomas Patricia), who had been teaching in a Catholic high school in Los Angeles, decided in January 1969 to leave the convent after 12 years as a nun. After a great deal of soul searching, she felt constrained by convent life from accomplishing some of the things that she wanted to do with her life. She returned to San Jose, took an apartment and landed a job tutoring adults (primarily immigrants) in basic education skills. My mother, while having mixed feelings about her leaving the religious life, was delighted to have her nearby again, as were Pat and Frank and their family. Mom had sold her home at 2247 Serra Avenue in Santa Clara and had taken at apartment nearby in the Summerwood complex on Saratoga Avenue.

In February 1971 Mary Lu married Bill Swain, an engineer, and they purchased a home in San Jose.

On February 11, 1970, I celebrated my 40th birthday. Timmy, not quite four, and prompted by his mother, came down to breakfast and wished me a happy birthday. "How old are you?" asked Timmy. "Forty," I said. "Wow!" said he, "that's really old." I agreed and said, "Tim, you probably don't know anybody else in the whole world who's that old." And he replied, "I don't even know anybody who's six."

Later that evening, after everybody else had gone to bed, I got out a bottle of scotch at midnight and sat down to contemplate my life at age forty: where I had been, where I was going, what I expected to accomplish, and the Great Meaning of Life. At 12:15 I fell asleep.

Out in the real world, protests against the war in Vietnam were accelerating rapidly, especially on college campuses all around the country. Richard Nixon in his memoirs records that in the academic year 1969-70 there were 1800 campus demonstrations, 7,500 arrests, 462 injuries, 247 arsons and 8 deaths.

By 1971, the situation had gone from bad to worse. A national day of protest was proclaimed for Friday, May 1, and the call went out for 100,000 protesters to "take over" the nation's capital. There had been a great deal of violence in many of the campus protests, including arson and widespread destruction of property, and more of the same was expected in the march on Washington.

The Attorney General and the criminal division of the Department of Justice were heavily involved, along with the Pentagon, the White House, and the local governments and police of the District and surrounding Maryland and Virginia communities, in the preparations to combat the onslaught. The National Guard was called out, as was every available officer of the District police department, which was well trained and experienced in riot control. Some of the problems we faced included where to confine the thousands of persons who might be arrested; how to insure that each person accused of a crime was properly identified, along with the officer making the arrest, for purposes of possible prosecution; and how to protect the civil rights of peaceful protestors and prevent police brutality. Will Wilson, head of the criminal division, was in charge of this aspect, and several of us accompanied him to numerous meetings with other federal and local officials.

On the morning of May 1, we came down to Justice before dawn. National Guard troops and local riot police were stationed at all the bridges into the city as well as around the Pentagon and White House and other targeted areas. Over the years, there had been numerous "marches on Washington" on behalf of one cause or another (such as the civil rights march in August 1963 when Martin Luther King, Jr. delivered his famous "I Have a Dream" speech), but this one was different, in that its stated intent was to take over the city and bring everything to a halt: traffic, commerce, and government operations.

The day was chaotic but relatively little permanent damage was done. There were attempts to storm the federal court house and other federal buildings, but all were repulsed. Television images were mainly of gangs of college-age kids running in all directions, with the police in hot pursuit. Trash cans were dumped in the streets and a few cars were overturned, but there was no wholesale smashing of store windows such as had occurred during the "Days of Rage" at the 1968 Democratic convention in Chicago. My colleagues and I spent the day at Justice with relatively little to do beyond watching the action in the streets below, and listening to reports as they came in from around the city.

As it turned out, Susan was closer to the action than I was. While driving our three children in the Georgetown area, she was attempting to cross Wisconsin Avenue when she was stopped by (as she described it at the time) "a gang of young hippies with long hair, looking like flower children." One male tried to open the car door, and she shouted "Don't you <u>dare</u> harm my children!" and stomped on the accelerator and sped away.

By the end of the day, about 10,000 demonstrators had been arrested. Most of them were taken to the Washington Coliseum, a large indoor arena, where they were given sandwiches, water, and blankets and held overnight. The next day, a Saturday, most of the local judges were called into special session, including Tim Murphy, who had been elevated to the bench in 1967, where during the course of the day most were released upon payment of a $10 bail fee. The primary purpose of the arrests was not prosecution, but to get those who had broken the law off the streets.

Not surprisingly, all of this resulted in thousands of lawsuits against the government and the public officials in charge of maintaining law and order, including Will Wilson, for alleged violations of civil rights. The cases dragged on for years. After I had left the government and entered private practice later in 1971, Wilson hired me as his personal lawyer to monitor his interest in these cases, although he was officially represented by the Department of Justice. As I recall, most of the cases were eventually dismissed, a few were settled, and Mr. Wilson suffered no personal liability.

We were outgrowing our townhouse at 1803 37th St. NW, so in November 1970 we purchased a four-level, 6 bedroom, 4 bath house with a large back yard at 4817 V St. NW, in the Foxhall/Reservoir Road area, about a mile west of Georgetown University. It also had a maid's quarters on the lower level, so we were able to hire the wonderful Nora James from Trinidad-Tobago, who lived with us for three years. The children loved Nora, as did we, and her presence gave Susy some freedom to pursue a number of other activities including her public relations work with Stanley-Williams Presentations. Also, just a block away was Our Lady of Victory parish and school, in which we enrolled Patrick, followed by Tim and Katy. All in all, the house was perfect for us, and we made it our home until we moved to California in 1994.

Reaching mid-life, I also purchased a little red MGB convertible, and each day in good weather when I came home from work I would find three little kids and an Irish setter eagerly waiting for a spin around the neighborhood, the three kids in the back and Christopher Clancy in the front (no seat belts then).

Christopher Clancy

Susan had brought cats into the marriage, but we had never had a dog. Patrick, at age six, began agitating for a canine pet. Susan and I talked it over and decided that an Irish setter would be a nice addition to the family. They are a handsome breed, with their shiny reddish-brown coat and feathery tail. They are handsome, intelligent, and fun-loving, not to mention being Irish. We saw an ad in the paper for a two-year-old male. The owner seemed eager to emphasize that her apartment was too small for "Christopher," and seemed relieved that we had a nice yard for him.

"Christopher" did not seem an entirely appropriate name for an Irish setter, so after we closed the deal and brought him home to our little family we added the name "Clancy."

Christopher Clancy bounded with glee into our lives. He was boisterously carefree, joyful, and high-spirited. "Rollicking" may be an understatement. He did indeed love children, and in his exuberance regularly knocked them to the ground. He loved nearly everybody, including Butterball, the family cat, previously master of the domain, who most assuredly did not return the affection.

The only real problem with Christopher Clancy was that he loved to run great distances and at great speeds. Running with abandon seems to be a common trait in this breed. One time in Manhattan we observed a blind man walking with his seeing-eye dog, an Irish setter. Suddenly something spooked the dog and he broke into a run, the poor man hanging on for dear life, yelling and cursing as he went.

Christopher was also an accomplished jumper. Our 4' chain link fence in the back yard presented no challenge at all, and before long Christopher regarded our entire block as his private steeplechase course, much to the chagrin of many a startled neighbor.

Under the pressure of increasing hostility from all sides, I went one Saturday morning to Hechinger's hardware and purchased an install-it-yourself 6' reed fence. Christopher watched intently as I spent the rest of the day putting it up. Immediately after I got the last section in place, Christopher, with a good running start, cleared the fence like an Olympic hurdler.

One Sunday afternoon, we all, Christopher included, took a drive up to Fort Frederick, one of Maryland's better known historic sites from the Revolutionary War. Like all such forts, it was surrounded by high walls. As we went through the gates and entered the parade ground Christopher broke loose, galloped across the grounds, up the ramp, and disappeared over the wall, two stories above the ground.

We rushed to the top and peered anxiously over, expecting to see the dead body of our beloved companion. Just then somebody looked behind, as Christopher came running up the ramp again at top speed, ready for another leap into oblivion.

Like all good Irishmen, Christopher Clancy held his grudges. For no valid reason, he took a dislike to a small and ancient dog belonging to our neighbor Dick Slater, two doors away. The poor old dog was so decrepit that Slater had to carry it across the street to do its business in the weeds. If Christopher happened to be out at the time, he never failed to harass the two of them.

The final straw came when the phone rang early one cold February morning. Susan picked up the receiver and was greeted by a stream of invective the likes of which she had never heard before. It was Slater—"in my pajamas and slippers," he screamed—calling from the fire house a block away. It seemed that Christopher Clancy had escaped from our yard and had camped himself on Slater's front porch, teeth bared, barring entry to Slater and his dog.

Not long thereafter we sadly but realistically found a nice new home for Christopher Clancy, way out in the country, surrounded by lots of open land where, God willing, the wind was always at his back.

Shortly thereafter, we obtained Beaujangles, a wonderful little *Bichon*, who remained with us for the next eleven years.

Skulduggery in the Big Easy

Since the memory of man runneth not to the contrary, Louisiana politics has been fabled in story and song for its outlandish public figures and its tradition of public corruption. Huey Long, the "Kingfish," ruled the state in the nineteen twenties and thirties, both as governor and U.S. senator, dispensing largesse to the public with roads, schools, and housing, while at the same time benefitting handsomely from the contractors who did the work. The Kingfish was a benevolent despot who ruled with an iron fist and an open palm, until his assassination in 1935.

Huey Long's brother Earl served as governor three times in the 40's and 50's until, if memory serves me, he was committed to an asylum. In addition to having a notorious affair with a New Orleans stripper named Blaze Starr, Earl had ridden his white stallion into the governor's mansion, which caused the locals to comment that it was the first time there had been a *whole* horse in the governor's office.

More recently, there was Edwin Edwards. He served four separate terms as governor from 1972 to 1996. During all of this period he was indicted at least four times for corruption, and on each occasion was either acquitted or the jury was deadlocked. Finally in 2000 he was convicted under the RICO statute for corruption in connection with granting of casino licenses, and was sent off to prison.

In keeping with the bizarre state of Louisiana politics, District Attorney Jim Garrison of New Orleans achieved notoriety in the mid-1960's by developing several simultaneous conspiracy theories concerning the assassination of John F. Kennedy. According to Garrison, there may have been at one time or another up to 16 marksmen in Dealey Plaza, working either for a homosexual ring seeking a thrill, or for the Pentagon, or the CIA, or sinister forces in the military-industrial complex, all somehow connected to Lee Harvey Oswald, who for a time had lived in New Orleans. In 1967 Garrison indicted Clay Shaw, a reputable gay New Orleans businessman. Shaw was ultimately acquitted, whereupon Garrison indicted him for perjury at his trial. Eventually a federal court put a stop to all further proceedings against Shaw. Garrison's crackpot theories were given new life in Oliver Stone's 1991 movie, "JFK".

During all of this time the self-righteous crusading Mr. Garrison was on the take from the illegal gambling industry in New Orleans, receiving up to $4000 every two months as protection money. The bag man was his former chief investigator, a colorful figure (though "colorful" is a redundancy in New Orleans) named Pershing Gervais. Before going to work for Garrison, Gervais had been fired by the New Orleans police department. Gervais had—not once but twice—stolen payoff money collected for the department and used it to finance free-spending trips to New York City.

At the time we set up the strike force in New Orleans in 1970, Gervais had been under intense scrutiny by the IRS. Finally, he decided to cooperate, declaring that he had recently lost a son in Vietnam and he wanted to amend his life to honor his child. Gervais stated that he had been the conduit for protection money from the gambling industry since 1961, during all of which time he had delivered the payoffs to

Garrison and to the present and former chiefs of the vice squad in the New Orleans police department.

John Wall, a shrewd and experienced prosecutor whom we had sent down from Boston to head up the New Orleans strike force, told Gervais that a case could not be made on his word alone. Then Gervais consented to be wired for sound for future meetings with Garrison. Electronic eavesdropping with the consent of one party is legal and the evidence is admissible in court. Meetings and lengthy conversations between Gervais and Garrison, highly incriminating to Garrison, were recorded during the payoffs in March and May 1971.

Then on June 30, 1971, after Gervais had picked up the latest payoff from the gambling operators, the FBI recorded the serial numbers, marked the bills with powder, and listened in as Gervais delivered the envelope in the bedroom of Garrison's home. Garrison placed the money in a dresser drawer.

Later that evening arrest and search warrants were obtained and in the early morning hours Garrison was arrested. The powder was on his hands and the marked money was still in the drawer. Also arrested were the two vice squad officers (whom Gervais had also paid off that evening) and six gambling operators.

All of this and more was contained in a 113-page affidavit supporting the arrest warrant. We wanted the public to know the extent of our evidence, to forestall an anticipated claim of frame-up by Garrison.

I personally wrote the press release on the arrests, taking care to give full credit to the FBI and the IRS, as well the Customs Bureau, the Secret Service, the Labor Department, and the Postal Inspection Service, whose agents on the strike force had contributed greatly to the investigation. But believe it or not, I got a complaint from the FBI the next day because the IRS had been named eight times in the release and the Bureau only five.

The arrests caused a sensation in New Orleans and the press had a field day with the affidavit. Garrison, after an unsuccessful attempt to get an injunction against its publication, then went on the offensive, claiming that the bribery charges were a "complete frameup" resulting from his investigation of the JFK assassination. "I predicted some months ago that I would be charged with some federal offense," Garrison said. "I have pounded away at the warfare complex of this government and have not given up." He added, "I guess this is better than being shot. I'm ahead of the game." (New Orleans States-Item, 7/1/71). According to the Associated Press, he said "I have pounded at the Pentagon and the Central Intelligence Agency and this had to happen sooner or later. I decided I would keep pushing until they killed me or put me in prison." (San Jose Mercury-News, 7/1/71)

The case was tried, at his insistence, by Gerald Gallinghouse, the U.S. Attorney. Gallinghouse was not overly competent as a trial lawyer but was dedicated and honest, and he was politically ambitious. However, in New Orleans the deck was stacked against the federal government. In most courtrooms the tapes and the marked bills would seem to guarantee an easy conviction. But in New Orleans things are hardly ever what they seem. By the time of the trial Pershing Gervais had been gotten to, and he recanted, claiming he had been forced by what he called calculated harassment to work and lie for the government, though he never denied that the taped conversations and the delivery of the money occurred. Both John Wall and I gave statements describing Gervais' completely voluntary cooperation.

Then Garrison presented his "retaliation" defense, and his lawyers asked the good folks of New Orleans to come to the aid of their beleaguered hero and not permit him to be sacrificed to the evil and powerful men in Washington bent solely on revenge for his valiant attempts to uncover the truth about the Kennedy assassination.

The jury swallowed it hook, line, and sinker, and after due deliberation acquitted Garrison of all charges.

And then things returned to normal in the Big Easy. That is, until the horror of Hurricane Katrina on August 28-29, 2005.

By the spring of 1971 I had come to a decision that I had been considering for several months. It was time to leave the government and take a shot at private practice. I had almost done so a year earlier. Bob Peloquin, in private practice after leaving the Buffalo strike force, and Tom McKeon, another associate from the Hoffa squad and then head of the Detroit strike force, who also had left the government, decided to form a corporation to be called International Intelligence, Inc. Intertel, as it came to be known, would be an investigative services company with a specialty in advising and protecting businesses and governments against the encroachment of organized crime. It would be staffed by experienced former government agents, many of whom had worked on the strike forces. Their first client was Resorts International, owner of a new luxury hotel and casino in the Bahamas. Resorts had the support and cooperation of the government of the Bahamas, whose gambling casinos were under attack from organized crime figures like Meyer Lansky who had been driven from Cuba after the Castro revolution. Another promising client was Howard Hughes, who was beginning to buy up hotel casinos in Las Vegas in opposition to the mob-controlled casinos.

Peloquin and McKeon had asked me to join them in what promised to be a highly exciting new venture, and I was tempted. But there was a greater loyalty which kept me at Justice another year. Bill Lynch, the chief of the organized crime section, had been taken off the job to try the high-profile case against the Berrigan brothers, the anti-war priests who had resorted to violent means, including the destruction of FBI files in Media, Pennsylvania.

With Lynch gone, and with only two other deputies to supervise the work of 140 lawyers in Washington and 17 other cities, I decided that it would be unfair to abandon the important work of the section and the progress we were making.

But by the early summer of 1971 Lynch had returned and with an additional year of experience, the strike forces were well established and things were going more smoothly. I also felt that if I was ever going to try private practice I had better get started. I was 41, supposedly at the height of one's energy and skills. I had been a prosecutor for ten years, and was eager to try my hand at criminal defense work, which I had found both challenging and enjoyable in the Marine Corps, and civil litigation, as well as the other areas of a general law practice. Susan was a bit apprehensive about my going into practice on my own, with three small children to support, but as usual was supportive of my decision. So I announced that I would be leaving the Department in mid-summer. Upon my recommendation, Marvin Loewy was designated as my replacement.

But first I was given one final assignment. There were two major prosecutions being considered by the Department. Prosecutive memoranda had been submitted by the U.S. Attorneys in San Francisco and Chicago respectively, and as is usual in high-profile cases, final approval had to be given by the Attorney General upon recommendation of the criminal division. The first involved Mayor Joseph Alioto of San Francisco, accused of public corruption. In the second, Otto Kerner, the former governor of Illinois as well as chairman of the commission that had studied the urban riots in the 1960's, and currently a judge on the federal court of appeals for the Sixth Circuit, was accused of accepting a bribe to vote in favor of an appellant before his court.

As an experienced prosecutor supposedly possessed of some wisdom in such matters, I was asked to study carefully the evidence in each case, and to render an objective opinion as to whether the cases should go forward. After thorough analysis, I concluded that there was an airtight case against Alioto. As to Kerner, I concluded that the evidence was not sufficient to warrant an indictment.

Ultimately the decision was made to indict both. Alioto was acquitted, and Kerner was convicted. So much for my judicial wisdom. Actually in the Kerner case, observers said that he was well on the way to acquittal until he took the stand, and was caught in one lie. It is axiomatic in criminal trial practice that if jurors catch the defendant in one lie, no matter how unimportant to the whole case, he will be convicted. This is why most defense lawyers are extremely reluctant to put their clients on the stand.

On August 19, 1971, I closed out my career as a federal prosecutor, and had the opportunity to express my appreciation to friends and colleagues in the Department and the other federal agencies with whom I had such great times, 85 of whom attended a lavish gathering in my honor held in the Grand Reception Room of the State Department. The attendees included Will Wilson, head of the criminal division, as well as his two predecessors for whom I had worked, Fred Vinson and Jack Miller. I was excited about launching a new career, yet there was some sadness in knowing that never again would I have the comradeship of such an outstanding group of dedicated public servants.

19.

PRIVATE PRACTICE

I began my law practice with David Blum, with whom I had become acquainted in Puerto Rico. Dave had been in the Labor Department at that time but had since transferred to the Department of Housing and Urban Development in Washington and had become well versed in federal housing law. Dave and his wife Harlyn had become close social friends of ours, and Dave was also eager to try his skills in private practice. We rented space in the Federal Bar Building at 1819 H St., NW, two blocks from the White House, and set up shop as Kennelly & Blum. Shortly thereafter we were joined by John Wall, who had just left the New Orleans strike force, and for a while we were Kennelly, Blum & Wall. But after a few months John found that most of his clients were back in Boston, so he returned to his home town and continued a successful criminal practice there.

It was at this time that I began riding a bicycle to my office. It was an easy commute, less than four miles, and it kept me in good shape during the good weather from April through November. I continued this practice for the next ten years.

I also formed a corporation, Kennelly Associates, Inc., for consulting work in the area of organized crime prevention.

I had been advised that the first six months of private practice might be very private indeed. Undaunted, I really looked forward to being completely on my own, and not being responsible to anyone for my time, except of course the four starving mouths at home, not including canines and felines. One afternoon I actually walked over to the lobby of the Mayflower Hotel and read a newspaper, without feeling guilty.

It was not long before things began happening. The auditing/consulting firm of Peat Marwick Mitchell & Co. had received a large contract from the Law Enforcement Assistance Administration to conduct training programs in organized crime enforcement for state and local police, prosecutors and judges. They asked me to be their technical consultant and I eagerly signed on. It was what I knew best and it provided enough income for the first six months of practice. There were three conferences of one week each, in Williamsburg, VA, at the University of Notre Dame, and in San Diego. Working with the PMM staff, I devised the curriculum and selected all the resource persons, who were experts in their subjects and were people with whom I had previously been associated. In each conference there were about 60 attendees, a cross-section of state and local police officers, district attorneys and judges, all from urban areas across the country where organized crime was a problem. It was also a great opportunity for an exchange of ideas. A New York police detective could get to know his counterpart in Philadelphia, or a district attorney from Detroit could get the insights of a judge from Chicago. Our curriculum included all the usual areas in which the mob was active, from gambling and loan sharking to infiltration of legitimate business. We also discussed enforcement procedures such as intelligence gathering, networking with other agencies, and witness protection problems. We even had a section on computer crime, in 1972, the first time this had been covered in a law enforcement conference, as far as I know.

As a result of the success of the above conferences, Kennelly Associates, Inc. was the successful bidder on another such week long seminar in Columbus, Ohio, for officials just from that state. This time Susan and I handled it alone. I set it up, using the same curriculum and most of the same resources, and Susy, in addition to helping with the administrative details, handled all the public relations. Thanks to her expertise and charm, we got coverage in all the media nearly every day. It was great fun working as a team.

Other Kennelly Associates contracts included some consulting work on organized crime enforcement for the Quebec Provincial Government. This consulting work was a big help while I was getting started in the law practice.

How Can You Defend a Person If You Know He Did It?

On the legal side, the practice was developing nicely. Most of my white collar criminal defense work was by way of referrals from other attorneys whom I knew. In Washington at that time there were more than 16,000 members of the District of Columbia Bar (not all of whom practiced regularly in Washington, of course) but surprisingly, there were only about 25 of us who were doing white collar criminal defense work (as opposed to street crimes, which were handled mostly by a coterie of lawyers whose offices were near the courthouse—known as the "Fifth Street Lawyers."). And nearly all of us were former federal prosecutors and were sole practitioners or in small firms. The big prestigious firms considered it unseemly to have a criminal law practice—until Watergate came along! We all knew and respected each other, and referred clients to each other. For example, if a defense contractor was under investigation for fraud, each corporate officer under suspicion would need his own lawyer, because of possible conflicts of interest. Whoever got the case first would farm it out to the others among us, as needed.

In addition, some former Justice officials joined law firms that referred out all criminal defense work. In this manner I received a number of good clients from Fred Vinson, former head of the criminal division.

White collar criminal investigations are high-profile and usually get a lot of publicity because they involve public corporations and their officers, or government officials. Because they are high-profile, indictments in these cases customarily must be approved in advance by the Attorney General. And the AG almost always accepts the up-or-down recommendation of his Assistant AG in charge of the criminal division. A great many potential defendants therefore like to hire a former federal prosecutor, who has access to the Department and is respected there, to plead his cause in the hope of staving off an indictment. Every trial lawyer is asked to name his or her most famous clients, but the lawyer's most successful cases involve clients nobody ever heard of, because he has kept them from getting indicted and has kept their names out of the press.

This is not to say that the decision-makers in the Department show favoritism to their former colleagues. But it does mean that the lawyer is more likely to get a chance for a hearing and an opportunity to plead his client's cause, before indictment. If I call and ask for a meeting, they know that I am going to be up front and truthful with them, that I have important factors for them to consider, and that I'm not going to waste their time with a lot of baloney about my client. It may also be the opportunity to discuss the possibility of the client becoming a witness instead of a defendant; or if all else looks hopeless, the chance to talk about a possible plea bargain. In any case, it is an important phase in the whole process of criminal jurisprudence.

Which brings us to another question asked of every criminal defense lawyer: "How can you defend a person if you know he did it?" It's a simple and legitimate question deserving a straightforward and honest answer. But the answer is a little more complicated.

The most obvious answer of course is that in our system of justice if an accused person chooses to exercise his constitutional right to a fair trial, the government must prove each and every element of the offense beyond a reasonable doubt, and it is the defense lawyer's obligation to hold the government to that standard. He does this by cross-examination of the government's witnesses and by presenting evidence on behalf of his client, which must not be false evidence; nor must he ever permit any witness, including his client, to lie on the stand. Finally, there must be a unanimous verdict by a jury of twelve. These are things we all learned in school.

But the good defense lawyer must examine the case more deeply. For instance, even if it appears that his client "did it," does what he "did" constitute the crime for which he has been charged?

To illustrate: In 1972 Fred Vinson asked me to represent a man named Knute Knighton, who was the Washington government affairs representative for a Dallas corporation named Resalab, Inc. Resalab, a relatively small company, had won a major contract from the Federal Aviation Administration to install new runway lighting systems at about a dozen major airports. There had been fierce bidding on the contract, and Resalab had won over much larger corporations such as Lockheed and General Electric. The FAA official authorized to make the final decision was one John Mercer. After the award it had come to the attention of the Department of Justice that Knighton, during the bidding process and prior to the award, had offered Mercer, and Mercer had happily accepted, numerous perks from Resalab. These included not only drinks and dinners and theater tickets, but a free golfing weekend at the famous Pebble Beach course in Carmel, including transportation from Washington in the Resalab corporate jet. Not only that, but the records showed that Resalab was not the lowest bidder. Resalab and Knighton were charged with offering, and Mercer was charged with accepting, bribes to award the contract to Resalab.

When I got the case our chances looked pretty bleak. But I had learned, going back to my Marine Corps days, that in trial work preparation means everything. It is a truism among trial lawyers that a case is won or lost before you ever enter the courtroom. Eloquent summaries rarely do the job.

So I examined every single document in the FAA's voluminous file on the matter, and I interviewed employees involved in the contract award process. Lo and behold, it turned out that although Resalab was not the lowest bidder, it was found to be the lowest <u>responsible</u> bidder, meaning that other lower bidders had not submitted proposals that, for one reason or another, would be in full performance of the contract. Further, the recommendation to award the contract to Resalab was made by a committee. There was no evidence that either Mercer or Resalab had influenced the committee in any way. Mercer's sole participation in the process was to sign off on the recommendation of the committee. These facts were not uncovered by the prosecutor in his preparation; he had looked primarily at the gratuities and the award. Nor, for that matter, had it been discovered by my co-counsel representing Mercer.

All of the above was revealed through cross-examination of the government's witnesses. As a result, the judge dismissed the charges at the conclusion of the government's case and our clients went free. The prosecutor, a friend of mine named Bob Ogren, was furious, but the judge was right. Was justice done? You bet. The facts did not fit the crime charged. The gratuities given and received did not cause the award of the contract. Our clients were unethical and lucky, but they were justifiably acquitted of the crime charged, and were protected by double jeopardy from being charged under any other statute.

Another example of looking behind the question of whether the client "did it" involves the question of specific intent. With very few exceptions, every felony case requires proof that the defendant had the specific intent to commit the crime charged. In most cases the specific intent is obvious. He robbed the bank. He stabbed his victim in the heart. But not in all cases. Cconsider the charge of tax evasion.

My client was Gayle Rogers. She was the partner of Robert Williams, a portrait painter. Williams was very talented and was becoming spectacularly successful, mostly doing portraits of well-to-do families throughout the south. He had started slowly a couple of years earlier, but his fame spread by word of mouth, and he was getting as much business as he could handle. Williams was also functionally illiterate, and Gayle acted as his business manager. Gayle was very bright and had a Ph.D. but it was in philosophy, not business, and accounting was not high among her skills. She did keep records of all his income and expenses, but in a very haphazard fashion, using shoe boxes as her most sophisticated filing method. She took her summaries to an accountant who prepared Robert's tax returns. She expressed her feelings of inadequacy to her accountant, but he said she was doing just fine and did not offer to take over the bookkeeping.

When the IRS showed up for an audit, it turned out that she had failed to report over $60,000 in income one year and over $70,000 the next. Her own records showed the income received, according to the IRS, but she had failed to report it, either to the accountant or to the IRS. The auditor recommended that Mr. Williams and Ms. Rogers be charged with tax evasion for both years, a felony carrying a maximum of five years imprisonment on each count.

She brought me all of her records. They were a mess What came across to me, after innumerable hours of tedious study, was that she really had made a good faith and sincere effort to keep everything straight. But her efforts were those of a philosopher, not a bookkeeper.

A taxpayer under investigation for a criminal tax violation has the right of appeal at three levels of the IRS: the District, the Region, and finally the National Office. If the taxpayer is rebuffed at all those levels, the National Office then sends the matter to the U.S. Attorney for indictment.

Williams' attorney and I were unsuccessful at three levels of the IRS. Gayle came to each of the meetings and tried to explain how her errors had occurred, although she herself did not fully understand how it had happened. But the IRS officials could not accept that anyone could overlook that much income (out of gross receipts of $200,000 to $300,000 per annum). I think they also felt that her failure to hire a bookkeeper was proof of her intent to evade.

Normally when a tax case is referred to the U.S. Attorney's office for indictment, the prosecutor correctly assumes that the case is a strong one, having been thoroughly reviewed at three levels of tax lawyers and other experts at the IRS. But in this case I was fortunate to get the ear of a very able and conscientious Assistant U.S. Attorney named Bill Pease, who agreed to sit down with me and go through the tortuous step-by-step process whereby one could finally understand how the errors occurred. Ultimately he agreed with me that the errors were accidental and there was no indication of an intent to deceive or evade. After a great deal of deliberation and consultation with his superiors, they agreed that there was insufficient evidence of a specific criminal intent, and they declined to indict.

Our clients were more than happy to arrive at a civil settlement, paying all taxes due plus penalties and interest. It was one of my most satisfying cases, because my client's name never appeared in the press.

Some of my lawyer friends who regularly did tax work said they had never heard of a tax case being dismissed by the U.S. Attorney after referral from the National Office of the IRS. It is always satisfying to receive praise from one's peers.

Here is the irony of this case. While all this was going on, Robert Williams was commissioned to do the official portrait of the Attorney General, Edward Levi, and the portrait hangs in the halls of the Justice Department to this day.

In interviewing new clients, I never asked if they were guilty. For one thing, I didn't care. Guilt is determined by judges and juries, not advocates. My job was to make sure that my clients' rights were defended and protected. But also, a client may not really know whether or not he is guilty; in fact, he may even *think* he is guilty when in fact he is not.

Here is another example. My client, whom we shall call Dr. Paley, was the only doctor in Ronceverte, a small coal-mining town (pop.1500) in West Virginia. Many of his patients suffered from the occupational hazards of coal mining, and most were on Medicare or Medicaid, being either retired or with low incomes. Therefore he received reimbursement from the federal Health Care Finance Agency, which oversees Medicare and Medicaid.

It was Dr. Paley's custom to take extensive lab tests, to rule out diseases such as diabetes, renal failure, thyroid problems, and others. Dr. Paley found a laboratory in Tennessee which could perform a battery of these tests for about $27. However, he submitted bills for this work to the HCFA for around $350 and was regularly reimbursed in full. When Dr. Paley's records were examined by HFCA auditors, they concluded that his fees for lab work were excessive, compared to what he had paid, and they referred the matter to the U.S. postal inspection service for using the mails to commit medicare fraud.

The postal inspector assigned to the case obtained from Dr. Paley a list of all of his patients, and then sent a letter to each of them stating that Dr. Paley was under criminal investigation and requesting them to fill out an enclosed questionnaire. Not surprisingly, this created panic in the town and almost without exception, the patients immediately terminated their relationship with the doctor. In fact, his income dropped to nearly zero and he was forced to leave town and take another position in Maine. As a result, the town was left without a local doctor.

The matter was referred to the United States Attorney in Charleston, West Virginia, for indictment, and at this point Dr. Paley came to me. I asked him how he arrived at the $350 figure. He said that he called the nearest hospital in the region and asked how much they would charge to perform each of the requested lab tests. They came up with a total of $350 and so that is the amount he submitted to the government, even though he had found a laboratory in Tennessee which would do the whole battery for $27. Is this legitimate? Dr. Paley had no idea whether this was permissible under the regulations or not. He just reasoned that if the hospital could charge that much, so could he.

It turned out he was right. The regulations are dense and confusing, but they provide that doctors shall be reimbursed in amounts that are "fair and reasonable in accordance with the usual custom and practice in the community." Further, the medical profession itself decides what is fair and reasonable in a community. In Ronceverte the medical profession (*i.e.* the hospital) had apparently decided that $350 was fair and reasonable.

In other words, the doctors themselves set their own fees, and as long as they all adhere to the standard they set for themselves, the government *must* pay them accordingly. Talk about price fixing!

I could not believe what I was reading, and neither could the U.S. Attorney at first, until I finally located an expert in the field who agreed that indeed this was so, and Dr. Paley—though it certainly looked like gouging—was not in violation of any law or regulation.

The charges were dropped, and my client was more than happy to pay my fee. But I often wondered thereafter what the people in Ronceverte were doing for medical care.

When I first entered private practice, Susan was wary about my taking on defense work because she had always known me as a person "in pursuit of justice." But she came to realize that justice is multidimensional, and each of its sides must be vigorously pursued by able advocates and jurists, in order for genuine justice to be done.

On Teaching Justice to Children

At some time during this period I decided that it was time for our children to learn something about the concept of justice. So on one occasion when Susan had taken her mother to New York for a few days and I was left alone with the children, then about 7, 6, and 5, I seized the moment.

"What do you think is meant by justice?" I asked, and Patrick ventured, "Freedom. The right to do whatever you want." Not bad.

I responded, "Does that mean you have the freedom to throw a rock through Mr. Lacovara's window next door?"

"Oh no," chimed in Katy, "that wouldn't be fair."

"Very good," said I. "Justice has to do with fairness; being fair to all people." And they all nodded in agreement.

Flushed with success in teaching commutative justice—man's relations with his fellow men—I decided to press on with distributive justice, man's relations with his government.

"Now suppose," I said, "that the government decided that only people with white skin could get jobs. Would that be fair? Would that be just?" And three little heads shook in disapproval.

"Why not?" I asked.

And Tim said, and all agreed, "Because that would mean that people with white skin would have to do all the work."

Guys on the Street Need Lawyers Too

I also had some interesting street crime cases. All criminal lawyers are urged by the bar association to take "court-appointed" cases, representing indigent defendants, in return for which the court pays the lawyers a small fee.

In some ways street criminals are easier to deal with than businessmen or public officials. Robbers and muggers know they're crooks. They aren't trying to fool anybody; they tell their lawyers the truth and just ask them to do the best they can. The white collar guys, on the other hand, cannot possibly think of themselves as criminals. They are respectable citizens. Criminals are people who rob banks and steal purses from little old ladies. Therefore these pillars of the community will do everything possible to evade the truth if it makes them look bad. They want their lawyer to think highly of them, and are afraid that if he doesn't he won't willing to give his all for them. I used to say, "Don't expect me to fall in love with you; all I want is the truth, so I won't be surprised in the courtroom." It seldom worked.

My most memorable street-crime client was Clifton Bullock. Clifton was a very bright and articulate man in his late twenties, born and raised locally, who had written a couple of unpublished novels. Unfortunately Clifton had a penchant for bank robberies and prison escapes. He carried a .22 caliber bullet lodged in his heart from one of his escapades (I saw the X-ray). When I was assigned to represent him upon his most recent capture, he was already under cumulative sentences of life plus forty years.

A couple of weeks before his trial there was a daring escape attempt from the D.C. jail. I followed the story on TV and in the press with only mild interest until I discovered that the ringleader was my client, Clifton. It seems that he and his cellmate had recruited ten other eager inmates. They overpowered two guards, locked them in the cell, and then, armed and wearing the guards' uniforms, managed to gain entrance to and take over the command center. The plan then was for two of them to go out the gate, commandeer two cars, drive back in and pick up the others. All went according to plan until the two drivers, unable to resist the call of freedom, neglected to return. A few days later one was recaptured in Cleveland and the other in Dallas.

In the meantime Clifton and his cohorts, realizing their plight, took some of the guards as hostages and engaged in a running two-day battle from cellblock to cellblock until they were finally cornered, tear-gassed, and recaptured.

I now found myself representing a client charged with eighteen counts of kidnapping (moving the guard/hostages against their will), assault with deadly weapons, attempted homicide, and attempted escape.

Clifton, looking forward to a couple of weeks out of his cell and in the courtroom with a suit and tie, insisted on pleading not guilty and going to trial. Actually I was able to get him acquitted on nine of the eighteen counts, which made not the slightest difference in the long run. The judge awarded him an additional life sentence plus twelve years, and sent him off to the federal prison at Marion, Indiana, the government's replacement for Alcatraz. But Clifton thought I was the greatest trial lawyer ever, and sent me Christmas greetings for several years thereafter.

My name apparently went into the system's computer as representing anyone named anything like Clifton Bullock, and so several months later I was appointed to represent one Clifton <u>Bullet.</u> This fellow was a gentle giant, reminding me of Lennie in *Of Mice and Men*. He was charged with robbing a liquor store, his first venture in crime. Unfortunately, he and his buddies chose the very store where he had a part-time job. But Clifton figured a ski mask would disguise his 6'5" 300-lb. frame. The owner, upon hearing Clifton announce "Stick 'em up!" said, "Clifton, what do you think you're doing?" They were all captured a short time later, with the guns and loot in their car. There was a search-and-seizure problem which justified going to trial, but the judge didn't see it as a problem, and Clifton spent the next five years in the care of the federal government.

One day there walked into my office Bill Anders, the astronaut who was the lunar pilot on Apollo 8 and who took the famous photo of the "earthrise" as seen from the moon. Bill was accompanied by his 18-year-old son, Daniel, who had been arrested for possession of marijuana. Daniel, a high school senior, had just been accepted for admission to the United States Military Academy at West Point, and a drug bust would ruin his chances for entry and perhaps jeopardize his entire career.

Here were the facts: Daniel and a buddy were in a car, with Daniel at the wheel, late at night in one of the inner city areas of Washington. As they pulled up to a stop light, a police cruiser pulled alongside, and the police officer noticed that Daniel was smoking a weird-looking pipe, of a kind, according to the officer, that is often used by pot-smokers. So he pulled the boys over, arrested them for possession, and seized the pipe. The pipe was sent to the laboratory and was found to contain marihuana seeds. Daniel was charged with possession of marihuana.

The legal question was whether the officer had probable cause, within the meaning of the 4th Amendment, to believe that a crime was being committed in his presence which would give him the authority to make an arrest without a warrant. The officer admitted in his report that Daniel was not driving erratically; nor could the officer detect any odor, as the windows of both cars were closed. It all depended on whether the appearance of the pipe was sufficient probable cause, based on the officer's experience.

I visited the most upscale pipe and tobacco shop in Washington, located on Pennsylvania Avenue a half-block from the White House, and persuaded the owner to loan me ten of his most unusual-looking pipes, all from his display case, all expensive and all available to the general public. Placed among them, Daniel's pipe was virtually indistinguishable from the others.

Upon viewing the display, the judge granted my motion to suppress the evidence and the charges were dismissed. The judge also ordered the arrest to be expunged from the court records. Daniel, a chastened young man, went on to West Point and I hope to a distinguished military career.

Bill Anders gratefully provided me with a large copy of his earthrise photo, inscribed "To Patrick, Tim, and Katy Kennelly, with best wishes—Bill Anders, Apollo 8." Bill later went on to become CEO of General Dynamics.

In 1972 my military career came to an end. I had remained active in the Marine Corps Reserve off and on throughout the years, but finally my work, travel, and family responsibilities made it impossible to continue my reserve obligations, and I had to drop out. On 4 August 1972, I was honorably discharged from the United States Marine Corps with the rank of major. The Marine Corps did wonders for me, and I have always been grateful for and proud of my military service.

20.

WATERGATE

At breakfast on the morning of June 18, 1972, I noted a small story on the front page of the Washington Post about a break-in the previous night at the headquarters of the Democratic National Committee, located in the Watergate hotel-apartment-office complex. Five men were caught at the scene, all wearing business suits and all with pockets full of hundred dollar bills. Police had seized a walkie-talkie, cameras, numerous rolls of undeveloped film, and electronic devices capable of bugging both telephones and room conversations. Two of the men were named McCord and Barker, and the other three appeared to be Cuban-Americans from Miami.

How curious. Burglars in business suits with C-notes in their pockets? And why burglarize the DNC?

Curiosity heightened when it was disclosed that Mr. McCord was employed as the security officer for the Committee to Re-elect the President, gleefully termed CREEP by the press.

John Mitchell, who had left his post as Attorney General to direct Richard Nixon's second presidential campaign, immediately issued a press release from California stating that "this man" [McCord] was the proprietor of a private security agency who had been hired by the committee to assist in the installation of its security system. Mitchell added: "We want to emphasize that this man and the other people involved were not operating either on our behalf or with our consent.

There is no place in our campaign or in the electoral process for this type of activity, and we will not permit it or condone it."

Ron Zeigler, White House press secretary, termed it a "third-rate burglary attempt."

Curiosity became intense a few days later when it was revealed that there were at least three others involved in the burglary. An ex-FBI agent named Alfred Baldwin had been found at the other end of the walkie-talkie manning an observation post in a room on the eighth floor of the Howard Johnson motel, directly across the street from the DNC offices. Baldwin revealed that there had also been a command post in a room in the Watergate hotel, which had been occupied by the group's leaders, named G. Gordon Liddy and E. Howard Hunt. Both Liddy and Hunt were employed by the Committee to Re-elect the President, and both had previously been on the White House Staff as aides to Bob Haldeman, Nixon's chief of staff, and John Erlichman, Assistant to the President for Domestic Affairs.

What the public did not know, and would not know until the national frenzy known as Watergate had run its course, was that the entire burglary and bugging operation had been conceived by G. Gordon Liddy and had been approved in advance by Mitchell while he was Attorney General. Nor was the public aware that the operation was financed by CRP from contributions secretly raised by Maurice Stans, the committee's finance chairman and former Secretary of Commerce, and Herbert W. Kalmbach, deputy finance chairman and personal attorney to the president.

The public was also unaware that this was not the culprits' first foray into the Democratic headquarters. In fact they had broken in a few weeks previously and installed bugs in the offices and on the phones, and had photocopied numerous documents, all for the purpose of spying on the activities of the Democrats in preparation for the upcoming convention and campaign. This last entry was made to correct a malfunction in the listening devices. Further, they had also made an aborted attempt to break into the campaign offices of George McGovern, the leading candidate and eventual Democratic presidential nominee.

Perhaps most devasting of all, Americans did not know that this group had been in operation for some time while Liddy and Hunt were on the White House staff. They were known as the Plumbers, to find the source of leaks of in-house information, which had infuriated the president. Their most audacious caper was the burglary of the office of the psychiatrist of Daniel Ellsburg in an attempt to discredit Ellsburg's credibility. Ellsburg, it will be recalled, was the former Pentagon analyst who provided the New York Times with the secret government history detailing the growth of American involvement in Vietnam that came to be known as the Pentagon Papers.

Mitchell's disclaimer was the first step in a gigantic cover-up. When it eventually came to light that Nixon had recorded all of his conversations in the oval office, and the Supreme Court directed that the tapes be turned over to the Special Prosecutor, the tapes revealed that on June 20, 1972, Mitchell and Nixon had a phone chat about the break-in. On that same day Haldeman and Nixon discussed the matter in a 45 minute conversation, of which 18 minutes was somehow deleted. Immediately thereafter John Dean, the White House counsel, was assigned to ensure that no taint of the scandal would touch any member of the White House. The gradual unraveling of this blatant cover-up would ultimately lead to the resignation of Richard Nixon on August 9, 1974, and to the ultimate imprisonment of all of the aforementioned characters, plus several others. In all, 40 people would be indicted in the scandal.

G. Gordon Liddy was a familiar name to me. I had met him several times during my days at Justice. A former FBI agent and DA in Poughkeepsie, NY, and an unsuccessful Republican candidate for Congress, he had come to the attention of John Mitchell, who arranged a job for him with the Treasury Department in Washington. His title was Special Assistant to the Secretary for law enforcement (organized crime). In that capacity he had come to Buffalo to visit the strike force on one occasion, and I found him to be likeable and enthusiastic. But he considered himself an action guy, disdainful of what he considered bureaucratic caution, and suggested we adopt methods against the mob which were, let us say, of questionable constitutionality.

Later as a supervisor in Washington I attended several multi-agency committee meetings at which Liddy was present. There too he displayed a zeal for combating organized crime, coupled with a note-worthy lack of good judgment. His proposals caused eyes to roll. Liddy was charming and witty, so that one could never be sure whether he was a serious fanatic or just playing at cops-and-robbers. He was the quin-tessential likeable rogue.

Eventually he was requested by his superiors to look for employ-ment elsewhere. He came to Bill Lynch looking for a job with one of the strike forces. We made some inquiries and confirmed that in law enforcement circles he was considered a cowboy. We already had a cou-ple of loose canons in the field, and we didn't need another, so we politely sent him on his way.

It was then that, through the good offices of John Mitchell, he was sent over to the White House, and the rest, as they say, is history.

United States Attorney Harold Titus assigned the Watergate burglary case to three of his top prosecutors, Earl Silbert, Seymour Glanzer, and Don Campell. I knew both Silbert and Glanzer from my days at Justice, and Don Campbell had been one of our original lawyers on the Buffalo strike force. They began a grand jury investigation and called numerous witnesses, including John Mitchell, over the course of the summer. They made some progress in tracing the hundred-dollar bills to various sources dunned by the CREEP fund raisers, but made little progress in getting to any higher-ups above Liddy and Hunt. Everybody was stonewalling. They found it curious that no one among the defendants was willing to talk. Ordinarily in a multi-defendant case at least one of the culprits, on the good advice of his attorney, is willing to cooperate in exchange for a promise of leniency. Silbert had no way of knowing that some of these defendants and their families were receiving financial support, and their lawyers' fees were being paid, in return for keeping their mouths shut.

Moreover, there was nothing in the prosecutors' careers to prepare them for the reality that a former Attorney General of the United States would come before a grand jury and commit perjury, much less that he would have authorized the commission of felony burglary. But perjure himself is exactly what John Mitchell did.

And so the prosecutors were left with the only other alternative, namely, that after conviction the defendants might be willing to or could be coerced into spilling their guts.

Thus on September 7, 1972, the Watergate grand jury indicted Liddy, Hunt, McCord, Barker, and the three Cubans. At their arraignment before Chief Judge John Sirica, all pleaded not guilty. Liddy was represented by his best friend, Peter Maroulis of Poughkeepsie. Because Maroulis was not a member of the D.C. Bar, the judge ordered Liddy to also retain a local attorney to represent him.

On the following Monday I received a call from Bill Bittman, my friend from Justice days who had convicted Jimmy Hoffa in Chicago. Bittman was representing Hunt and had recommended me to Maroulis as local counsel for Liddy. Would I be willing to take the job?

Though I disagreed with Liddy's politics, I had no antipathy toward him personally, and as a lawyer I was eager to do whatever I could to help him. Mainly, I was thrilled to become part of the biggest show in town.

The next day I debriefed Liddy. He revealed Mitchell's involvement. He did not tell me Nixon was involved (I don't think he knew himself) but he told me about others in high places in the White House. That evening I came home stunned and sickened. I was bound by the attorney-client privilege not to reveal what I had been told, but Susy could see that I was concerned. I was able to convey to her that this thing was bigger than anybody realized, and that it was not going to go away soon.

Then came the matter of how best to defend Liddy. Since Maroulis was unfamiliar with federal practice, I filed the usual flurry of pre-trial motions which all defense counsel must do in order to protect the record on appeal and to demonstrate that they are putting forth their best efforts on behalf of their clients. (Incarcerated convicts have a remarkable tendency to file motions for a new trial on the grounds of "incompetent counsel".) They were all denied, as expected.

Pre-trial conferences among the lawyers and clients, which sometimes can be exciting and contentious and occasionally even productive, were in this case singularly unproductive. Bittman, representing Hunt, was a superb lawyer, and therefore realized the hopelessness of the case. McCord was represented by Gerald Alch from Boston, a partner of F. Lee Bailey. Alch was also experienced and realistic. Maroulis was unfamiliar with the ways of Washington but knew that Liddy was a loyal soldier and would never talk or plead guilty, and had hired Maroulis solely to walk him through the trial. Barker and the Cubans were represented by Henry Rothblatt of New York, who had gained a reputation as the author of several books on criminal trial practice, but who in fact turned out to be a blundering loudmouth.

All of us realized that our clients were caught red-handed and none would testify. And all planned to go to trial.

Various theories of defense were advanced and abandoned. Obviously the Adolph Eichman defense of "just following orders" was not available; first, because it's not a valid defense, and second, because you can't make the argument if you're not willing to say who gave the orders. Alch and Rothblatt decided they would argue that McCord, Barker, and the Cubans were good fellows and had no criminal intent.

As to the clients themselves, I had come to know Liddy well enough to know that he was reveling in his role as the stand-up guy willing to fall on his sword for The Cause. He was of German descent, and clearly had a great admiration for Germanic self discipline and iron will. By his own admission, he had fortified his will power by training himself to hold his left arm over a lighted candle until the flame seared his flesh. I would not call him a Nazi sympathizer, but at one point I jokingly said to him, "You know, Gordon, you were born thirty years too late and in the wrong country. You would have been a great storm trooper." Liddy loved it.

Hunt, a retired CIA spy, was also resigned to the fate of a spy who gets caught. McCord, a former CIA electronics expert, and a sullen loner, seemed to have the idea that somehow those who got him into this mess would put the fix in and get him out of it. The Cubans, hired by Barker who was also from the CIA, had apparently been given the impression that the break-in was a lawful CIA operation aimed at restoring freedom to Cuba. They may have actually believed it, but no jury would find it credible.

A few weeks before the trial, Susan's mother came from Omaha for a visit. Saintly woman that she was, she expressed concern that her son-in-law would be defending such a reprehensible man as Mr. Liddy. While she was visiting, Liddy came to the house one day to pick up some legal papers. I introduced them to each other, and then left the room to go to my desk. In my absence, Gordon proceeded to charm all the hostility out of Mother Powers. He had attended Catholic schools. He had pictures of his five lovely children. He even knew people she knew in Omaha, and Irish at that.

After he left, Mother Powers exclaimed, "Isn't it a shame that such a nice man is in all that trouble!"

In November Richard Nixon was reelected in a landslide over George McGovern, taking every state except Massachusetts and the District of Columbia.

The trial began on January 8, 1973, the honorable John J. Sirica, Chief Judge, presiding. It was held in the ceremonial courtroom to accommodate the huge crowd of press, media, and spectators. Time Magazine carried a picture of Liddy and me entering the courthouse (Time, 1/22/73, p.19).

When, as is customary, the defendants were introduced, Liddy stood, smiled broadly, and gave a stiff-armed wave to all the crowd, which looked ominously like a fascist salute. Not a good beginning. Judge Sirica, looking grim and determined, moved things right along. Howard Hunt, who had been staggered by his wife's death in a plane crash three weeks earlier, decided that he had no stomach for a trial and no chance of acquittal. He entered a plea of guilty to all counts and was discharged from the trial.

When it came time for Henry Rothblatt, representing the Cuban-Americans, to give his opening statement, he conceded right off that his clients were caught in the act. His defense was lack of motive, he said. Lawyers call it the "my-client-is-a-good-guy-so-leave-him-go" argument.

Referring to one of his clients, he said, "The evidence will show that Sturgis is of impeccable character and of highest patriotic background. During World War Two he volunteered and joined the <u>Marines</u>, and after serving through World War Two in the Marines and was honorably discharged, he immediately went into the <u>United States Navy</u>! [voice rising] Served honorably in the United States Navy and then went into the <u>United States Army</u>!!" [voice at fever pitch].

At this point Judge Sirica interrupted and said, "Now Mr. Rothblatt, let's just get down to the business of why he went into the Watergate."

The next day all of Rothblatt's clients engaged a new attorney and pleaded guilty to all counts.

That left only Liddy and McCord. The trial dragged on for three weeks. Fortunately I was not required to be there every day, as Maroulis was handling everything. There was not much for him to do actually. At the end, on January 30, the jury took all of about 45 minutes to return verdicts of guilty on all counts.

Sentencing of all defendants took place on March 23, 1973. The courtroom was packed. Judge Sirica first read aloud a letter he had received from McCord, which in substance stated that McCord would be willing to talk in exchange for leniency. This sent the reporters in the courtroom racing for the phones. Sirica postponed sentencing for McCord.

Judge Sirica then imposed on Liddy a sentence of twenty years. This was exceedingly harsh for a first offense breaking and entering charge, even from "Maximum John." In his book, Sirica says he had "given up on Liddy." As to the other five, he imposed maximum sentences but made them provisional and subject to later reduction, depending on their cooperation with the prosecutors and with the Senate Select Committee on Watergate, which had been convened under Senator Sam Ervin. Liddy was immediately remanded to Danbury Federal Prison in Connecticut.

It is not my intent here to recount the rest of the Watergate saga, which has been referred to variously as "the case of the century," "a central chapter in the story of 20th-century America," and "the most important scandal in our history." For those too young to remember, I recommend two books among the dozens that have been written. The first is *All the President's Men*, by Carl Bernstein and Bob Woodward, the two young Washington Post reporters who dogged the story from the beginning and who claim to have received insider information from the unidentified informant known as "Deep Throat." [Simon &Schuster, New York. 1974]. The other, which is much more entertaining, is by my old friend from Justice days, George V. Higgins. Its title is *The Friends of Richard Nixon*, written in his inimitable and witty crime-thriller style [Little, Brown and Company, Boston. 1974].

As for Liddy, he was next brought before Siblbert's grand jury, granted immunity from further prosecution and ordered to testify under penalty of contempt of court. I pleaded with him to help himself, pointing out that the others had done so and the whole case was beginning to unravel. It would proceed to its ultimate conclusion with or without his help. He had demonstrated his loyalty to the president. Now it was time to think not only of himself but also of his wife, who from this point on became the sole support of their five young children. (All assistance from CRP had long since ended).

Needless to say, following his own peculiar code of *omerta*, he refused, and was promptly sentenced to an additional 18 months for contempt of court, to be served prior to the longer term.

Seeing that I could be of no further service to him, I then filed a petition with the court asking to be relieved as his local counsel on the grounds that he had persistently refused to follow my advice. One of my motives was also to be free of the daily harassment I was getting from the press and media. There were a lot of young reporters who were building their careers in the Watergate case—people like Sam Donaldson, Connie Chung, Leslie Stahl, and many others. Like good reporters, they were aggressive and persistent. Would Liddy talk? When would he talk? What would he say? Who would he name? They would call at all hours of the day and night, workdays and weekends at my home. I tried to be polite and courteous, but there was nothing I could give them, and it was becoming increasingly annoying both to me and to Susan. I think the final straw was a call in the middle of the night from Seymour Hirsch of the New York Times, who then hectored me for not giving him coherent answers.

It happened to be a slow news day when I filed my petition, and it made the front page in the Washington papers and others around the country, including a banner headline in the Los Angeles *Herald-Examiner*. They carried my statement about Liddy: "He's a man of singular fortitude—with the emphasis on singular. He's going up the river, but he's not taking any captains or lieutenants with him."

No lawyer is ever disappointed to see his name in the paper. It's good for business. Sure enough, the very next day a lady walked into my office saying she had a problem. She had not filed any tax returns in ten years and she needed a lawyer. I agreed. It turned out that her problem was not serious. She would have been entitled to a refund in seven of those years, so we were able to work things out with the IRS to her ultimate benefit. But as she left the office after that first meeting I couldn't resist asking, "How did you happen to select me as your attorney?"

"Oh," she said, "I just opened the yellow pages, closed my eyes and put my finger down and it landed right on you." Never underestimate the power of advertising.

Liddy also refused to testify before the Senate and House committees investigating Watergate, and refused to be interviewed by the Watergate Special Prosecutor. He served hard time. He was unpopular with prison authorities but extremely popular with other inmates, because he assisted them in their legal petitions and also filed petitions on behalf of inmates when he saw their rights being violated.

At one point he discovered that the Bureau of Prisons had appropriated $100,000 to be spent on the law library at Allenwood federal prison, where he was incarcerated. But the warden had refused to spend the money. Liddy brough a class action suit against the warden on behalf of his fellow inmates. He won the suit. The warden then spent the money on *furniture* for the library.

As a result of his advocacy, Liddy was moved from one prison to another, spending time in nine different places of incarceration, until he finally received executive clemency from President Jimmy Carter and was released on September 7, 1977, having served four and a half years.

*   *   *   *

After his release he returned to his home in suburban Maryland and gave his first interview to our son Patrick, who was doing an eighth-grade paper on prison reform.

*   *   *   *

I did some *pro bono* legal work for Liddy after his release. It seems that during his incarceration, to pass the time, he had developed pen pal relationships with a number of lonely women. To him it was a lark, but to them it was serious and they were now demanding his personal attention. To fend them off, I composed a number of letters of discouragement, using every ruse I could think of, short of suggesting that he had contracted rabies in prison. He was grateful.

Sometime thereafter he began his lecture tour of college campuses, which proved extremely popular, and he was able to command $4000 for each appearance. He spewed his right-wing claptrap, but emphasized to young people the importance of personal strength. Though I had no use for his message I did not begrudge him the income. He had earned it.

A couple of years later, at one of his lectures, a man approached him and said, "I think we have a friend in common." It was Paddy Calabrese, our first relocated witness from Buffalo, who had attended the lecture. Shortly thereafter I received a framed picture of the two of them, inscribed, "To Tom, from your pals Gordon and Paddy."

Watergate provided lots of business for a multitude of lawyers. Between the Watergate Special Prosecutor and various Congressional committees, it seemed as though every aspect of government and politics was under investigation, and Washington was under a blizzard of subpoenas. To the average citizen, there are few things more frightening than the receipt of a government subpoena, and the first reaction is to send for a lawyer, preferably one experienced in such matters.

The Washington Evening Star and Daily News ran a story on May 8, 1973 entitled "'Hoffa Squad' Is Back." It opened, "The Watergate scandal is rapidly taking on the appearance of a 'class reunion' for the Justice Department attorneys who banded together more than a decade ago to investigate and prosecute James R. Hoffa, then president of the Teamsters Union." It went on to point out that Walter Sheridan had been hired by George McGovern to check on Watergate developments; that Thomas Kennelly was local counsel for Gordon Liddy; that Bill Bittman was representing Howard Hunt; that Charlie Shaffer, who with Jim Neal had prosecuted Hoffa in Chattanooga, was the lawyer for John Dean; and that Bill Hundley, former head of the Organized Crime Section, was counsel for John Mitchell. Later Jim Neal came out of private practice to become the chief prosecutor in the trial of Haldeman, Erlichman, Mitchell, *et al.*

The Wall Street Journal headlined a front page story on November 12, 1973: "It's an Ill Wind, etc.: Watergate is a Boon For a Lot of Lawyers;" and the sub-headline was "Ironically, Those Representing GOP Defendants Tend to Be Kennedy-Trained Democrats." The story went on to state: "Among those profiting the most from the Republican fiasco are Democratic barristers trained as prosecutors by Robert F. Kennedy's Justice Department a decade ago. They are now in private practice defending the accused. It then named nine lawyers, all Democrats, including myself, who had come out of the Kennedy Justice Department and were now representing Watergate figures. In addition, Archibald Cox, the Watergate Special Prosecutor, had been Kennedy's Solicitor General, and four lawyers on the Special Prosecutor's staff had also worked for Kennedy.

Why was this so? A Republican lawyer is quoted as saying, "Republican lawyers don't come to Washington to work for the Justice Department and then stay here. Republicans go back home." One Democrat recalled that when Bob Kennedy became Attorney General he launched a campaign to bring "the cream of young, talented, professional prosecutors" into the Justice Department. The story's reporter speculated that criminal law attracts relatively few law school graduates, and they tend to be Democrats. Bill Hundley put it more succinctly: "All those white-shoe Republicans go into corporate law."

Whatever the reasons, it was true that nearly all of my white-collar clients throughout my career, in civil cases as well as criminal, were Republicans, and conservative ones at that. I should add that I liked them all, and several became lasting friends.

Susan and I were on vacation in Ireland on the night that Nixon announced his resignation. The next day I struck up a conversation with the ticket taker on a Dublin bus. "You know why they forced Nixon out, don't you?" he said.

"Tell me," I replied.

"Because he's Catholic," said my informant.

Gordon Liddy finally wrote his autobiography, entitled *Will*, in which he told all. [St. Martin's Press, New York. 1980.] He sent me a copy, inscribed "For Tom Kennelly, who has been for years my counselor, my colleague and, most important of all, my good friend. Gordon Liddy."

Thanks, Gordon. You are indeed an unforgettable character.

21.

WASHINGTON LIFESTYLE

By the nineteen seventies Susan and I had acquired a large circle of friends and acquaintances developed from our various contacts in the community: friends from Marine Corps days; former colleagues from Justice and other lawyers with whom I associated in private practice; journalists, including investigative reporters whom I had come to admire and respect, like Bob Jackson and Ron Ostrow of the Los Angeles Times and Nick Horrock of Newsweek; and drama critics and other media people whom Susan had met in connection with her public relations work and journalism; alumni from St. Thomas, including former classmates who had been friends for years and also recent alumni I met as head of the St. Thomas alumni chapter in Washington; Catholic University alumni both from Susan's student days and her long service on the university's alumni board of directors; actors and musicians from her days at Arena Stage and the American Light Opera Company; friends from our two parishes (Holy Trinity and our new parish, Our Lady of Victory); parents of our kids' schoolmates, and neighbors.

As the nation's capital, Washington attracts interesting and stimulating people, many of whom are engaged in one way or another in the making and reporting of the national and international news that appears everyday in the media. More than in any other American city, in Washington the local news *is* the national and international news. Washingtonians, like New Yorkers, are also great theater-goers and sports fans. Thus it is that when friends gather together in Washington, government and politics, as well as theater and sports, are the main topics of conversation.

Our friends typically included legal or administrative assistants to Congresspersons or Senators or Cabinet officers; general counsels of government agencies or private corporations, officials of foreign governments, and reporters and columnists. As such, they all, and their spouses, had something new and exciting—and preferably provocative—to contribute to the sparkle of conversation that characterized the Washington dinner and cocktail party.

Our neighborhood, just west of Georgetown, was a microcosm of the Washington scene. Next door was Mamadou Toure, an official of the World Bank, from Mali. On the other side of us were Phil and Madeline Locavara and their family. Phil, at age 29 and with seven children, had come to Washington to serve as Deputy Solicitor General at Justice. Later he became Deputy Watergate Special Prosecutor under Leon Jaworski and made the argument that persuaded the Supreme Court to order disclosure of the Nixon tapes, leading to Nixon's resignation. Up the street was Jim Belson, a judge on the Court of Appeals for the District of Columbia. Another neighbor was Dr. Mike Maginnis, deputy secretary of the Department of Health, Education, and Welfare. Around the corner was Andy Tully, a syndicated columnist in over two hundred newspapers and author of some seventeen books. Andy once wrote a column about one of our parties, at which he met Jill Wine Volner, the bright and attractive young prosecutor who had just completed her famous cross-examination of Rosemary Woods, private secretary to President Nixon. Andy's charming wife Molly worked for a congressman. Andy, a crusty but delightful Irishman, found it difficult to write his columns with a small boy around the house, and so their son John spent a great deal of his time at our house, and we were always pleased to call him our "adopted son."

Also nearby were the Belgian and German embassies, and we became acquainted with many of their staff members through the parish or our children's schoolmates.

The preferred method of entertaining was in the home, as Washington nightlife in those days was non-existent, with strict liquor laws (no drink could be consumed while standing up) and midnight closing hours, even on Saturday. Dinner parties of six or eight were the most common and always the best, and I am still of that opinion, because everybody can get involved in the animated conversation. But large Saturday night parties were common too. We were all in our thirties and forties and young and vigorous, and though most of us had small children, we looked forward to comparing all of the week's political gossip, and to contributing our own inside word. These parties often lasted well past midnight. I remember one memorable occasion when the Walter Sheridans were the last to leave our house at about 4 AM. Two hours later the first of our kids awoke, and probably one of their six as well. On Sunday afternoon Nancy Sheridan called and said, "I've just re-read your invitation, which says REGRETS ONLY. I'm calling to send mine."

Before we were married Susan had initiated the custom of having a Tree Trimming party just before Christmas every year, in which each guest was invited to bring an ornament and to help decorate the tree while enjoying the conviviality and spirit(s) of the season. We continued that custom every year for all the time we lived in Washington, and still have some of the ornaments from her first year. After moving to California in 1994 we decided that we were a bit overloaded with ornaments and instead we now have an annual St. Patrick's Day party. Nevertheless, as we trim our own tree each Christmas, each ornament reminds us of good friends and great parties over the years.

Washington also afforded many opportunities to hear and meet officials, dignitaries, and other notables from all over the world. Susy was a member of both the National Press Club and the American News Women's Club, which regularly held receptions and luncheons to meet and hear from the people who were making news at the time. On one occasion we attended a small breakfast gathering with John Denver, who had no greater fan than my mother. He graciously signed and subscribed a life-size poster of himself "to Olive Kennelly," which remained on her bedroom wall, I believe, until the day she died.

Susan's freelance public relations work brought her in contact with a great variety of clients, all seeking to get their activities publicized in the press and media, and she was very good at it. There was the nation-wide Ukrainian community, celebrating its centennial in the U.S., which included a White House Conference. She also did the publicity for a French musical making its world premier in Washington. Another client was TransAfrica, a lobbying group for issues involving Africa and the Caribbean. One time there was a conference held by the Bah'ai Religion in D.C., a pleasant group of folks with headquarters in Iran, who preach peace and have been around since the 19th century. (Susan to me: "How can I get publicity for such a nice quiet group of people? If only they'd run around nude or practice self immolation or something....")

In 1979, during the momentous visit to Washington of the newly elected pope, John Paul II, Susan worked as a volunteer handling press relations for the hundreds of media reps attending the event from all over the world. This got our family front row seats for the Holy Father's outdoor Mass celebrated on the National Mall before at least 500,000 faithful.

Susan's most interesting clients, as far as the rest of the family was concerned, were the entertainers who appeared under the auspices of Stanley-Williams Presentations, drawing capacity crowds to Lisner Auditorium on the campus of George Washington University or to Constitution Hall or the Kennedy Center. The performers, most of whom were delightful to know, included the Clancy Brothers and Tommy Makem, the Chieftans, Joan Baez, Judy Collins, Tom Paxton, Pete Seeger, Arlo Guthrie, Jacques Brel, Gilbert Becaud, Simon & Garfunkel, Tammy Wynette, Eddie Arnold, and Flatt & Scruggs & the Foggy Mountain Boys.

One evening Pete Seeger came to dinner at our home, along with several members of the Washington Folklore Society. After dinner Pete and his friends got out their guitars and banjos and played and sang long into the night. They played all the old favorites for which Pete had become known—some of which he had written—and a few that are never performed on a public stage. We got the kids out of bed to enjoy this very special occasion in our lives. Later Patrick said, "I love you, Mommy. You've got the neatest friends."

We also enjoyed going to sporting events together, to see the Redskins, the Senators (before they were sold and became the Texas Rangers), the Baltimore Orioles, and the Bullets (now the Wizards).

On one memorable occasion I took all three kids to see the Baltimore Orioles play the Boston Red Sox. During the course of the game I went to the refreshment stand to pick up three cokes and a beer. Climbing the steps back to our seats, and carrying the tray of drinks, I suddenly felt something whiz by my ear. A split second later the drinks went flying. A foul ball had landed smack in the center of my tray and was now lying at my feet. Suddenly there was a scrum for the ball, which immediately disappeared. All I got out of it was four spilled drinks, a crowd laughing uproariously—including my kids—and not even a game ball. Rodney Dangerfield, I know how you feel.

It was also at this stage in our lives that we began getting into volunteer activities. I served for a year as president of the Home & School Association at the kids' school (what parent hasn't?), while Susy applied her skills to numerous fund-raisers, both at their elementary school and at Gonzaga High School (for Patrick and Tim) and at Georgetown Visitation Preparatory School (for Katy).

In our parish there was a wonderful lady named Margaret Teachout, who organized a Day of Recollection for the Blind. Each year she and her fellow volunteers, including myself, arranged a special Mass at Our Lady of Victory for a couple of dozen blind and low income (mostly African American) residents of all faiths in the community. The church service was then followed by a sumptuous meal in a fancy Georgetown restaurant. For many of those folks it was the highlight of the year. Through this program I met a number of unforgettable people, the most memorable being Caleb J. "Dusty Roads" Rowe. Dusty was a former jazz musician from Chicago, who now lived alone in an apartment in one of the poorest sections of Washington, subsisting on a meager social security stipend and contributions from his friends. Although blind and elderly, Dusty was unfailingly exuberant and optimistic and was deeply religious. He was an inspiration to our entire family and we always enjoyed getting together with him two or three times a year until his death in the early 1990's.

Knowing the devastating effects of Cystic Fibrosis on Pat and Frank's family, I was happy to serve for several years on the local board of the Cystic Fibrosis Foundation, and was able to secure some research grants for the foundation, used by doctors at Georgetown University Hospital in the fight against that terrible disease. I also served on the citizens advisory board of D.C. Village, a public assisted living facility for low income and elderly residents of the District.

On Prejudice

My description above of the "Washington scene" is somewhat misleading. I was referring to that portion of Washington which lies west of Rock Creek Park, where nearly all of the whites and most of the affluent African Americans reside. Washington's population is 75% African-American, and nearly all of them live east of the Park, subsisting in substandard and overcrowded housing, with the attendant high crime rate and drug problems found in all inner cities.

While most residents of the District are accustomed to this situation (perhaps too inured to it), it can come as a jolt to folks coming from small towns in mid-America. On one occasion Susy's cousins, the Kenney family, with children about the same age as ours, came to visit us from Plainview, Nebraska. They are wonderful, open people, but Nebraska does not have many African Americans, and they had certainly never been to a city which is 75% non-white. Their comments reflected their astonishment, so much so that after they departed, Susy and I felt compelled to discuss with our children, who were then about 13, 12, and 10, the issue of race and prejudice.

I asked, "Do any of you feel that you are superior to anybody else because the color of their skin is different, or they belong to a religion that is different from yours?"

They all shook their heads, and Katy spoke up first. "My friend Camille lives next door to some Jewish people. I've met them and they're really nice."

"Yes." added Tim, "and my friend David is a Methodist, and that doesn't make him any different from me."

What neither Katy nor Tim mentioned is that both Camille and David are Aftrican Americans. We stopped worrying.

22.

A HELPING HAND FROM THE MOB?

W e'll call him Sal Torricella. Sal was from Detroit, where he had been in the insurance business for many years. He had also been a loyal contributor to and a worker for the Republican party in Detroit, a city which had a chronic shortage of Republicans. And so after Nixon's victory in 1972, Sal was rewarded with a rather high-ranking job with the Small Business Administration in Washington, in charge of the Office of Bond Guarantees. The SBA would assist eligible small businesses, particularly those in the construction business, by guaranteeing performance bonds, thus allowing the bidder to obtain the bond at a lower cost.

When Torricella came to me in early 1975 he was in trouble. The Detroit Strike Force had placed an electronic surveillance bug in the office of Nick Licavoli, head of the Detroit mob. The FBI overheard a conversation in which Licavoli told one of his underlings that he had to help his *paisan* Sal Torricella. He said Toricella had been promised a bribe of $20,000 to guarantee a bond for some contractors in Cleveland but they hadn't paid up. Licavoli said he would contact [the Mafia boss] in Cleveland and ask him to lean on these guys. A week or so later the FBI heard Licavoli comment that the matter involving Sal had been taken care of.

Torricella vehemently denied the accusation. He readily admitted to me that he and Licavoli had grown up together in the same neighborhood in Detroit. They still met socially on rare occasions, but he denied that he had ever asked Licavoli for help on anything, and he denied ever asking for or receiving a bribe from anyone.

I was granted a hearing with my old friends in the Organized Crime Section, Bill Lynch and Ed Joyce, along with John Newcomer, head of the Detroit Strike Force. They said there was enough in the overheard conversations for them to identify two owners of a small business in Cleveland who had indeed received a bond guarantee in connection with the grading of a proposed shopping mall, and had defaulted on the bond. The implication was that had it not been for the bribe, the guarantee would not have been granted.

There was very little I could offer on behalf of my client at that time, and in due course, he and the contractors were indicted in Detroit for bribery and conspiracy.

More than two years elapsed before the case came to trial, mainly because of the procrastination of the presiding judge, the honorable Damon Keith, who denied my motion to dismiss for lack of a speedy trial. I have faced many outstanding judges in my career, and some less so, but I can truthfully say that Judge Keith was the only judge I ever encountered who was both stupid *and* lazy. He seemed not only unqualified but disinterested in his work. At one point during the trial he left the bench to take a phone call in his chambers, instructing counsel to "carry on"; and so for about twenty minutes we continued the trial with no presiding judge.

Moreover, he was thoughtless. Notwithstanding that Torricella and I were from Washington, and the two other defendants and their lawyers had to travel from Cleveland, he held court only from 9:30 to 1:00, Tuesdays through Fridays. One week we met only for two days and the following week not at all. As a result I spent most of the summer of 1977 commuting to and from Detroit. It was costly for the defendants and inconvenient for the jury, but the judge was unmoved.

The government's case was mostly circumstantial—except for the tapes. The head of the SBA's regional office in Chicago testified that

Torricella had personally come to his office to push for approval of the bond guarantee in question. We countered that by showing that it was Torricella's custom to do this in many instances. He was a "hands-on" director who traveled to many local SBA offices to try to change the mindset of local SBA bureaucrats who too often were like bankers who will only grant you a loan if you can prove that you don't need it.

Concerning payment of the $20,000, the government was able to show via bank records that between the two taped Licavoli conversations, the contractors issued several checks to cash in one day totaling $20,000, but they could not trace the money thereafter. (The contractors did not testify).

It was clear that the Licavoli tapes were crucial to the government's case. If the jury was permitted to hear them, a conviction was almost a certainty.

The observant reader will note that the tapes were hearsay; that is, they were statements made by a third person outside the courtroom and not subject to cross-examination. And everybody knows that hearsay is not admissible evidence and therefore the tapes should be excluded. However, there is an exception to the hearsay rule which says that any statement made by any co-conspirator made during the course of the conspiracy is admissible against all other conspirators; and here all the defendants, including Licavoli, were charged as co-conspirators.

But (here comes another rule of evidence) in order for Licavoli's statements to be admissible against Torricella as statements of a co-conspirator, it must first be proved by independent evidence that Torricella was part of a conspiracy which included Licavoli. Aside from the tapes themselves—and they were not independent evidence—there simply was not evidence of any connection whatsoever between the two.

Judge Keith, over my vehement objections, ruled the tapes admissible. And so for a whole day the jury listened to the tapes and read the transcripts. Doom seemed inevitable.

The next morning Judge Keith announced to the jury that he had thought it over during the evening, and concluded that the tapes should not have been admitted. "You never can rely on what a member of the underworld says," he casually observed. "He might have all kinds of motivations. Therefore I'm instructing you to disregard what you have heard on the tapes." Finally, he had made the right ruling, if for the wrong reason—and too late, I thought. How can you expect human beings to forget what they have listened to for a whole day? I felt vindicated but incensed at the same time.

Following my usual instincts, I did not put Torricella on the stand, a risky move but I thought the right one. I did, however, through his accountant, lay out his entire financial status, which showed that he lived within his means, with no unusual debts or obligations, nor any unusual expenditures, as one might expect from someone who came into a $20,000 windfall.

In the end, the jury came in with verdicts of not guilty as to all defendants. They had done their duty and disregarded the tapes. It was one of the most difficult cases in my career as a defense attorney, and probably the most thrilling verdict. Though I am unsure whether or not my client "did it," I am certain that justice was done. The government had not proved the guilt of the defendants beyond a reasonable doubt with sufficient admissible evidence, as it is required to do in our Anglo-Saxon system of justice.

But Torricella's ordeal was not yet over. After his indictment, he had been relieved of his position and placed in a meaningless job in the SBA, pending the results. Now, with the acquittal, he was entitled to be restored to his appointed position. But the SBA Administrator initiated proceedings to have him fired, on the ground that dismissal from a government job did not require proof beyond a reasonable doubt. This is exactly what had happened to my client Sergeant Pimentel in the Marine Corps, who had been given an undesirable discharge even though he had been acquitted of charges of homosexual activity. So I had to file an appeal with the Office of Personnel Management (formerly the Civil

Service Commission), and after many months and much additional expense, Torricella was vindicated and restored to his old job.

23.

A NEW LAW FIRM

By the summer of 1975 Dave Blum and I decided, after four years of sharing offices, that our practices were so divergent—he in housing law and I in criminal and civil litigation—that neither of us could provide any benefit to the other. We could not help out with each other's clients, nor could we share ideas, legal theories, or strategies with regard to our clients, something which is important among professionals in any field. So we decided to split up, and I joined the small firm of Diuguid & Siegel, which became Diuguid, Siegel, & Kennelly, located at 1000 Connecticut Avenue, on Farragut Square, not far from the White House. John Diuguid and I had served together in the Organized Crime Section at Justice, and his practice was similar to mine. Tom Siegel, about ten years younger than ourselves, specialized in health care law In 1977 we were joined by Howard Epstein, five years younger than I, who had served in the Civil Division at Justice.

From the moment he joined the firm Howard and I became the best of friends. He was like the brother I never had. Though he was as devoted to Judaism as I to Christianity, we discovered early on that we shared the same values and interests. Howard was always enthusiastic and animated, with a great range of interests, and had a wonderful sense of humor, which I much admired. He was also an excellent lawyer with good insights and instincts, which made him an expert negotiator, a valuable asset for a lawyer. He loved his family, the arts, and sports. He and I shared season tickets for the Georgetown basketball games for many years, and in 1985 we drove all night to Lexington, Kentucky, to see Georgetown play (and lose 63-62 to Villanova) in the NCAA championship game.

Howard and I remained the closest of friends until his untimely death from cancer in 1990 at the age of 54.

Never Go Trap Shooting With Your Wife

When Ed Derwinski came to my office in 1976 he had been serving as a Republican member of Congress from Chicago for twenty years. Stocky and affable and in his early fifties, he came wondering if he could sue someone, not as a member of Congress but as an aggrieved citizen. He had the following complaint. Ed's wife Pat and their 16-year-old son, Robert, were competitive trapshooters. They traveled to trapshooting contests all around the East and won many prizes. Ed had no interest himself in shooting at clay pigeons, but he enjoyed watching his wife and son compete. One Sunday afternoon they were competing at the Bull Run Trapshooting Park in Manassas, Virginia. Trapshooting competition, I learned, consists of five shooters standing in a horizontal line, shotguns in hand, and facing toward the outfield. One by one, each participant has a chance to shoot at a clay pigeon mechanically flung through the air from left to right across the front. Needless to say, the contestant who has, after several rounds, destroyed the greatest number of the little clay saucers, wins the prize.

On the day in question, Pat Derwinski was in position #1, son Robert was in position #3, and other contestants were placed in #2, #4, and #5. Ed was seated in the bleachers, about 25 yards behind the line. Pat fired first, then reloaded, locked, and cradled her weapon, as required by the rules. Contestant #2 then did the same. But when Robert fired, his shotgun suddenly exploded in his hands, and he fell back. Pat, seeing this, turned, screamed, dropped her gun, and ran to Robert's side. When she dropped the gun it was pointed backward. When it hit the ground it fired, discharging about 200 small pellets directly at—guess who?—her husband. No one else was injured. Derwinski was struck on his right side, from his shoulder to below his knee. Luckily, the pellets missed an artery. He was not gravely wounded, except for the pellets which were too numerous to be surgically removed, the partial loss of one finger, and damage to his right hand which prevented him from making a tight grip. However, the latter was a significant problem for a politician about to embark on a hand-shaking re-election campaign.

The son, miraculously, was uninjured. Howard and I had tests run on the son's shotgun which showed that the cartridges he was using were overloaded with powder, causing a high risk of exploding when fired. It also turned out that mother and son had fashioned the cartridges themselves, with a machine they had recently purchased. We could not determine at that point whether the machine had a design defect, or whether mother and son had operated it improperly.

Potentially Ed could sue his wife and/or son for negligence, either in their fashioning the cartridges which initiated the series of events, or in her dropping the weapon, and actually their family liability policy would probably have covered the damages. However, it did not seem terribly discreet for a politician seeking reelection to be suing his wife and son.

Next we turned to her shotgun. Laboratory tests showed that even when locked, if dropped from a height of 24 inches or more, and if it landed upside down, as it did in this case, it would discharge every single time. This was clearly a design defect. I found a design engineer who was able to create a mock-up showing exactly where the flaw occurred and how it caused the weapon to fire when dropped.

Manufactured products carry by law an implied warranty of "fitness for use," which is stringently applied in the case of dangerous weapons. They must be designed so as not to accidentally discharge under foreseeable circumstances. And the courts have held that dropping a weapon is a foreseeable circumstance. Simply put, a weapon that fires when dropped, even if locked, is a defective weapon. Further, this warranty of fitness for use is imposed not only on the original manufacturer but on every subsequent dealer.

Pat Derwinski's shotgun was an expensive Perazzi, manufactured in Italy, for which she had paid $4000 from a used gun dealer at a gun show in northern Virginia. We traced its provenance, and found that the Virginia dealer had purchased it from a dealer in North Carolina, who had purchased it from another dealer in Rhode Island, who had imported it from the Perazzi company in Italy.

We sued them all. Initially Perazzi denied liability, but after the usual round of pretrial discovery, along with protracted negotiations, on the day of trial we finally, with Howard's great skills as a negotiator, reached a settlement for a handsome sum, to which all of the defendants (or their insurance companies) contributed. The Congressman was satisfied, and eventually he regained the full use of his hand. However, I imagine those pellets are still coming to the surface from time to time.

Late in 1977 Ed Derwinski came back to me. This time he was in trouble as a Congressman. Strongly anti-Communist, he was a staunch advocate of military and economic aid to South Korea to repel any attack from Communist North Korea. He had strong ties to South Korea, having visited there several times and having received a medal from the South Korean government and an honorary degree from one of its universities.

Derwinski was the ranking minority member on the House Subcommittee on International Organizations, which was investigating activities of the Korean Central Intelligence Agency (KCIA) against South Koreans in the U.S. who opposed South Korea's president. At one point a KCIA agent secretly offered to cooperate with the committee in return for asylum. The next day agents of the Korean government arrived at the defector's home with intent to seize him and return him to Korea, but thirty minutes earlier the FBI had taken the defector and his family for safekeeping. U.S. intelligence agencies then informed the subcommittee that someone had leaked to the Korean government news of the planned defection. The spotlight fell on Derwinski, and the Department of Justice convened a grand jury to investigate the disclosure of classified information. The story made the front page of all the papers.

The federal authorities learned about the leak through secret sources that they would be reluctant to disclose, namely, electronic surveillance of the Korean Embassy by the National Security Agency. They were hoping Derwinsky would admit his involvement and they would not have to disclose the source. So I advised the congressman to assert his 5th Amendment right against self-incrimination in the grand jury. It was a risky move because although grand jury proceedings are secret, leaks sometimes occur, and it would not bode well for a politician if the folks back home knew he had taken the 5th. But I saw no alternative, and with some reluctance, that is what he did. There were no leaks, and the matter was quietly dropped by the government without further publicity.

Derwinski won reelection, and remained in Congress until in 1981 when President Ronald Reagan appointed him to his cabinet as Secretary of Veterans Affairs.

One of Life's Embarrassing Little Moments

Who among us is ever able to say "I am caught up with the news"? There was one moment in my life when I could.

It was a winter day and I was heading up Connecticut Avenue from my office on my way to lunch. I stopped to purchase a newspaper at a sidewalk rack. Then I closed the rack on the tail of my overcoat. I could not extricate myself. I had no more coins, and the coat was too good to leave behind. I was reduced to begging a quarter from a passerby in order to release the trap. I offered him the paper, but he declined, saying the chuckle was worth the money.

24.

FAMILY ADVENTURES, VENTURES, AND MISADVENTURES

Trial work is a young man's game, and I played it as hard as anybody. But regardless of the long hours and consecutive days of work, usually I was able to arrange my schedule for an active summer vacation. Susy felt that vacations should be an adventure, and I agreed.

One of our first family vacations was two weeks at Montego Bay, Jamaica, when the children were 4, 3, and almost 2. We rented a house with a staff and a pool, and had a wonderful time exploring the island.

We were not much for lying on the beach in the sun. Among other reasons, it is, as the doctors say, "contraindicated" for fair Irish complexions. But we both loved hiking up and down mountains, and still do. It was one of the first things that we discovered we had in common. As I described earlier, she introduced me to Estes Park after the Brighton Bank trial. As soon as the boys were 5 and 4 we initiated them to the exhilarating joys of the scent of pines, sparkling mountain lakes nestled beneath ancient glaciers, the wild and barren tundra above the tree line, and the spectacular vistas from the top of rugged mountain peaks. Katy joined in the fun as soon as she was old enough, and all the children took to the mountains like ducks to water.

In 1976 we lost one of the persons indirectly responsible for our love of the mountains: Susan's dear mother, Sue Morearty Powers. She died of a sudden heart attack in her home on September 7, 1976, the eve of her 82nd birthday. In good health and high spirits, she was preparing to fly to Washington to celebrate her birthday with us. We had last seen her in August en route home from one of our vacation trips to the West. She was a woman of great courage, generosity, and unshakeable faith. It was her firm belief that "death is not extinguishing the light; it is putting out the candle because the DAWN has come." We like to think that her sudden death, without pain or suffering, was God's last great gift to her; but we and the children missed her greatly.

When the children were 8, 7, and 5 we decided it was time for a family camping experience. None of them had expressed any interest in summer youth camps, nor were my memories of "camping" happy ones. They had to do with night exercises in the Marine Corps in the driving rain and mud. Nevertheless, we were determined to expose the kids to the alleged joys of camping. So on the Memorial Day weekend we rented one of those pop-up trailers—the kind that after a two-hour struggle open up into an eight-room canvas mansion—and headed off, along with Christopher Clancy, the Irish setter, to a campground in the Pennsylvania Dutch country.

It was a total disaster. It rained buckets the entire weekend, in 40-degree weather. The campground became a sea of mud. We mostly huddled in the leaking tent, the five of us and Christopher, who occasionally had to be walked, only to return and shake his wet body all over the rest of us.

That first experience was so bad that we said that camping has got to be better than this. So we tried again that summer. While Susy went out to pick up the rental trailer, I placed all our camping gear and provisions in the front yard, ready to be loaded. Before she arrived with the trailer, everything disappeared from the yard. The young boys playing next door said they saw a man and woman load everything into the trunk of their car. Eventually it was returned by the "thieves," an older man and woman, who said they thought it was trash left for pick-up (and presumably realized it wasn't when they got home and unloaded the unopened booze and camera, among other things). So off we went to hike in the mountains of West Virginia and explore the caves and horse country of Kentucky.

After struggling with the pop-up trailers for a couple of years, we rented RV's and began making longer cross-country trips. In 1979 we purchased a 22-foot Shasta motor home and christened it the Irish Rover. For the next four summers we traveled the length and breadth of the United States and Canada, from New England to California, and from Nova Scotia to British Columbia. We planned our routes so as to visit every possible national park, historic site, big city, and ghost town along the way. We camped, hiked, fished, read, visited friends and relatives, and learned as much as we could about our great country and Canada. Before departing, each child was charged with learning as much as possible about the states and provinces assigned to him or her. They took great delight in informing the rest of us, as we approached one of "their" states or provinces, about the history, the capital, the major industries or farm products, the state flower and bird, and the sights to be seen. It gave them something to do in anticipation of our vacation, and was informative for all of us.

Our children still remember these trips as some of the best times of our lives together. Our memories are filled with mountains, waterfalls, grand cities, battlefields, camping under the stars, and catching the succulent Kamloops trout in British Columbia. We remember signs like "Dismal Canoe Trips" (on the Dismal River in Nebraska), "Drummond: Bullshippers Capital of the World" in Montana, and the "Ricochet Pizza Parlor." We will not forget Belgrade, Montana, where late at night we selected as our campsite the parking lot behind the town library, which turned out to be adjacent to the railroad tracks, as we discovered when the "Midnight Special" came roaring through! And to this day, whenever we sing the hymn "I Am the Bread of Life" in church, Susan and I remember the night we all sang that hymn, with Patrick playing the guitar, as we sat around the campfire in the Grand Tetons.

Probably our most exciting vacation experience together was in the summer of 1981; we went white-water rafting through the entire

Grand Canyon for eight days and 275 miles of wilderness adventure. My sister Mary Lu, good scout that she is, joined us. Susan best described it in her Christmas letter that year:

"It was beautiful, scary, awesome and unforgettable, alternating between freezing fierce rapids and blistering desert sun. Perhaps the greatest sensation was that of being totally removed form the ordinary sense of time—we moved with the River, awakened when the sun came over the canyon wall, spread sleeping bags beneath a million stars and saw our world illumined with a full moon.

"With a marvelous conglomeration of fellow adventurers, we found lush tropical waterfalls and fern grottos a mile below the surface of the earth; scaled steep cliffs to hidden Indian ruins, met a Big Horn sheep in one encampment and even got shipwrecked while going backwards down a raging rapid right into the canyon wall. (We spent the next eight hours repairing the raft at aptly-named Furnace Flats, 115 degrees.) Now who else do you know who has been shipwrecked in the middle of a desert?"

Truly the Grand Canyon raft trip was the experience of a lifetime.

We sold the motor home in 1983, because after four years of adventures we had gone just about everywhere it could go; and the kids were now in their middle teens, longer than most families are willing and able to travel together.

But this was not the end of our joint ventures.

Doonesbury

In 1983 we all agreed to invest in the Broadway musical "Doonesbury". It seemed like a sure thing. Gary Trudeau's satirically political comic strip was wildly popular, running in over seven hundred newspapers here and abroad, with a readership of 60 million. Actually we felt fortunate to have the opportunity to invest in the show, through our friendship with John McMeel, owner of United Press Syndicate, which owned the strip. John was also investing in the show. He invited us to the workshop presentation in New York in June 1983 and we loved it. Together we bought a partnership interest for $20,000—a small part indeed of the $2 million cost of the show, but we were excited to be in the ranks of Broadway "angels."

All of us were present on opening night, November 21, 1983, at the Biltmore theater. Patrick came up from Duke University, Tim was already in New York at Columbia, and Katy came with us from Georgetown Visitation. We thought the show was great, and the audience seemed to agree. After the show we attended the opening night party at Gallagher's restaurant, met the cast and other celebrities and investors, and had our picture taken with Gary Trudeau. It was all very exciting.

But the reviews were mixed. The Wall Street Journal and The New Yorker thought it was great; it got so-so reviews from The New York Times, Newsweek, and USA Today; and it was panned by The New York Post and Time Magazine ("too cutesy"…"not enough satirical bite"). It ran for nearly four months and then closed on March 6, 1984. The economics of show business are such that although it was averaging 85% of capacity each performance, it was losing $30,000 a day. We went back for closing night, and shared in the after-curtain libations and lamentations with Trudeau and the cast.

In January in New York we met with the producer, Jim Walsh, a man of great experience and outstanding integrity. He told us that with the investment funds remaining, a road show was being mounted, again with high hopes. It opened in Rochester, then played five nights in Washington in October, where we again enjoyed the road company as much as the original cast. But the show closed in Los Angeles on November 4, 1984, half way through its run, due once again to mixed reviews and insufficient ticket sales. Thus all the investors came up empty, but we five never regretted it for a minute. It was a hell of a lot more fun than many a stock market venture with the same result. And we still have the LP record album of the show.

25.

A MELANGE OF CLIENTS

I have heard many lawyers say they enjoyed the practice of law, except for the clients. I do not agree. I really enjoyed working with most of my clients. I cannot think of a single one that I disliked (though perhaps some have been conveniently forgotten). This may be due in part to my determined avoidance of domestic relations cases. Two of the lawyers in our office handled divorce cases, and it was my frequent observation that in nasty divorces, the only thing the two parties seemed to agree on was that both of their lawyers were no damn good.

As a small firm in general practice, we did a little of everything in addition to criminal and civil litigation: contracts, real estate closings, labor-managements, sometimes on one side and sometimes the other, and an occasional tax return. I wrote a few wills, but never felt confident about it; in fact with each will I said a little prayer that my clients would outlive me so that I would never know the fruits of my labor.

In personal injury cases I always represented plaintiffs, as the insurance companies are represented by larger firms who specialized in insurance defense work. I did not particularly enjoy personal injury practice for several reasons. For one, it is always taken on a contingent fee basis. If successful, the lawyer gets one-third of the award (or 40% if it requires a trial), but if the award is for the defense, the plaintiff's lawyer gets nothing. So it's a crap shoot. If a small firm becomes overweighted in contingent fee cases, it can present a real problem in budgeting office expenses, not to mention putting regular meals on the table. Further, personal injury cases can take an inordinate amount of time to reach resolution, whether by settlement or trial. I have always felt that they could be resolved fairly quickly, once the question of liability becomes clear and the extent of the injuries is known, if both sides would be willing to sit down and discuss the matter reasonably. Eventually this does happen, but not until there is a year or more of dancing around the fire; in legal terms it is called bills of particulars, requests for admissions, interrogatories and answers thereto, and endless depositions. Ralph Nader calls this outpounding each other—both sides piling up pounds of paper work. This is not the fault of the plaintiff's lawyer, who is eager to get the matter resolved and get paid off. The defense lawyers, on the other hand, are paid by the hour by the insurance company, and can demonstrate the excellence and thoroughness of their work by its enormity, which has added advantage of pressuring their opponent into submission, while at the same time enriching the law firm. At least that's my take on it.

One result is that many plaintiff's lawyers have to turn down small but worthy cases. A person's injuries, caused by the negligence of another, may be worth $25,000, but if the lawyer has to spend $20,000 of his time to get it resolved, he cannot afford to take the case; his only alternative is to take it on as a charity case (and all of us do from time to time) or accept an early settlement for whatever he can get for the client.

Many people are under the mistaken impression that insurance companies are willing to settle every claim, however questionable, for "nuisance value," just to get rid of it. Nothing could be farther from the truth, in my experience. I found that whenever there was any doubt about the defendant's liability, his insurer would fight tooth and nail to the bitter end. Perhaps those really famous plaintiff's lawyers have better luck who have established a reputation for winning enormous verdicts. But they are few and far between.

One of my favorite litigation clients was Irv Meyers, a really nice guy who had been done wrong. Irv for twenty years had been manager of a large photo processing laboratory in Washington. He had established an outstanding reputation for the lab, despite working for a tyrannical and irascible owner, Byron Roudabush. One day, in a fit of pique and for no discernible reason, Roudabush fired Irv and banished him from the premises. Irv had nearly two years remaining on his current employment contract. We sued for wrongful termination. This so incensed Roudabush that he posted a notice on the company bulletin board, visible to vendors: "It's a good thing we got rid of Irv Meyers. He brought nitrate film into the lab, and we might all have burned to death." Nitrate film was an old type of film used up until about the 1940's, and is still found in places like the National Archives, and it is indeed highly flammable. But there was no truth whatsoever to the allegation. So we threw in a count of libel.

In the trial we brought in witness after witness, customers of the lab, who testified to Irv's competence and reliability, and who added their comments about the incompetence and unreliability of his successor. The successor manager, a young hot shot brought in by Roudabush, took the stand and bragged about his experience and accomplishments. I had done a thorough background investigation on him, and it turned out that his resume was a pack of distortions and exaggerations. Cross-examination was what I enjoyed most about trial work, and this was a banner day. He was forced to admit that he had no previous experience whatsoever in this business. Further, his numerous previous business ventures, which he had proudly discussed on direct examination, all turned out to be total failures, including bankruptcy, and in fact he had once been convicted of fraud.

The jury awarded Irv the full amount due on his contract, plus $50,000 for libel. Irv and I remained friends for a long time, and later I represented his daughter in a personal injury case which we settled to everyone's satisfaction.

There was one client who became a good friend even though I lost his case. Al Duduk was an official with the National Transportation Safety Board, and he had first come to me when there was an apparent screw-up concerning tire safety tests, and Al was under investigation as the person responsible. It turned out he was totally blameless, and he received an apology from the Board. Later Al came back to me with a possible medical malpractice claim. It involved surgery to correct an anal fistula (don't ask). Suffice it to say that we went to trial and lost the case.

During this period, Al had begun taking instructions in the Catholic faith, and at his baptism he asked me to be his sponsor. I was very honored. A year or so later Al died of cancer, and his widow gave me the great honor of being the eulogist at his funeral. It was one of those moments that made everything right with the world.

26.

NIXON, THE WEATHERMEN, AND THE FBI

Today in 2005, four years after the devastating terrorist attacks on the Twin Towers and the Pentagon on September 10, 2001, and with our country deeply involved in a War on Terrorism, it is hard to believe that there was a time when the Director of the FBI and two of his top assistants were prosecuted for attempting to protect Americans from terrorists. Yet that is exactly what happened in 1978. The Director was L. Patrick Gray III, successor to J. Edgar Hoover, and the other two were Mark Felt, Associate Director, and Edward S. Miller, head of the Bureau's Intelligence Division. They were charged with authorizing searches without warrants in the hunt for known fugitive anti-war terrorist bombers five years earlier. I represented Ed Miller.

Today when we think of terrorists we think of Islamic fundamentalists, particularly of Al-Queda, led by the arch terrorist Osama Bin Laden.

But in the late Sixties and early Seventies, during the height of the Vietnam conflict, there was the Weatherman Underground. They were anti-war extremists who engaged in widespread terrorism, including sabotage, bombings, and even murder.

A radical wing of the Students for a Democratic Society, the Weathermen had instigated the "Days of Rage" at the Democratic convention in Chicago in 1968. They took their name from Bob Dylan's anti-war song "Blowin' in the Wind" ("You don't need a weatherman to know which way the wind blows"). After a townhouse accidentally blew up in midtown Manhattan in March 1970, killing three bomb-making members of the group inside, the Weathermen went underground and became fugitives, harbored by a loyal group of supporters, all of whom referred to themselves as members of the Weather Underground. They were mostly white middle-class college men and women who were into drugs, obtained guns, and prepared, as their literature put it, "to establish another front against imperialism right here in Amerika [their spelling]—to bring the war home."

Violence was their method. They set off bombs in public buildings and business establishments, including bank and airline offices, all over the country. At least 52 bombings were officially recorded during the 1968-73 period. Their targets included Police Headquarters in Manhattan, the U.S. Capitol, the State Department, and the Pentagon—none of which caused extensive damage but resulted in a great deal of panic and anxiety. Bomb scares were a regular occurrence in many public buildings in Washington. Moreover, the Weathermen were engaging in a series of bank and armored car robberies to finance their activities, some resulting in homicides.

Numerous Congressional hearings were held on terrorist activities and specifically the WUO, by both the Senate and the House. These revealed, along with other intelligence available to the FBI and other agencies, that members of the group had extensive contacts with foreign entities eager to foment unrest and violence in the United States. Many Weatherman members had received training in guerilla operations in Castro's Cuba; there was also extensive travel to and contacts with the Soviet Union, North Vietnam, the Palestine Liberation Organization under Yassir Arafat. and Libya.

In short, the Weatherman Underground Organization posed, in the opinion of many in and out of government, a genuine threat to our homeland security. This placed enormous pressure on the FBI, both from the White House and from an angry and apprehensive public. The Bureau's traditional methods of information gathering were proving ineffective, all in the face of mounting public pressure to pursue and apprehend these fugitives.

Every new Bureau agent learns at the FBI Academy the technique of surreptitious entries, commonly known as Black Bag Jobs, because of the bag of tools used in the old days for carrying lock-picking tools. In effect they were searches without warrants. Although black bag jobs were not publicized, from the days of Franklin D. Roosevelt they had been deemed to be outside the purview of the 4th Amendment, because they were used in intelligence gathering rather than in ongoing criminal investigations. They were also employed by other agencies, including the CIA. Further, in the FBI they could be authorized solely by the Director without obtaining higher approval from the attorney general or the president. They were effective in tracking pro-Nazi activities in the U.S. before the war, were frequently used to enter embassies to obtain and break codes during the war, and after the war were employed in the effort to trace the activities of alleged Communists and white supremacists. My client, Ed Miller, during his younger days in the Bureau, had conducted numerous surreptitious entries to gather intelligence concerning our national security, and had received commendations for his work.

Black bag jobs were utilized not only to conduct searches, but to implant electronic listening devices. It is almost impossible to install a bug without a break-in.

As noted previously, President Johnson in 1966 issued an executive order prohibiting the use of electronic surveillance, because its illegality had jeopardized criminal investigations in Las Vegas. Hoover had followed suit by formally prohibiting further use of bag jobs.

The presidential order prevailed until 1968, when Congress, as part of the Safe Streets Act of 1968, authorized the use of electronic surveillance in criminal cases, under strict judicial supervision.

But the issue of the use of bag jobs, for intelligence gathering only, remained murky. It is known that Hoover, prior to his death in

1972, authorized a few surreptitious entries for gathering intelligence concerning the Soviet Union, and it is also known that the CIA routinely used these techniques for the same purpose.

The Supreme Court in 1972 held that warrantless entries for electronic surveillance in *domestic* national security cases were illegal. By implication, it seemed to hold that warrantless entries in *foreign* national security cases were permissible. However, the Court did not define the line between foreign and domestic national security; nor did it specifically deal with entries which did not involve electronic surveillance. And, incredibly, no directives or guidelines were promulgated by the Department of Justice or the FBI following the Court's decision.

Two or three months later, on May 2, 1972, Hoover died. Nixon appointed L. Patrick Gray III from his former position of Assistant Attorney General to become the Acting Director of the FBI. All this time the White House and the public were breathing down the Bureau's neck to find and apprehend the Weatherman fugitives.

There is some dispute as to what happened next. It is undisputed that in September 1972, at a meeting of all Special Agents in Charge of all Bureau field offices, Gray emphasized the importance of tracking down the Weatherman fugitives, using such terms as "hunt to exhaustion," "no holds barred," and "use all available means." Felt and Miller remember asking Gray privately if this meant that bag jobs could again be used. Gray answered in the affirmative and directed them to so inform the field agents, providing that each request from the field had to be specifically approved by both Felt, as Associate Director, and Miller, as head of the Intelligence Division. Gray later denied having had this conversation.

Between September 1972 and May 1973, Felt and Miller, believing they had the authority to do so, approved a total of seven requests from Bureau field offices in New York and New Jersey to conduct surreptitious entries of homes of close friends and relatives known to have had prior contacts with the Weather Underground fugitives. No electronic surveillance was involved. As it turned out, none of the searches uncovered any useful information. Incidentally, Felt and Miller also approved field requests for seven such searches in connection with an investigation of suspected members of *al-Fatah*, the terrorist arm of the Palestine Liberation Organization.

All of this was revealed in 1976, long after Felt and Miller had retired from the Bureau and Gray had been forced out as a result of Watergate. It came to light after the end of the Vietnam war when several Congressional committees and the Department of Justice under President Carter's attorney general, Griffin Bell, were doing a retrospective on intelligence gathering excesses by several federal agencies during the Vietnam era, and especially during the Nixon years. The excesses were aimed at protesters and dissidents of all types, in the name of protecting our national security. Two years of investigation followed.

When Ed Miller came under scrutiny, he called Henry Petersen and asked for a recommendation for a lawyer. Ed told me that Henry said, "There is only one person I would recommend, and that is Tom Kennelly." This pleased me greatly, as Henry was my boss at Justice and I had great admiration for him.

I felt that it was unfair to lump Felt's and Miller's specific actions in the Weatherman investigation with the clear abuses against religious groups and other pacifists, including Martin Luther King, Jr., that had occurred and were being ballyhooed in the press. In attempt to stave off prosecution of my client, in March 1978 I wrote a long legal memo to the Assistant Attorney General in charge of the Criminal Division in which I contended that Mr. Miller acted only on the express authority of his superior and believed that the authorization was both warranted and appropriate to deal with the Weather Underground bombings that prevailed at the time.

I concluded my memo as follows:

"It appears that this country has emerged from the turbulence and violence of the 1968-1973 era; many of the actions and counteractions undertaken by responsible government officials during that period to deal with extremely urgent and dangerous problems no longer are considered necessary. Prosecution now of government officials who spent their careers protecting and defending the Constitution and apprehending that small minority who acted to endanger the constitutional rights of the majority of Americans can serve no useful purpose today."

But the pendulum had swung back, and the public, still reeling from Watergate, was in a mood to "indict an era" and to purge what were now perceived as earlier misdeeds.

The Indictment

On April 10, 1978, a federal grand jury in the District of Columbia returned a felony indictment against Gray, Felt, and Miller for conspiracy to violate the civil rights of the subjects of the Weatherman searches. It is interesting to note that it did not include the *al-Fatah* searches, an implied admission that foreign intelligence searches were not subject to the 4th Amendment.

As anticipated, the indictment made front page headlines around the country. Further, it led to a flood of commentary on the news and op-ed pages, from both right and left, on the vital and age-old issue of our nation's duty to protect its citizens versus the citizens' constitutional right against invasion of their privacy.

The conservative Washington periodical Human Events (owned and published by a distant cousin of Susan's from Omaha) declared: "Atty. Gen. Griffin Bell's new prosecutorial actions relating to the FBI can bring only further shame, not honor or credit, to the Carter Administration's Justice Department.... [I]n carrying out an assignment to track down terrorists who were fugitives from justice, [they] had employed the same techniques that had been used by the FBI and other security agencies for many years."

The Washington director of the ACLU had a different point of view: He stated to the Washington Post: "I am astounded that in all the end-justifies-the-means excuses given for FBI conduct, no one refers to the law—the constitutional rights of the citizens whose houses were bugged or whose phones were wiretapped."

In fact, no houses were bugged or phones tapped. In the same story, a former FBI agent had this to say: "To 'break in' in order to apprehend a terrorist is a different intent than breaking in, say to *steal*. The FBI should not have to stand by while people are blowing up buildings."

The Washington Post's editorial page took a more lofty view: "The indictment is an effort to exert governmental influence over the FBI and to ensure that its top officials are held responsible before the law for the actions they take. The bureau was never intended to be 'independent' of the law.... It is not easy to square the commands of the Constitution with the reality of police work, especially in the field of counterespionage. Nor is it easy to punish agents, either criminally or administratively, for acts they committed in good faith and for the protection of the American people. But if the acts were illegal—a point not yet established in court—the motivation behind them is irrelevant." Next to the editorial was a Herblock cartoon depicting two FBI agents carrying a black bag, standing in front of a picture of a scowling J. Edgar, and saying "We broke the law? We are the law!"

Anthony Marro in the New York Times raised the dual questions of whether heads of agencies have known of previous break-ins for years and have given tacit approval for reasons of "national security," and whether charging specific individuals at this time constitutes selective prosecution. "Evidence that two and perhaps three recent Attorneys General knew about break-ins and ignored them makes it easier to claim that the prosecution of these defendants is as selective and discriminatory as to be unconstitutional."

This last issue of who knew what and when, as it developed, literally pitted neighbor against neighbor in the area where Susan and I lived. In a motion to dismiss the indictment on the grounds of selective prosecution, I offered evidence that Robert Bork, who became Attorney General in October 1973, had been informed of the FBI's Weatherman break-ins several months earlier and had condoned them, taking no action. Bork's wife was a member of our parish and a good friend of Susan, and the Borks, who lived nearby, had been dinner guests in our home. On the other hand, Phil Lacovara, our next-door neighbor, testifying as a former Deputy Solicitor General, told a Senate criminal justice subcommittee: "People who are somehow connected with intelligence information think they have something like a license not only to kill, but to lie, steal, cheat, and spy."

I have mentioned these issues at length because these are the very issues that are again being debated after 9/11. We are told that we are in a war against terrorism and that certain of our traditional civil rights must be restricted in order for the government to protect us against those who would stop at nothing to destroy our way of life. There is no question that extremist Islamic terrorism poses a threat; but are the means being employed to combat the threat necessary and constitutional? As I write, legislation has been introduced in Congress which would grant the FBI the power to conduct the same activities, in the name of national security, for which Gray, Felt, and Miller were prosecuted.

Reasonable people differ on whether this is right or wrong. Perhaps a changed world does require a change in traditional views of protection versus freedom. But I believe we must always be vigilant, to protect not only our national security but our civil liberties. Justice Louis D. Brandeis wrote nearly 80 years ago: "Experience should teach us to be most on our guard to protect liberty when the government's purposes are beneficent.... The greatest dangers to liberty lurk in insidious encroachment by men of zeal, well meaning, but without understanding."

The arraignment of our clients took place on April 20, 1978. Normally it is a routine procedure in which the defendants enter pleas of guilty or not guilty and a trial date is set. This arraignment became an unforgettable experience for the defendants and for us lawyers. As we approached the courthouse steps on Constitution Avenue we were greeted by more than five hundred special agents and former special agents of the Bureau, standing in silent vigil in support of their leaders. There were no signs or placards or shouts of protest, unlike that day in May seven years previously when Weather Underground supporters and other anti-war activists attempted to storm this same courthouse. As the defendants and their lawyers walked across the plaza and up the steps they were greeted by loud and sustained applause. Those present came from as far away as Boston, New Haven, Baltimore, and Richmond, as well as from Washington, D.C. Statements of support were read by representatives of current and former agents. It was a very emotional experience for all of us.

Our defense of Ed Miller was based not on any argument that the FBI had an absolute right to conduct searches without warrants. It was based on a lack of criminal intent and a lack of clarity in the law at the time of the alleged offenses. The Fourth Amendment does not require that every search be backed by a warrant. Law enforcement agencies have traditionally assumed that searches in national security cases are among the exceptions not requiring a warrant, and there was very little case law on the subject. Then, as previously noted, in June 1972, three months prior to the events in question, the Supreme Court held that searches in "wholly domestic" national security matters required prior presidential authorization. But the Weather Underground was well known in law enforcement circles to have had numerous contacts with hostile foreign powers and international terrorist groups, sufficient for a jury to conclude that the Weatherman investigation would fall within the purview of a foreign national security matter, or at last that our clients had reason to believe so.

Miller's lack of criminal intent was further demonstrated by his belief that he had received from Gray the necessary approval to authorize the searches, and that no higher approval was necessary. I was confident that the evidence would show (and it eventually did) that going back to the days of FDR in the 1930's, J. Edgar Hoover had the power to authorize bag jobs without seeking approval from any higher authority. Presidents and Attorneys General were well aware of this. Even if it could be argued that Miller should have been aware of the Supreme Court decision three months earlier (despite the absence of any guidelines from either the Bureau or the Department), he was right to assume that Gray, a lawyer (as Miller was not), having just been appointed by the president, would have obtained the requisite authorization.

The above outlines of our defense were jointly agreed to by myself and Felt's counsel, Brian Gettings, a good friend and outstanding trial lawyer with whom I had been associated in the Organized Crime Section. Gray's lawyer was Alan Baron, a former Assistant U.S. Attorney in Baltimore, whom Brian and I knew and admired both as a trial lawyer and as a friend. But Gray's defense was in direct conflict with ours. Gray flatly denied he had ever re-instituted bag jobs, denied that he had ever authorized Felt or Miller or anybody else to use them, and denied that he knew they had been conducted. These contradictory defenses made it impossible to try the three defendants in a joint trial, and Chief Judge William Bryant granted Gray's motion for a severance. The government elected to try Felt and Miller first.

Howard Epstein and I worked together on Miller's defense, and Brian Gettings was assisted by his partner Frank Dunham, together with Mark Cummings, a bright and enthusiastic associate, and Cathy Worthington, a sparkling young paralegal.

In order to prepare our defense we needed to examine extensive files from the Bureau and the Justice Department documenting the historical use of bag jobs authorized by the Director with the knowledge and consent of Attorneys General. Further, in order to document the links between the Weather Underground and hostile foreign powers we needed to look at files not only in the Bureau but in other intelligence gathering agencies, including the CIA and the National Security Agency. Opposition from the prosecutors to our request for access to this information was fierce and persistent. They told the court that we were seeking files that were highly classified and could not possibly be made public. We were attempting to compromise national security. We were resorting to "graymail," that is, hoping to force the government to dismiss the case rather than disclose needed evidence which, they claimed, wasn't really needed.

It was the custom of Chief Judge Bryant at the outset to grant our requests to examine these files. Then the prosecutors would announce that they had complied in part, but would offer further resistance to the rest of it, or would provide the documents in such "redacted" form, with much of the material blacked out, that they were virtually incomprehensible. This would lead to further wrangling and further delays in starting the trial.

On one occasion it was revealed that 1500 FBI file folders pertaining to the Weatherman investigation had been lost while in the possession of the Justice Department. Some 22 FBI file cabinets had been seized by the Justice Department for safekeeping when the investigation of possible illegal bag jobs began. It was apparently feared that Bureau agents would destroy incriminating evidence. But when the files were finally returned to the Bureau they were lacking 1500 of the earlier inventoried folders.

On each of these occasions we moved to dismiss the indictment for lack of ability to prepare a defense, and on each occasion Judge Bryant, after much soul searching and stern admonitions to the prosecutors, denied our motions.

All of this wrangling was extremely nerve-wracking and frustrating, and led to eight postponements of the trial during a period of two and a half years. All of us lawyers had other cases and matters to handle as well, and it made it extremely difficult to schedule our calendars. It was also frustrating for our families We were all working long days and hours—frequently fifteen to twenty days straight of working till late in the evenings getting ready for trial, only to have it postponed again. Extended vacations were out of the question. Susy and our kids began to refer to it as the "damn trial."

Even with all the foot-dragging by the prosecutors, we were faced with the prospect of examining an estimated 300,000 documents. The Department provided each of our law offices specially constructed 600-lb. safes for the protection of classified documents. In addition each of the lawyers had to obtain special security clearances above the level of Top Secret (something called an SCI clearance); further, some of the documents, and some of the witnesses, could only be examined in a vault surrounded by foot-thick concrete walls contained within the Justice Department.

To our rescue, for review of the files, came the Society of Former Special Agents of the FBI, a deeply devoted and fiercely loyal group of former agents. They provided us with fourteen volunteers, retired special agents, who worked full time for many months, analyzing and summarizing the contents of the documents. In addition, they were available to conduct witness interviews, or could call upon other retired agents anywhere in the country to do so. It was like having our own private FBI at our beck and call. This effort was coordinated by a retired agent named J. Allison Conley, and Al Conley and his associates were among the most dedicated and experienced investigators I have ever met.

The Society also organized a legal defense fund, and contributions from their members, along with those from active duty agents and some help from the William Simon Foundation, paid all the legal fees of all three defendants. We all agreed to work at a discounted rate—$50 an hour—yet the total fees came to close to a million dollars.

Trial preparation included interviewing potential important witnesses around the country. In the winter of 1978 Brian Gettings and I embarked on a trip to the west coast to interview some former Nixon staffers to see what they knew about bag jobs. We left on a Monday for Los Angeles to interview John Dean, then to San Francisco where we met with Jeb Magruder, then on to Seattle to interview William D.

Ruckelshaus, a Deputy Attorney General during the Nixon era, and finally to Phoenix where we talked to Robert Mardian, a CRP fund raiser, and Richard Kleindienst, John Mitchell's successor as Attorney General. We left Phoenix at midnight on Friday.

I got home at 9 AM Saturday, exhausted, only to have son Timmy, then in the eighth grade at St. John's Prep, remind me that I had promised to take him to the basketball game between St. John's High School and its hated rival, De Matha. The game was to start at noon. So off we went. What Timmy hadn't mentioned was that the first game was the freshman game. This was followed by the junior varsity game. Finally there came the varsity game, which went into two overtimes. Finally at 6 PM we emerged from the gym, only to find that we had been hit by a blizzard in the interim and I had to drive home in two feet of snow. Such are the vicissitudes of family life. I must say, though, that I really enjoyed the time with my son.

We Interview Richard Nixon

We needed to know whether Nixon, now in retirement, had approved or was aware of any FBI bag jobs carried out while he was in office. Nixon indicated his willingness to meet with us. So in December 1978 the lawyers for all three defendants went to interview him in his suite in the Waldorf Towers in Manhattan.

I had developed a thorough dislike of Richard Nixon over the years. It began with a book by Jerry Voorhees, a fine Congressman who was defeated for reelection in a smear campaign by Nixon in 1948. My dislike continued with Nixon's slimy mud-slinging defeat of incumbent Senator Helen Gahagan Douglas in 1950, and through his "Checkers" speech as Eisenhower' running mate in 1952. I was ecstatic when John Kennedy beat him in 1960 and appalled when Hubert Humphrey, another of my heroes, lost to him in 1968. And of course Watergate confirmed what I had known all along, that Richard Nixon was a sleazy scumbag. There was nothing since his resignation in 1974 that had caused me to change my opinion.

Therefore when we went to his suite I expected to find the nervous, wary, shifty-eyed Richard Nixon that had always been in my mind's eye.

It was one of the most disorienting experiences in my life. He welcomed us with genuine warmth and cordiality, and asked us all to join him around a large coffee table, where refreshments were served. He spoke of his admiration for the Bureau and of his dismay that our clients were being prosecuted. He offered to help in any way he could. He looked us directly in the eye and answered each of our questions fully and directly and without a hint of evasiveness. On a couple of occasions he even put his feet up on the table, totally relaxed.

He said that no, he had not been asked to approve any surreptitious entries, but had he been asked to do so, he would readily have given his approval, especially against the Weather Underground, which was causing a national crisis. He was aware that in the past, both in his and previous administrations, it was the custom for the FBI Director to authorize such techniques in national security cases without the necessity of seeking higher approval.

His answers were honest and complete, and we could not have asked for more. Notwithstanding that no other president, sitting or retired, had ever testified in a criminal trial, when we asked him if he would be willing to do so (even though we had not yet decided whether this would be a good idea), he readily agreed.

As we were nearing the end of our meeting of an hour or so, he remarked that he had been reading about our courtroom battle over the lost 1500 file folders. "How could the government lose 1500 files?" he exclaimed. "Unbelievable!" Then he added, "And to think they were all over my ass for a lousy 18 minutes of tape!"

Some of us had brought along copies of his just-published Memoirs, which we asked him to sign. He inscribed mine, "To Tom Kennelly With Best Wishes from Richard Nixon."

As we departed the Waldorf Towers that day, I had to admit to a certain liking, and also a bit of sympathy, for this man Richard Nixon, not to mention a certain amount of awe at having had a personal meeting with a former president of the United States. Heady stuff for a boy from Dubuque, Iowa.

Prior to the trial I also interviewed Dr. Timothy Leary, the former college professor whose advocacy of free drugs for everybody made him the guru of the Flower Children of the Sixties, but also led him ultimately to prison. He was potentially an important witness for us because while serving time in California he escaped, supposedly with the help of the Weather Underground, which delivered him for safekeeping to Yassir Arafat and the Palestine Liberation Organization. This would show a strong link between the WUO and *al-Fatah*, the terrorist arm of the PLO, at that time ensconced in Libya.

The interview with Leary took place at the Los Angeles airport, in that strange-looking building over the parking garage that resembles a ship just landed from outer space. I had always wondered what purpose that building served other than as a logo for the airport. It housed a coffee shop. Dr. Leary, who had long since returned to the U.S. and completed his term, was friendly if a bit loopy, and not very helpful. He remembered the escape but professed to have no idea who it was that spirited him off to Libya. As far as he was concerned, it could have been men from Mars.

Scratch one witness. I wondered if he had chosen the space ship-cum-coffee shop by design.

The Trial

It finally got underway on September 15, 1980, two and a half years after the indictment. The jury was the standard mix one would find in the District of Columbia, mostly African-American working class with a few Caucasian white-collar types, including one or two professionals of each race. Fair enough, but D.C. juries are not notably friendly toward cops who are charged with violating the rights of citizens.

The prosecutors, John Nields and Frank Martin, called as witnesses the persons whose residences had been searched, and they presented a sympathetic picture of decent citizens whose privacy had been violated without their knowledge by intrusive federal agents. They also put on the agents who conducted the searches and their supervisors, who testified that they received their authorizations from Felt and Miller. One of the agents was prompted to testify that while conducting the searches he felt more like a burglar than a law enforcer.

The trial also included the testimony of five former Attorneys General, another first in courtroom history. Herbert Brownell, AG under Eisenhower, testified that he was aware that Hoover conducted bag jobs and believed that Hoover had the discretion to do this without first seeking his approval. Nicholas Katzenbach, Robert Kennedy's Deputy AG and successor to Kennedy, testified that he had not personally been aware of any bag jobs while he was AG, but he admitted that he was present when Hoover informed Kennedy of the use of such techniques. Ramsey Clark, AG under Lyndon Johnson, who after leaving Justice became an advocate and counsel for many civil libertarian causes and clients (and now Saddam Hussein), vigorously denied ever authorizing or hearing about any bag jobs while he was in office, and said he would have prohibited their use in any case.

John Mitchell, who succeeded Clark, and Richard Kleindienst, Mitchell's successor, which brought us up to the time of the entries charged in this case, both testified as to their belief that surreptitious entries in national security cases were within the authorized purview of the Director of the FBI.

Another interesting witness was O. Roy Cohn, who achieved notoriety as counsel to Senator Joe McCarthy during the Army-McCarthy hearings in 1954. Cohn later became a flamboyant trial lawyer in New York, who died of AIDS and became a character in Tony Kushner's play "Angels in America." Early in his career he had worked in Justice under Brownell and he testified as to several bag jobs authorized by Hoover and known to Brownell.

One afternoon as the testimony droned on during the eight-week trial, the courtroom suddenly erupted with a loud whooshing sound. The first thought in everyone's mind was that the Weathermen had planted a bomb. In an instant Judge Bryant was off the bench and heading for his chambers, with all counsel and clients right on his heels. The spectators tumbled over one another fleeing the courtroom. It was then discovered that one of the janitors had inadvertently turned on the central vacuuming system.

Then it was announced that Richard Nixon would testify the next day. Long lines formed outside the courtroom early in the morning, but I arranged places for Susan and all of the children, who at this time were 15, 14, and 13.

It was a dramatic moment because it was Nixon's first public appearance in Washington since his resignation. It was also the first time a former president had testified in any courtroom. After a short examination by the prosecutor, in which he stated that he had not authorized any surreptitious entries in the Weather Underground investigation, I then questioned him for about 45 minutes, giving him the opportunity to help our cause as much as he could by repeating what he had told us in the Manhattan interview: He believed that at the time the FBI director and his deputies had general authorization from the president to order break-ins in the interest of national security. In any event, in view of the national crisis at the time, he would readily have given his okay had he been asked.

We hoped his testimony would bolster our defense that our clients, under a great deal of pressure in a time of national crisis, were performing what they perceived as their authorized duties to the best of their ability. But it is difficult to gauge what effect Nixon had on the jury, given the lingering effects of Vietnam and Watergate. It was a calculated risk. We hoped the jury's reaction would be different from that of one of the spectators, who during Nixon's testimony jumped to her feet and shouted "Baby killer!"

Finally, the jury heard from John Barron, a writer and expert on international protest movements, who had compiled all of our "foreign contacts" evidence and demonstrated with charts the myriad links and entanglements of the Weathermen with Castro's Cuba, North Vietnam, the Chinese People's Republic, the Soviet Union, and other international terrorist groups from whom Weathermen had received training and financial support.

But it was all to no avail.

John Nields, in his closing argument, played the patriot game. He told the jury that they were the bulwark between government oppression and personal freedom. He reminded them that the Fourth Amendment was not the creation of ivory-tower intellectuals, but was an expression of our deepest instinct. He urged them, through their verdict, to send a message to the world, loud and clear, that a man's home is his castle, and that his constitutional rights are not to be trampled upon by officious government agents, however well intentioned. It was the sort of thing I probably would have said myself had I been the prosecutor, and it was very effective.

On our side we were up against insuperable obstacles. Lets face it, a sneak search of a person's home without his consent and without a warrant looks like a crime, sounds like a crime, and feels like a crime. In this light, defenses like mistake of law and lack of specific criminal intent, though valid, are a tough sell. Further, we had an uphill battle on the foreign national security *vis-a-vis* domestic national security issue. Weathermen bombers are terrorists alright, but American college dropouts on drugs sound a lot more like *domestic* terrorists than agents of a foreign power.

And Judge Bryant's instructions to the jury sealed our fate. Bryant, who in his former career as a criminal defense attorney was known to rail against the FBI, decided to simplify things for the jury. No need for them to bother with complex issues like mistake of law and specific criminal intent. Over our vigorous protests, he instructed the jury that if the searches were not specifically authorized by the president, the defendants must be found guilty.

The jury was out less than a day. On November 8, 1980, eight weeks after the trial began and one day after Ronald Reagan defeated Jimmy Carter and was elected president, Felt and Miller were convicted.

Amazingly, on sentencing day the judge was lenient. Facing imprisonment of up to five years, Felt and Miller were sentenced to pay fines of $5000 and $3500 respectively. That was it. No further explanation.

After the convictions, the government dismissed the indictment against L. Patrick Gray III.

Shortly after completion of the trial, Susan and I hustled off to Hawaii for a week of rest and recuperation. According to her, I had worked every weeknight and every weekend, save one, for seven months.

I wrote a letter of thanks to Mr. Nixon, and he responded with a personal note thanking me for my thoughtfulness. He closed by saying: "While the verdict was disappointing, I am hopeful that the appeal will be successful. Mr. Felt and Mr. Miller have served the nation with great dedication for over thirty years and they have my deep respect."

The Pardon

We filed our notices of appeal and were compiling our lists of what we believed to be judicial errors, particularly regarding the jury instructions. We were heartened by a report of a committee of the American Bar Association in January 1981 which pointed out that there were three possible grounds of appeal in our case: 1) the jury instructions 2) the lack of guidelines and 3) the denial of access to more than 1000 pages of files showing possible foreign connections of the Weathermen.

Then in mid-January 1981, I received a call from Edwin J. Meese III on behalf of President-elect Ronald Reagan. Reagan was to be inaugurated on January 20. Meese was his campaign manager and had been designated by Reagan as the next Attorney General. Meese told me that the president-elect was outraged by the convictions and intended to grant a presidential pardon to both Felt and Miller. Would we kindly prepare and submit the necessary application papers to the Justice Department for forwarding to the White House?

Howard and I were ecstatic, and we immediately called Brian Gettings and his associates with the good news. Passing the word to our clients was one of the happiest moments in our careers. After an excruciating ordeal of more than four years, there would finally be a happy ending. We wasted no time in preparing the applications.

We were advised that the pardons would be announced on March 30th, 1981. However, on that day a young man named John Hinkley shot President Reagan as he emerged from speaking to a labor audience at the Washington Hilton Hotel. Reagan recovered after a sojourn in the hospital. Hinkley was found not guilty by reason of insanity and was confined to St. Elizabeth's Hospital for the mentally ill in Washington, where he remains to this day.

Felt and Miller received full and unconditional presidential pardons on April 16, 1981. Once again there were lead headlines and pictures on the front pages of all the papers. The statement by the president included the following:

"The record demonstrates that they acted not with criminal intent, but in the belief that they had grants of authority reaching to the highest levels of government....

"America was at war in 1972, and Messrs. Felt and Miller followed procedures they believed essential to keep the Director of the FBI, the Attorney General, and the President of the United States advised of the activities of hostile foreign powers and their collaborators in this country....

"Four years ago thousands of draft evaders and others who violated the Selective Service laws were unconditionally pardoned by my predecessor. America was generous to those who refused to serve their country in the Vietnam War. We can be no less generous to two men who acted on high principle to bring an end to the terrorism that was threatening our Nation."

We couldn't have said it better ourselves.

Brian Gettings and I were invited to present a seminar about the case at the annual meeting of the Society of Former Special Agents of the FBI held in Atlanta in November 1981. With Al Conley, coordinator of the volunteer investigative team presiding, we described to an overflow crowd of more than 1600 members, spouses, and guests, the long legal battle, and expressed our deep gratitude for the unwavering support we had received from the Society. We received plaques of appreciation from the Society for "compassion, legal professionalism, and concern for national security and justice through your stalwart defense of W. Mark Felt and Edward S. Miller." They are among our most valued treasures.

There remained one final task. Despite the presidential pardons, the convictions remained on the record. With Brian Gettings taking the lead, we were determined to get the convictions expunged and the indictment dismissed. We agreed to make the effort without further compensation. It took some creative legal thinking, as there was not a great deal of precedent for expunging convictions that were on appeal; but a more sympathetic Reagan Justice Department finally concurred that the pardons rendered the appeals moot. Upon submission of a joint memorandum, the Court of Appeals agreed, and it ordered the trial court to dismiss the indictments, which Judge Bryant promptly did, on November 28, 1983. At long last, after seven years of agony, Felt's and Miller's combined records or more than 55 years of service to the Bureau were clear of any taint.

As a result of the complications of this and other similar cases, Congress and the Justice Department finally codified and regulated the procedures for disclosing classified documents to defense attorneys in national security cases. Further, Congress created a special court, known as the Foreign Intelligence Surveillance Court, which meets to consider applications for search warrants and electronic surveillance in national security investigations. It is an *ad hoc* court, composed of specially selected U.S. District Court judges, as needed, who meet secretly in that soundproof vault in the Justice Department where I had studied all the secret documents.

Epilogue: Deep Throat and the Aftermath of Watergate

As noted earlier, the Watergate story was pursued vigorously by Bob Woodward and Carl Bernstein, two *Washington Post* reporters, who seemed able to obtain more inside information than any other media hounds. Their work eventually won them the Pulitzer Prize for Public Service and secured their place in journalism history. In their book, *All the President's Men,* they revealed that they were greatly aided by a source known as "Deep Throat," who had inside information, provided them with leads, and told them to keep digging, while at the same time the White House was trying desperately to cover up the story. The reporters had promised not to reveal the source's name until after Deep Throat's death.

For thirty-three years there was been great public speculation on the identity of Deep Throat. Hundreds of articles were written, and numerous books, whose authors all have claimed to know who it was, and dozens of people have been named. It has been one of the intriguing mysteries of our time.

Then on May 31, 2005, *Vanity Fair* magazine released an article which stated that Mark Felt had in recent years confided to family and friends, "I'm the guy they used to call 'Deep Throat.'" After publication, the revelation was confirmed by Felt and his daughter, and was verified by Woodward and Bernstein. The mystery was over.

The next day, curious about how Mark Felt had obtained inside information from the White House and why he had revealed it to the *Post*, I called Ed Miller. Ed told me that he had kept in touch with Felt over the years. Mark had suffered a stroke about two years previously, and at age 91 had no clear present recollection of the Watergate events. Ed had known that Mark was Deep Throat. Based on my conversations with Ed, this is my take on how Mark Felt became Deep Throat.

On May 2, 1972, J. Edgar Hoover, after ruling the Bureau with an iron hand for 48 years, died—an event which my witty friend George Higgins described as "an uncharacteristic submission to the authority of a superior deity." (*The Friends of Richard Nixon,* 1975).

Felt, ranked #3 in the Bureau (next to Hoover's lackey, Clyde Tolson, who was ill and retired shortly after Hoover's death), was close to Hoover and had every reason to expect he would be appointed Acting Director. Instead, Nixon chose as acting director L. Patrick Gray III, a career Navy submariner who after coming out of the Navy became a Nixon loyalist in Nixon's 1960 campaign, and who at the time of Hoover's death was serving as Assistant Attorney General in charge of the Civil Division. Gray had no law enforcement experience whatsoever.

Less than a month later, on June 17, 1972, the Watergate break-in occurred. Gray, ever the loyalist, assured the White House that he understood the sensitivity of the situation and promised at all times to keep in mind the greater good of the Administration (John Dean later testified to this). Dean, as White House counsel, called every day to see how things were going. But Gray was spending most of his time traveling around the country visiting the FBI field offices, to the extent that he became known around headquarters as "two day Gray." In his absence, Felt was in charge of operation, and he took the calls from Dean and Fred Fielding, Dean's assistant. They apparently assumed that Felt was Gray's alter ego.

What they didn't know was that Felt was a Democrat with a strong dislike of Nixon. In addition, besides being unhappy about being passed over, he was deeply resentful at the White House's attempt to prostitute the Bureau, which he deeply loved and to which he had devoted his entire career.

Dean (probably unintentionally) provided many of the leads for the investigation. Whenever Dean advised against following too far the trail of the money paid the burglars because it would cause embarrassment to GOP fund raisers, or warned against following up rumors about other break-ins, Felt knew *just* where to go. Felt knew that Gray would drag his feet, but he also had been around long enough to know that a story in the press would necessarily put pressure on the Bureau and it would have to follow up on the leads presented in the stories, and Gray could not stop it.

Felt and Woodward had become acquainted when Woodward was covering the attempted assassination of George Wallace, also in May 1972 (and according to Woodward, even before that).

The rest is history.

Ed reminded me of a final bit of irony. After his testimony on behalf of Felt and Miller in their trial, Nixon sent them each a personal note and a bottle of champagne.

27.

CHRISTMAS IN APRIL

Trevor Armbrister is a journalist with a keen eye, a clever pen, and a catchy name. When I met him in the early 1970's he was a senior editor with Reader's Digest, writing on numerous social and political issues. Trevor has also written several books. We first met when he was completing *Act of Vengeance*, the story of the Yablonski murders, for which Tony Boyle, head of the United Mine Workers, was ultimately convicted, thanks to the outstanding prosecutorial work of Chuck Ruff and Tom Henderson whom I supervised in the Organized Crime Section at Justice.

Eventually we were to learn that Trevor, in addition to his writing talents, is possessed of a big heart and an indomitable optimism. He had written a piece for the Digest in November 1982 about a volunteer program in Midland, Texas, called Christmas in April. Led by a man named Bobby Trimble, members of a church in Midland each year repaired and renovated the houses of elderly, physically challenged, and low income homeowners. Whatever needed doing—a new roof, new plumbing, a wheelchair ramp—volunteers took care of it. They did it all for free and they did it all in one day, the last Saturday in April. One of the recipients was so overjoyed that she said, "This is like Christmas in April," and the name stuck.

Trevor came back from Midland and said if they can do it in Midland, we can do it in Washington. He began drumming up interest in the members of his church, St. Columba's Episcopal. He was eager to "reach across the Park," on the east side of Rock Creek Park, where most of the African Americans live, in the long blocks of three-story brick row houses which are common in Washington. The homeowners purchased them during or just after World War II when there was an influx of African Americans to Washington seeking employment, but because they are now elderly or infirm or living on limited incomes, there is no money for repairs and maintenance. The neighborhood is deteriorating and becoming crime-ridden, and these good people, who have worked hard and kept the faith all their lives, are in great need of help to keep their homes warm and dry and safe during their remaining years.

Trevor saw a Christmas in April program in Washington as a way to help these people. Starting with his parish, St. Columba's Episcopal, he talked to everyone he met, including a group of us at a Christmas party given by Tom Henderson, and we were hooked. Its greatest appeal is that everyone is willing to help his neighbor one day a year. All it needs is someone to get them organized. It's like an old-fashioned barn raising.

Of course most of us who agreed to do the organizing—because we considered ourselves experienced at organizing things—had no experience whatsoever in performing major home repairs. We were lawyers and writers and publicists and bureaucrats. Trevor himself admitted that he didn't know a plumb bob from a pliers. But his enthusiasm was contagious, and he did manage to recruit some skilled volunteers, including a couple of contractors who got us the necessary building permits; two members of the Plumbers Union; and a homicide detective with the D.C. Police who arranged street parking for delivery trucks and volunteers. Trevor also coaxed and cajoled some bankers and business people to contribute the sum total of $11,000 to a program they never heard of, in order to buy paint, plasterboard, and other supplies, usually at discounts he had negotiated. The rest of us recruited friends from our own churches and other social contacts.

The biggest problem, to our surprise, was finding willing recipients. Most of the homeowners to whom we had been referred were extremely wary and suspicious. They had been ripped off so many times by con artists that they could not believe that a dozen or more people were going to come in on the last Saturday in April and in one day paint their rooms, fix the toilets and sinks, repair the wiring, and build ramps and railings, all for free.

We finally settled on 19 houses and had 350 volunteers, with varying degrees of skills, and launched Christmas in April, Washington, DC, on the last Saturday in April 1983. Each house had a house captain and an assigned crew. I was the captain at the home of a Mrs. Wright, with 19 volunteers, of all ages and backgrounds. Even those with no experience could paint and patch and haul trash. It was inspiring to see a banker and a common laborer working together to unstop a sink, and a judge and a taxi driver painting a wall together, and all with great enthusiasm. Everyone was amazed at how much could be accomplished with a couple of dozen people in one day. At the end of the day we had a big picnic for all volunteers and homeowners in Rock Creek Park. Everybody was given a Christmas in April cap. One volunteer said, "I've never worked so hard in my life for a free cap, but it was worth it." The recipients were profuse in their gratitude. The day was proclaimed a success.

In truth it was closer to a disaster. Enthusiasm did not make up for inadequate preparation. We had no idea of the scope of planning required. Some of the houses did not receive their materials until mid-afternoon. We did not have enough carpenters, plumbers, electricians, or drywall people. Nobody had enough tools. Some of the houses had too much paint, others not enough. Neighborhood hardware stores were overwhelmed. We were unable to do any roofs. Some of the house captains had overestimated what could be accomplished in a day. There was an uneven distribution of volunteers. And in spite of Trevor's valiant efforts, not enough money had been raised.

Reasonable people might have concluded that if there was to be a second year at all, at the very least it should be scaled down. But carried on a wave of Trevor's irrepressible optimism, we formed a board of directors, began preparations earlier, and in the second year we did 35 houses with about 500 volunteers. Things went somewhat better, except for one major glitch. At the end of the day someone, while attempting to hang a picture, punctured a water pipe. In the emergency, a non-union plumber was called, whereupon the Plumbers Union pulled out of the program.

But we began to get some publicity on television and in the press. A couple of suburban Washington communities, with our help, started their own Christmas in April programs. We got a big lift from President Reagan on June 29, 1984. While speaking in the State Dining Room at the White House, he commented that he had previously heard of the Christmas in April program in Texas and thought it was a great example of volunteerism. Then he added:

"And to show you how fast it all happened, I'm looking at television one day up there while I was getting dressed, upstairs, and I saw a television program and a fellow there with a painter's cap and a paint brush in his hand. And yes, he was a judge. [Tim Murphy] And what was he doing? Well, this "Christmas in April" and so forth. And I started to yell to Nancy that, 'Hey, they've got that town in Texas on the air.' I found out it was in Washington, D.C. [*Laughter*] They've adopted the program here, too."

In the third year, 1985, I was elected president and we took on 40 houses with 800 volunteers. That year we achieved a major break-through when Trevor recruited his fellow parishioner Patricia Riley Johnson, whom we hired as our part-time executive director. Patty Johnson, 39, a vivacious and enthusiastic wife and mother of four children, was just what the program needed, and she and I and the other leaders became an effective team. Patty has great organizational and people skills, good insights, and unlimited patience, as well as an Irish wit. We set up headquarters in the basement of her home, and she worked long hours with little pay.

We were beginning to become known as a legitimate operation in the neighborhoods, which made it somewhat easier to locate needy homeowners and persuade them to let us help them. But what we desperately needed was more recognition among the skilled trades. It was a challenge, to say the least, trying to recruit 35 or 40 plumbers, electricians, and carpenters to come and work for free on a Saturday in a high-crime neighborhood for an organization they knew nothing about. Then someone put me in touch with the local head of the International Brotherhood of Electrical Workers. When I described what Christmas in April was all about, and also mentioned that my father had been a loyal member of the I.B.E.W. for many years, he became an enthusiastic supporter. From that day forward he provided us each year with all the electricians we needed and persuaded electrical suppliers to donate all necessary supplies. He was well regarded in Washington, and his support helped us gain the participation of other skilled trades and vendors.

In my second year as president in 1986, we renovated 56 houses with 1200 volunteers. Gradually we were able to recruit roofing companies to install new roofs—and many were needed—for free or at steeply discounted prices. As always, the work was free to the recipients. Through year-round advance planning we gradually were able to solve the logistics problems, and we began to develop some how-to manuals both for ourselves and for other communities that were showing an interest.

We got another boost from President Reagan on May 24, 1986, when in his weekly radio address to the nation he talked about volunteerism and cited at length Christmas in April as a shining example.

Tom Henderson took over as president for two years in 1987, during which time we moved up to the 100-house level. I remained actively involved, primarily in recruiting skilled workers and in fund raising.

My admission to the Order of Malta was also of invaluable assistance to me in promoting the cause of Christmas in April. The Sovereign Military Hospitaller Order of St. John of Jerusalem of Rhodes and of Malta, commonly known as the Order of Malta, was founded in Jerusalem with the First Crusade in 1099 to care for the wounded in the Holy Land. It is the fourth oldest religious order in Christendom. By 1126, because of the need to provide armed protection against Muslim attacks, in addition to medical care for the sick and pilgrims to the Holy City, the Order assumed military functions in defense of Christendom.

Eventually it was driven from the Holy Land by the Muslims and was headquartered first in Cyprus, then on the Island of Rhodes, and then Malta. For three hundred years its powerful Navy fought epic battles against Muslim forces attacking Europe through the 1500's.

Today the Order of Malta, with its rich and colorful history, is headquartered in Rome and is still recognized under international law as a sovereign entity. It exchanges ambassadors and diplomatic representatives with over 80 countries, and is a member of the United Nations in a "Permanent Observer" status.

The Order's role today is entirely one of service to the sick and the poor, in keeping with its original purpose. Its work is carried out through persons distinguished in their profession who, in addition to being Roman Catholic, must have established a record of charitable works in the church and in the community, and must pledge continued service to "our lords the sick and poor." When I was admitted in 1982, through the good offices of my friend Tim Murphy, there were 10,000 Knights and Dames of Malta worldwide, including 1500 in the United States. The flag of the eight-pointed white Maltese Cross on a scarlet background stands out everywhere as a symbol of service to mankind.

In Washington the Order's charitable endeavors include supporting the work of Mother Theresa's community of nuns in one of the poorest sections of the city. Because of this, Susan and I had the great honor of meeting and conversing with Mother Theresa on her visit to

Washington. It was clear from the simplicity of her manner and her message that we were in the presence of a living saint.

Membership in the Order of Malta put me in contact with other like-minded members who were more than willing to assist Christmas in April, with contributions in cash and in kind, as well as hands-on assistance on Christmas in April day. In addition, two of our members from Kansas City, Dick Miller and John McMeel, decided to follow our lead and create a program in Kansas City, calling it Christmas in October, which continues to this day.

We were beginning to receive more national publicity, including laudatory stories in the New York Times and Time magazine. Along with it came inquiries from other cities. By 1988 there were a dozen or so other cities which had created Christmas in April programs with our assistance, and so we decided it was time to go national. We incorporated Christmas in April*USA, formed a national board of directors, including Bobby Trimble from Midland, and hired Patty Johnson as our national executive director (also moving our headquarters from her basement to donated office space in downtown Washington). We copyrighted the name, and for communities wishing to create their own programs, we set up admission standards and provided guidelines and manuals and all necessary hands-on assistance and advice. After a couple of years Patty Johnson was named president and has continued to guide the program for the past seventeen years.

In 1988, thanks to a recommendation from my Christmas in April colleagues, I was honored as one of "Washington's One & Only Nine," an annual award given by Washington's CBS affiliate Channel 9. The awards for community service were presented at a televised black-tie ceremony, with a generous stipend going to the charity each of us represented. It was an honor to be part of a group of eight others which included a man who volunteers 8-12 hours every day distributing food to the poor, a woman who operates a beauty parlor and provides a Thanksgiving dinner to over a thousand homeless persons every year, a 73-year-old retired Navy captain who helps disabled persons 40 hours a week, and a man who turned his residence into a shelter for the homeless.

Thanks to the tireless efforts of Patty Johnson and her staff and volunteers, Christmas in April*USA has now established local programs in more than 250 communities in every state in the union. In several cities Knights and Dames of Malta are sponsors and hands-on participants.

In 2000 the name was changed to Rebuilding Together in order to accommodate non-Christian groups and corporate sponsors who were eager to participate but had a problem with "Christmas." The work goes on, and in many communities the volunteers provide renovation services for more than one day, and in some cases throughout the year.

More and more I have come to realize that helping other people gives one great personal satisfaction. I think most Christmas in April participants would agree. You walk into a house at 8AM, look around, and you see holes in the ceiling and fixtures that don't work and rotted floors and a collapsing front porch and you think, "My god, how are we ever going to make this place look liveable in one day?" You meet the owners, a widow or an elderly couple or a man in a wheel chair, and they look hopeful but about as skeptical as you are.

Then you see the buckets of paint and brushes and rollers in a corner, and sheet rock and lumber stacked in the back yard and a new stove and refrigerator and a toilet in their cartons, and you and your twenty or so companions meet with the house captain. You get your orders and you begin. And then the plumber and the carpenter and the electrician arrive and before you know it the place is humming with activity. And at the end of the day you're exhausted but you can't believe your eyes, and neither can the grateful homeowner, and she has tears in her eyes, and she says, "It's just like Christmas!"

There's nothing quite like it.

*   *   *   *

Our household in the early Eighties witnessed many changes. The children had become young adults. Patrick and Tim graduated from Gonzaga High School in 1982 and 1983 respectively, and Katy from Georgetown Visitation in 1985. Each compiled outstanding records academically and in extracurricular activities, and all held down various part-time jobs on weekends and during the summers. We were proud of them. Patrick entered Duke University, Tim went to Columbia, and Katy was delighted to be accepted at Notre Dame. All chose liberal arts majors.

In 1980 Susan, after successful endeavors in theater, journalism, and public relations, launched a new career. She joined her friend Lorna Zimmerman in the travel business. With her wide circle of acquaintances and reputation for professional excellence, she soon numbered among her clients the presidents of Catholic and Georgetown Universities, Reader's Digest, and a number of other national organizations. She has continued as a travel consultant both in Washington and now in California for the past 25 years, during which time she and I have traveled extensively here and abroad. As a result, she is able to advise her clients from first-hand experience on destinations, itineraries, hotels, restaurants, and other sights to be seen (or skipped) almost anywhere in the world. She finds great satisfaction in creating both individual and group trips that perfectly meet the desires of her clients. It is greatly rewarding to be told by her clients that she has created "the trip of a lifetime." She has also found that the travel business can be extremely complex and challenging. It requires great people skills, infinite patience, and meticulous advance planning and attention to details, all of which she has in abundance.

28.

INTERTEL

After the excitement of the Felt-Miller trial had subsided, private practice became somewhat boring. The first Reagan administration (1981-85) was rather quiet in terms of public scandals or major investigations requiring the services of Washington trial lawyers. Primarily I was engaged in various phases of civil litigation, representing plaintiffs in personal injury cases, most of which resulted in settlement before trial. Our firm also did a considerable amount of employment termination work, which usually involved the question of whether a contract employee had been terminated arbitrarily or for cause. All in all, not a thrilling time in the law practice.

Meanwhile, my friends Bob Peloquin and Tom McKeon, whose invitation to join them I had declined in 1971 when they created International Intelligence, Inc. (Intertel), were going great guns. They were providing sophisticated worldwide investigative services for corporations and law firms, and had set up offices in half a dozen U.S. cities and in London, mostly staffed by former prosecutors as well as retired investigators from the FBI and other federal agencies, and from Scotland Yard. Some of them were my former colleagues from the Buffalo Strike Force. Intertel had gained a great deal of favorable publicity helping Howard Hughes drive the mob from the casinos he purchased in Las Vegas. Intertel was also retained by Resorts International to protect it from mob infiltration of its casino investments in the Bahamas and then in the newly developing casinos in Atlantic City.

Intertel advised corporations and their law firms on a variety of matters, with emphasis on management security and corporate litigation. Among other things, for corporations it conducted background investigations on high level executive candidates; or internal investigations of suspected fraud or corporate theft.

I had remained in close contact with Bob Peloquin and Tom McKeon over the years (and in fact I had hornswoggled them into becoming co-investors in the ill-fated *Doonesbury* venture), and had followed Intertel's progress with great interest. So in 1985 when the opportunity arose to become Intertel's vice president and general counsel, it seemed the right time to leave private practice and join them. I was 55 and hoping to retire at age 60 or shortly thereafter. I thought this would be an interesting and exciting way to end my professional career. And it was. My only regret was parting company with Howard Epstein, my partner and surrogate brother in the law practice.

It was understood that my duties as general counsel would not require my full attention, and that I would be able to join in the investigations. The Washington headquarters had a staff of about ten, including Peloquin and McKeon. Together the investigative experience of the staff totaled hundreds of years, and there was great camaraderie in the office. The chief of staff was Vadja Kolombatovic, originally from Yugoslavia, who had retired from the FBI as head of all the Bureau's legations in U.S. embassies throughout the world. Vadja spoke at least six languages and had contacts with law enforcement agencies across the globe. Among others with whom I worked closely were Gus Fipp and Jim Healy, both slightly older than I, and both of whom I had known from earlier days. I also knew most of the people in the other Intertel offices, and so for me it was like rejoining old colleagues.

My five years at Intertel provided a kaleidoscope of interesting assignments. I took part in investigations of everything from embezzlement at a furniture manufacturing plant in Secaucus, NJ, to a salmonella poisoning at a dairy outside of Chicago, to thefts by employees at a mobile home manufacturing plant in North Carolina, to an internal fraud matter at a major company in Austin, Texas, among others.

The most memorable year was 1987, when I spent six weeks in India, commuted semi-monthly to Las Vegas, and had four business trips to London.

The Bhopal Disaster

On the night of December 2-3 1984, a gas leak at a chemical plant operated by Union Carbide in Bhopal, India, killed thousands of residents and injured thousands more. It was the worst industrial accident in history.

Bhopal is the capital of the state of Madyha Pradesh in central India. The cause of the leak was never finally resolved. Union Carbide's investigation concluded that the disaster was probably the deliberate act of a disgruntled employee, but the evidence was circumstantial, and was disbelieved by the state and central governments of India, which placed all the blame on Union Carbide. American trial lawyers flocked to the scene, signing up plaintiffs by the thousands. Things got so out of hand that the central government took over the representation of all plaintiffs and denied visas to all American lawyers.

By the end of 1986, after protracted pre-trial litigation and negotiations, Union Carbide was ready to settle and to pay fair compensation to families of the victims and to the injured. The problem was, nobody on either side had been able to make an accurate determination of the number of dead, the number of injured, or the nature and extent of their injuries. Estimates of the dead ranged up to 5000 and of the injured up to 100,000.

Union Carbide's law firm in New York then retained Intertel to try to make this determination, gathering information from whatever sources might be available.

Jack Gibbons, head of our New York office, went over as the advance man, and I was asked to join him in late January 1987. Because of the ban on visas for lawyers, we were instructed to obtain tourist visas and to act like tourists, and to try to obtain the needed information as quietly as possible. We were not to let it be known generally that we were working for Union Carbide.

I had never been to India and had no particular desire to go there. However, after experiencing one of the biggest blizzards ever to hit Washington two days before my departure, it somehow seemed more enticing. I arrived in Delhi on January 28, a beautiful spring day.

My hotel, the Hyatt Regency, was in the suburbs, in a supposedly affluent area. But in a 45 minute walk around the neighborhood I saw incredible sights: people everywhere, bicycles, scooters, 3-wheeled motorized rickshas (a Delhi specialty—thousands of them). Grinding poverty—mud huts with tarp covers. Tiny children in rags, barely subsisting. The sacred cows really are there, wandering around, stopping traffic. Two men walking with cobras around their necks, perhaps off to their jobs as charmers. Women swinging picks and shovels, others carrying on their heads baskets of dirt from place to place. Row upon row of cow chips lying in the sun, for later use as cooking fuel. Many vendors with pots of things cooking God knows what. Women wearing brightly colored *sarees*, even the poorest, some with rings on toes, bells on ankles, and ornamentation on noses. Water buffalo pulling lawn mowers in a park, camels pulling work carts, many goats. An elephant, working.

The city itself is vast and sprawling, built over a period of a thousand years. The population in 1987 was 6-7 million; today it exceeds ten million. There are many architectural styles, but in all there is a pervasive sense of decay. Some things have been decaying for a thousand years, some 400, and some 20, but all is decaying. The British left a system of government, a civil service, and a judicial system. But they forgot to leave a bucket of paint.

However, the vibrancy of the city is in its people! The sights and the sounds are staggering! The sidewalks are filled with people wearing every possible kind of costume—business suits, turbans, pyjamas, robes, rags, loin cloths. The mixture of Hindus, Muslims, Jainists, Buddhists, and Christians is denoted by the goods, shops, foods, dress, and places of worship.

We were fortunate to have as our constant companion and guide Mr. Kalra, who had retired as principal assistant to the director of the Indian equivalent of our FBI. He was 76, a lawyer, distinguished and eccentric, an exact replica of the Alec Guinness character in Lawrence of Arabia. I never learned his first name, and we paid him in cash. He was to lead us to our contacts, people who might have the information we needed.

After a few days we flew to Bhopal, located on a high plateau and with a mild year-round climate. Viewed from the air, vast wheatfields give the countryside the appearance of Kansas or Nebraska. Bhopal is on a large lake, with many alabaster buildings, none more than 2-3 stories high. From a distance it looks like a Mediterranean resort. But as one drives in from the airport it becomes even dirtier and more squalid than Delhi. Thousands of people were living in lean-to's and straw huts. Yet there was the same hustle and bustle and frantic traffic as in the capital.

What is staggering about India is the constant collision between the old and new—"synthesis," Mr. Kalra called it. For example, a caravan of wagonloads of steel girders, each wagon pulled by a team of water buffalo. A street crew getting ready to pave a street at night, but completely in the dark—no lights of any kind. In this city of 750,000, a herd of at least 200 goats making its way along a busy street; an elephant grazing in somebody's front yard; a few stray hogs.

We drove out past the closed Union Carbide plant, just on the edge of the city. It was an extremely poor area, and still teeming with people. It is common in India for workers to set up housekeeping for themselves and families in fields or vacant lots near the job site, and as many members of the family as are able will work. There were still thousands near the closed plant. Shelter consisted of piled rocks or straw or cardboard, or for the fortunate ones, some sheets of corrugated tin. There was no water or electricity, running water or sanitation. When the plant closed after the disaster, many survivors simply faded away, but many others simply stayed, having nowhere else to go.

Two years after the disaster, the only visible signs of the catastrophe were a great many dispensaries, designated with a red cross, which also seemed to dispense haircuts.

It was time to get to work. But we soon learned that it would be at Mr. Kalra's pace. We gathered together at the hotel at 11AM. We talked about what needed to be done. After 20 minutes he announced that it was time to take a walk around the grounds of our stately old hotel—a former maharaja's palace on a hilltop. After a leisurely lunch we took a walk down to the lake. On our return (2:00) he assured us that he would start making the needed phone calls, right after his nap. All of this was interspersed with wonderful stories and comments on the history, poetry, and philosophy of India. At 4 o'clock he awoke from his nap and at 5:00 triumphantly advised us that two people were coming to dinner and we had an appointment with a third at 10:30 the next morning. At 7:00 he was sorry to report that the two could not come to dinner after all. But we did sit down and discuss all over again what we had accomplished (!) and what needed to be done. Thus ended our first day of work, five days after my arrival in India.

The next morning at 11 we arrived for our 10:30 appointment (probably a little early) at the office of the local manager of a major company. The executive, an old army buddy of our host, said with supreme confidence that there were three people who could provide us with the information we wanted. Unfortunately, #1 was in Bangalore, #2 had a slipped disk, and #3 was dead. But #1 would be back next week so we could try again.

A week earlier I would have been maddened at this pace, but I began to realize that it is easier to go with the flow than to try to change a thousand years of tradition. I was also told that the Hindi word *kal* means both "tomorrow" and "yesterday" which was helpful. And I learned that no polite Indian would ever, in answer to a question, reply "no" or "I don't know." It's more polite to evade, and if necessary, to make empty promises.

I noticed that nearly all the educated people we dealt with changed back and forth between English and Hindi when speaking with each other. Thus: "Now here is what we have to do: Lak deep singh hok bang krishnan no problem, agreed?" The whole thing was so comical that I was beginning to enjoy it.

After numerous fits and starts, we finally made some progress. We had lunch one day with a relative of Mr. Kalra's who was an M.D. and deputy chief medical officer at the hospital nearest the Union Carbide plant. She recounted with restrained but obvious emotion the events of the night of the disaster. The explosion occurred at 9-10 PM while she was on duty. All doctors were shortly summoned to all hospitals but it was several hours before the exact nature of the poison gas was identified as MIC and the proper antidote could be obtained and administered. There was chaos everywhere, people running in all directions—"mothers running one way and fathers another." Victims quickly filled the corridors, lobbies, and the outside compound. Thirteen thousand victims descended on this 300 bed hospital. There was no way people could be registered. The Red Cross and other organizations brought food and blankets. She and her staff worked around the clock for five days. They administered atropine injections, oxygen (both of which were soon depleted), cortisone for aching joints, and had people wash out their eyes, but little more could be done. After a week or so, most of the survivors just drifted away. She estimated that 2500 died and 30-40,000 were seriously injured. Strangely enough, nearly all the water buffalo died, and some goats, but dogs and fowl were not affected.

It was a very moving account.

Jack Gibbons returned to New York after two weeks, and I was on my own for the next four. I missed his experience, advice, and companionship. Mr. Kalra and I continued our quest, both in Delhi and in Bhopal. About every fourth day we would strike pay dirt. The rest of the time was spent in frustration. Promises not kept, appointments missed, phone calls not completed, phone calls not returned, blind alleys followed. "This is no problem. Call me next week and I will have the information for you." We were in the third week of that.

But the hours passed not unpleasantly, sipping tea in the cool breezes with good conversation about the culture and customs of India. It must have been like this in the days of the Empire; waiting for the messenger from the Punjab.

The Indian bureaucracy is legendary for making and keeping ledgers. For example, in order to retrieve lost luggage at the Delhi airport, at the "Mishandled Baggage Section," I passed through eight clerks, each one making entries in books and stamping papers; signed my name five times, and then was directed to find my own bag in a warehouse containing, I would estimate, at least 5,000 pieces of luggage, including some Gladstones from Victorian days.

They were good at ledgers, but they had not—at least not by 1987—developed the art of statistic gathering. That's what made our assignment so difficult. I went to the Bureau of Vital Statistics in Bhopal. I was shown a huge room full of death records going back god knows how many years, but there was no compilation of statistics with regard to years, ages, gender, or cause of death. My attempt to determine the disaster's effect on the birth rate, or whether there was a rise in birth defects, came to naught.

Meanwhile there was my obligation to play the tourist. In Delhi I moved to the ultra-luxurious Oberoi hotel and visited the city's many gardens, mosques, temples and museums. Mr. Kalra took me on a tour of the trial courts and the Supreme Court, and introduced me to the president of the Delhi Bar Association. I even visited the Delhi zoo, where I met the son of the zookeeper, who allowed (compelled) me to pet a Bengal tiger, drop bananas into the mouth of a rhino, and he saved me from a rock-throwing gorilla.

I boarded a bus for a weekend in Agra, and was captivated by the Taj Mahal, taking photographs at sunrise, high noon, sunset, and under a full moon. Each phase of daylight and moonlight gives a different shade to the white marble. Fabulous.

I flew to Kanha National Park—Kipling country, where he wrote his Jungle Stories—for a tiger hunt on the back of an elephant. We saw cheetah, wild boar, and monkeys, among other animals, but only the tracks of a tiger.

I flew to Jaipur and road an elephant to the Amber Fort.

One weekend I went to Nepal. Kathmandu is the most exotic place I've ever been. It's another world. In a single day one can visit Pashupatinath, Nepal's holiest Hindu temple; three miles up the road, Boudnath, one of the world's biggest Buddhist stupas. While in Nepal I hired a guide for a trek up into the mountains to the village of Nagarkot to view the Himalayas at sunset, and did a fly-by of Mount Everest. An amazing weekend.

Although six weeks was a long time to be away from Susy, and I missed the companionship of other Americans, I recognized my good fortune in seeing these amazing sights and having all these adventures without spending a nickel of my own money.

Mr. Kalra was very gracious in introducing me to his own family and to the Indian lifestyle. I was invited to a birthday party for his 11-year-old grandson. There were about 75 adults and children, all family members, all very gracious and hospitable, most Punjabi-speaking as well as English. They were upper middle class people, lawyers, engineers, small factory owners, doctors. There was also a young newly married couple, the product of an arranged marriage. I spoke to them at length, he from Delhi, she from Calcutta. They were introduced to each other a month before the engagement, and saw each other half a dozen times before the wedding ten months later, but were permitted to write and make phone calls. They seemed happy and indicated no resentment against the system. They lived with his parents, the usual custom. I asked if they ever planned to have a place of their own, and he replied, "I will never leave my parents." She was bright and attractive, and she said she occupied her day by helping her mother-in-law cook, reading magazines, and watching T.V.—"That is what brides do in India." At least upper middle class brides, I thought. I wonder if things have changed in the 18 years since then.

On another occasion I was invited to the Kalra home "to meet a few relatives" left over from a wedding the previous weekend. It turned out to be a dinner for 18. These same people then invited me to dinner another evening at the Gymkhana, Delhi's most exclusive private club, dating from British Colonial days. On each occasion there was animated conversation and savory food, eaten with great gusto, and great deference given to me. This family originated in the Punjab in the north of India, and it is said that Punjabis are exuberant people, and I believe it. They are not the stereotype shy and reticent Indian. My impression of the people of India, based on the ones I met through Mr. Kalra, is that they are an extremely gracious and hospitable people.

Meanwhile there were developments on the litigation front. There was one issue on which both the Indian government and Union Carbide agreed. Jointly they commissioned scientific demographic studies, which concluded that the maximum number of persons who could have been affected by the poisonous cloud was about 325,000. However, there were already more than 500,000 plaintiffs. Moreover, after about two years of pre-trial litigation, it came to light that the judge handling the case was himself a plaintiff. He hadn't found it necessary to tell anybody.

By the time I left India on March 13, we had compiled some fairly good statistics from reliable sources. This was further augmented by my replacement from Intertel, Bruce Holman, who was there an additional month or so.

Six weeks was the longest Susy and I had ever been apart, but we had a great reunion—in Hong Kong at the Shangri-La hotel. En route home we stopped in California for a visit with my family.

In a final report to our client, our best estimate, as I recall, was about 2000 killed on the night of the disaster with another thousand succumbing within a year thereafter, and about 20,000 injured. The case was settled a year or two later, and Union Carbide paid the government of India $325 million as compensation for all victims. The Indian government then authorized payment only to those who could prove their claims by medical or hospital records. This of course was impossible for many, if not most, of the victims.

On July 20, 2004, nearly twenty years after the catastrophe, the New York Times reported that the Supreme Court of India ruled that the $325 million in compensation should be paid directly to the victims and no longer held by the government. Even so, I doubt that much of it will ever reach the victims. Apart from the problem of locating them, the money must first be filtered through the corrupt hands of the Indian central bureaucracy, and then the equally corrupt hands of the Madyha Pradesh state bureaucracy. I would be surprised if one victim in ten ever gets a rupee.

Benny Binion's Horseshoe Casino

In Las Vegas, The Strip and Downtown are worlds apart. Both are glitzy, but The Strip is upscale glitzy and Downtown is blue collar glitzy. The Strip is exotic; Downtown is earthy. In recent years Downtown has added more lights and more flash, and better hotels like Steve Wynn's Golden Nugget, but in fact the two will never be equivalent, and shouldn't be. They attract two different kinds of gamers. Downtown is a no-nonsense place where you can get down to the serious business of high-stakes gambling without being bothered by pirate battles or roller coasters or fancy art galleries. And you can get a decent meal at a fair price, prepared by a non-celebrity chef.

One of the pioneer entrepreneurs in Downtown was Benny Binion, a maverick gambler and racketeer who was run out of Texas in the 1950's by crusading Texas Attorney General Will Wilson. That's the same Will Wilson who was my boss at Justice and later my client.

Benny Binion came roaring out of Texas and into Las Vegas and seized the moment. He took over the El Dorado casino on Fremont Street and renamed it "Binion's Horseshoe." In the lobby of Benny's place you can have your picture taken in front of a ten-foot high glass horseshoe containing one million dollars in cash—all in one hundred dollar bills. Benny's cowboy style—flashy and definitely non-chic—attracted just the clientele he was looking for. The Horseshoe became the anchor of Downtown. Benny was not bothered by the mob. Downtown held little attraction for them, and Benny would never have tolerated sharing the action.

In keeping with his boots and buckskins style, Benny disdained high-falutin' games like baccarat and *chemin de fer*. It was Benny who established the World Series of Poker in 1970, playing no-limit Texas hold 'em, years before its imitators began proliferating on television, and the original World Series is still held every year right there at the Horseshoe.

By 1987 Benny had turned over the operation to his son Jack, a shrewd no-nonsense businessman. The Horseshoe is said to be the last family-owned casino in America. Another son, Ted, had become a profligate playboy and drug addict. His connections with the underworld through his addiction eventually led to his murder.

Jack ran a tight ship, so tight that suspected cheaters and card-counters soon found themselves escorted by the beefy security squad to a "quiet room" and then to the back alley, from which they usually made their way to the nearest emergency room.

There was at this time in Las Vegas a branch office of the Los Angeles federal strike force, which I had helped establish in 1970. The main purpose of the Las Vegas office was to combat organized crime in the casinos, a noble purpose. However, by 1987 nearly all of the casinos were owned by major corporations, and Mafia control was no longer a significant factor. As a result, the Las Vegas strike force was looking for work.

It got wind of the Horseshoe's heavy-handed treatment of some of its patrons, and began an investigation of a possible "pattern of racketeering activity," *i.e.* systematic assault and battery upon customers of the Horseshoe. This was of serious concern to Jack Binion and his father Benny, because a conviction under the RICO statute could result in a government seizure and forfeiture of all of the assets of the business.

Upon recommendation of Binion's lawyer, Oscar Goodman (now the mayor Las Vegas), Intertel was brought onto the scene.

Old Benny, by this time in his dotage, was seldom seen on the premises, but he attended important meetings called by his lawyers and their agents. He looked like a Madame Tussaud version of Buffalo Bill, but he was an active participant, frequently barking out his opinions about meddling gummint lawyers and G-men and the exorbitant cost of defending his God-given right to run his own business. He reminded me of old H.L. Hunt in Dallas. In the end, though, it was agreed that Intertel would conduct a thorough study of the practices of the security department, past and present, and to see how they compared with the other casinos in town.

It was a long and tedious process, lasting several months and into 1988, and several of us took turns in teams of two spending a week per month in Las Vegas. At first we stayed in hotels on the Strip, but it got so depressing coming down to breakfast at 7:30 AM and seeing people shooting craps and drinking martinis that we finally rented a corporate apartment in a residential neighborhood.

Court records of civil and criminal complaints at the major casinos turned up some interesting tidbits. A golfer at Will Clark's Desert Inn golf course sent his ball over a high fence and into a neighbor's yard. The intrepid linksman scaled the fence and retrieved the ball, but failed to make it back to the fence ahead of the resident rottweiler. He was suing the Desert Inn for failure to post a warning sign.

At the Dunes, the security force was called to quiet an obstreperous over-imbiber. He reacted by mooning the guards, and *they* in turn responded by tasering the mooner.

Each place had its problems with suspected cheaters, but it did appear, at least from the records, that the Horseshoe was somewhat more forceful than the others. And there were some egregious incidents. It would be hard to justify beating up a man in a wheelchair, even if he was a cheater.

We interviewed all current security employees at the Horseshoe, but locating former employees was more of a problem. Las Vegas is a very transient city, with many people working for a few weeks or months in the gaming industry and then moving on. It also attracts a great many people who for a variety of reasons do not care to have their current addresses known.

On the flip side, we found that probably a majority of the permanent residents live their lives pretty much like their friends and relatives in Cleveland or Des Moines or Birmingham. They are in the PTA, their kids are in sports, and they go to the mall and the movies and to church. Except for their job in the gaming industry, they never go to the Strip or see any of the so-called fabulous shows.

Our investigation of the Horseshoe concluded that most of the excessive force could be traced primarily to two or three storm trooper-type supervisors on the security force. Jack Binion may have condoned these techniques or at least ignored them, but there was no indication that he had ordered or directed them. This enabled his lawyers to argue that the casino was not being operated through a "pattern of racketeering activity." Further, the treatment of cheaters was only incidental to the operation of the business, and not an integral part of it. That is, Binion was not operating with rigged games or skimming the profits to avoid taxes or engaging in other practices normally thought of as racketeering activities.

The upshot was that several employees were prosecuted for aggravated assault and battery, but the strike force decided there was insufficient evidence to warrant indictments under the RICO statute. The Horseshoe was saved, and Jack Binion was persuaded to lighten up on the security.

Machinations in Old London Town

In May 1987 the New York brokerage house of Donaldson, Lufkin, and Jenrette called us to say they had a problem in their subsidiary office in London. The London office was engaged exclusively in the commodities market, especially in metals futures. Their traders dealt in everything from aluminum to molybdenum to zinc. The problem was that about ten million dollars had disappeared from the firm's books. No one could account for the loss. Several employee traders were suspected. A thorough investigation was needed. DLJ was reluctant to report the matter to Scotland Yard, for fear of adverse publicity and public loss of confidence in the company.

In the United Kingdom, although there was an equivalent of our Securities and Exchange Commission, it had no authority over the commodities market, which was virtually unregulated. As a consequence, it tended to attract as traders very smart, fast-talking individuals unhindered by a strong sense of ethics, who decided they could make more money trading in metals futures than selling used cars.

Jack Gibbons and I flew to London and met with the Freshfiields law firm representing DLJ, in their offices in the City near St. Paul's. They gave us a brief summary of the problem and full authority to explore whatever avenues might look promising. We brought with us Jack Enright, Intertel's best auditor. Jack was a former IRS intelligence agent who knew how to follow a paper trail better than anyone I've ever known. Enright was not much for the London theater and concert scene, as Gibbons and I were, but loved examining records. In his career he had seen every kind of scheme and artifice to defraud that ever been conceived by the mind of man, and given the opportunity to ferret out skullduggery, he was like a bloodhound on the trail.

While Enright pored through mountains of trading records, Gibbons and I began interviewing employees, some of whom were more cooperative than others, and following leads developed from the interviews. We were assisted by a retired Scotland Yard detective.

Gradually we were able to ferret out a complicated scheme worthy of a James Bond scenario—except for the fast cars and beautiful women, unfortunately. It involved four traders who, together and with some assistance on the outside, had devised a network of phony trading accounts in such a manner that the gains in trades would be siphoned off to the phony accounts and then laundered before being returned to the culprits. The losses were debited to the company. In this way they had bilked the company of millions of pounds. The scheme included paper corporations in the Cayman Islands and the Bahamas and bank accounts in Zug, Switzerland. Our leads took us to the island of Mallorca where a former trader gave us a midnight statement at his resort villa on the far end of the island. There were also some colorful characters in London itself, including one who lived on Baker Street, a few doors from the fictional home of Sherlock Holmes, and another fellow with flaming red hair who ran a gay bar in Soho.

Three of the four suspects submitted to interviews but were masters at the art of circumlocution. The fourth, after a few minutes, begged off because of his bad heart, or in his parlance, his "dodgy ticker."

Our four trips to London were not without their benefits. Jack and I saw a number of West End plays, including "Les Miserables" and the original cast of "Phantom of the Opera." In June, Susy came over with me. At that time Patrick, who had graduated from Duke in 1986, was spending a year at the Free University in Berlin, and Tim, who had graduated from Columbia in January, was touring Europe. They joined us in London for a wonderful week of castles and concerts, plays and pubs,

In October, Susy returned with me again, and this time we brought my mother as a gift for her 87th birthday, staying at the renowned Brown's Hotel, where Susy knew the manager, having sent clients there. The two women toured London and environs while the rest of us wrapped up our investigation. Over high tea, our final witness gave us a very helpful inside view of the scheme, and it was agreed that we would obtain a written statement from him at his suburban home the next day.

That night London was struck by its first hurricane in 350 years, "since the reign of Queen Anne." We three slept through it all, although Mom said she thought she had heard some bumping sounds in the night. We awoke to find chaos in the streets—power lines down, windows smashed, debris everywhere, transportation at a standstill. The many parks in London suffered severe damage, and Kew Gardens lost over half its trees.

As a result, we could not get to our witness's home nor he to London, so we all returned to Washington.

We submitted our report to Freshfield's, but the outcome never became clear to us. The miscreant traders were terminated, of course, but it does not appear that any criminal proceedings were instituted, nor do we know if restitution was sought. In view of the fact that a high ranking DLJ officer in New York was the supposed overseer of the London office, we concluded that the company probably buried the matter in order to protect its public image.

There were subsequent assignments with my Intertel colleagues, of varying types and in diverse places, such as New York, San Francisco, Memphis, Nassau, and Vancouver. Each was interesting and challenging and the five years passed quickly, but by 1990 I had reached my hoped-for retirement age, and I had lots of others things I wanted to do with my life. One of them was to return to school.

29.

RETIREMENT, AND RETURN TO ACADEMIA

I had been thinking about taking some liberal arts refresher courses ever since our three youngsters had gone off to Duke, Columbia, and Notre Dame, and returned with fascinating accounts of their readings and studies. My professional career had been stimulating and exciting, but I began to look forward to a time of less pressure, more leisure, and an opportunity for more intellectual enrichment. It all came to head one summer when we five were on one of our motor home vacations and were visiting San Francisco. We went up to the Top O' the Mark for a drink and a fabulous view of "The City," as San Franciscans like to call their town. The kids had not seen much of each other, what with their summer jobs and social activities, and they were engaged in animated conversation. I looked at Susan and said, "They're not only talking about books I never heard of, they're talking about *authors* I never heard of. I'm paying six and a half bucks a drink and I can't even get in on the conversation." From that time on I vowed that when I retired I would go back to school.

And so in August 1990, six months after my 60th birthday, I said goodby to my colleagues at Intertel. We had enjoyed five years of adventures together, but I was looking forward to my new life.

The first thing we did was celebrate my mother's 90th birthday on September 10, 1990, by taking a three-day cruise from Los Angeles to Ensenada, Mexico. She, my two sisters and I and our spouses and our son Patrick, had a wonderful time together. Every night Mom engaged in her favorite activity, dancing. When the m.c. in the main lounge called her name to be recognized for her 90th birthday, the spotlight was unable to find her among the seated guests. She was out on the floor dancing the foxtrot with me. At a private party on her birthday, we all offered our toasts, and then awaited her words of wisdom. She said, "If I make it to 95, can we have another cruise?"

But God had other plans. Two years later she suffered a stroke, and after six weeks, she gained her eternal reward ten days after her 92nd birthday. She was a lady of unwavering faith and great courage, who enjoyed life, loved to dance and to laugh, and had a deep love for her family. She was an inspiration to all of us.

Georgetown University offers a Master's degree in Liberal Studies, just the program I was looking for. It requires ten courses, thirty credits in all, plus a thesis.

The courses are taught in the evenings and on Saturday mornings. There are a few retirees in the program, but mainly it attracts men and women in their thirties and forties, people in mid-career who find a need for the kind of personal enrichment offered by the liberal arts. It also attracts the University's very finest professors, who enjoy teaching mature and well-motivated students.

I applied and was accepted, to begin in the summer of 1990. Since we lived only a mile away, I could walk or ride my bicycle to the campus. I had my own carrel in Georgetown's vast library. My courses had enticing titles like Contemporary Values in British, Irish & American Drama; Plato's Ethics; United States—Latin American Relations; Soviet Russia and the Nationality Question; Fiction of Modern Ireland; and Art, Creativity, and the Sacred. Susan and the kids were very supportive and showed great interest in my studies, offering helpful advice from time to time, such as "Plato is great, but avoid Kant like the plague."

Papers of ten to thirty pages were required in each course, I took great pleasure in producing papers with titles like *The Gothic Cathedral as Medieval Metaphor*; *Sam Shepard and the Search for Communication in Love*; *The Great Gobachav/Yeltsin Debate*; and *The Religious Dimension in the Secular Paintings of Franz Marc and Georges Rouault*, two painters whom I had come to know and love through my friend Jackie Horner. My *piece de resistance* was a prosecutor's rebuttal to Socrates' closing argument in his trial. I got A's on every paper and thereby learned first-hand what grade inflation is all about.

For my thesis, I had the opportunity to indulge in a subject that has fascinated me for a long time—charismatic political leadership. In the early twentieth century the German sociologist Max Weber introduced the notion of charisma in the context of his theories on political authority. A charismatic relationship develops when the leader is perceived by his followers to have certain exceptional qualities which set him apart from ordinary men, as a result of which they are willing to offer their unquestioning loyalty. This relationship, Weber found, usually arises in time of crisis, when people are looking for messianic leadership.

Since Weber's time, history has witnessed the impact of both constructive and destructive charismatic leaders, from Mahatma Gandhi to Adolph Hitler. Recent scholars in a number of disciplines have found that although there are no universal attributes of charismatic leaders, they are generally perceived to be revolutionary, visionary, possessing heroic qualities, and authoritarian. Such messianic leaders generally emerge when economic conditions are frustrating and social structures have become fragmented.

Post-Soviet Russia was at this time undergoing the birth-struggle of democracy, featuring the titanic struggle between Mikhail Gorbachev, the hard-liner-turned-reformer, and Boris Yeltsin, the darling of the democratic hopeful. I thought it would be interesting to examine whether conditions were ripe for a charismatic leader in Russia; whether either of the aforementioned could be so described; or whether there was a new messiah on the horizon.

Through extensive research, I learned a great deal about both Russian history and charismatic leadership in general. I concluded in my 80-page thesis that although the conditions did indeed exist in Russia, neither Gorbachev nor Yeltsin filled the bill, nor did I see any other charismatic leaders either in the main stream or among the fringe elements. What Russia needed was heroic leaders, not necessarily charismatic leaders. Of course this was all before Vladimir Putin appeared on the scene, and his place in Russian history has yet to be determined.

It took me three years, until May 1993, to receive my M.A. in Liberal Studies, but it was one of the most stimulating and enjoyable periods of my life.

Community and church affairs had continued during my working years. Now retirement opened up additional time for these activities, including a food cooperative for the needy (called "Share" nationally), sponsored by the Order of Malta.

Our neighbor and good friend, political pundit Andy Tully, had developed Alzheimer's at about this time. His wife Molly and the wife of a former Assistant Attorney General formed a social club for men so that their husbands and other men with professional backgrounds would have an alternative to the usual day care facilities, which generally consisted of befuddled old men and women sitting around cutting out paper dolls and singing dumb songs.

The "Friends Club," whose members were a dozen or so men in the early and middle stages of Alzheimer's, plus male volunteers like myself and a social worker, met three mornings a week. We would socialize, reminisce, play simple games, and have lunch. The idea was to recreate as much as possible their experiences from the locker room at the golf club, to which their peers no longer invited them. It was (and still is) very successful. By attending once a week I learned a great deal about this tragic disease and how to deal with its victims, though each year I was frequently in mortal fear that one day someone would tap me on the shoulder and say, "Guess what! You're no longer a volunteer. From now on you're a paying member."

One of the most interesting courses I took at Georgetown was "Romantic Composers of the Nineteenth Century." Thereafter, by doing further research on the lives of these fascinating men and their music, I was able to put together a twelve-part lecture series for the enjoyment of the men of the Friends Club, playing the music and discussing the lives—including the triumphs, tragedies and foibles—of giants like Beethoven, Schubert, Mendelssohn, Brahms, Liszt, Chopin, Tchaikovsky, and others, including Italian opera.

The "golden years" were proving to be most enjoyable. I also had some time for tennis and skiing. For the latter I took Tim and Katy back to Vermont, where our friends, Ky and Rosemary McGrath, formerly of Washington, were operating the Inn at Long Trail near Killington. We three also flew to St. Anton. Austria, where I had learned to ski in 1959. In addition, Susan and I, thanks to her continued success in the travel business, have traveled to six continents.

But we now had an empty nest and had seen and done just about everything there was to do on the East Coast.

30.

THE MOVE TO PARADISE

When our children finished their education, none of them returned to Washington. By 1994, Patrick was in Brazil doing research for a Ph.D. in history from the University of Michigan, and was engaged to Myriam Campos, a psychologist from Rio de Janeiro and the mother of two young sons, Dimitri and Yuri. Tim had migrated to Los Angeles in the film business, working on various aspects of special effects and large format films. Katy, after Notre Dame, had entered law school at Northwestern, where her 3-person team had won the national mock trial competition. After graduation in 1993 she took a position with a litigation firm in San Francisco. So in addition to my two sisters, and several nieces and nephews and their children, we now had two of our three children living in California. Neither of us had lived close to our relatives during our married years, and the prospect of more frequent family gatherings, plus new regions to explore, was attractive. Some wise person once observed that humans, like plants, every once in awhile need to be re-potted.

My sister Mary Lu had divorced Bill Swain and married Dr. Stan Milstone, a warm-hearted and sensitive man who was welcomed into the family. They had moved from San Jose to the Napa Valley, where Stan, a psychiatrist, was employed at the Napa State Hospital and Mary Lu was teaching English as a second language at Napa Community College.

Whenever Susan and I would visit Stan and Mary Lu, we would say, "The Napa Valley is so beautiful, and the weather is so perfect, that if we ever leave Washington, this would be a great place to live."

A visit in February 1993 did the trick, with the golden mustard in full bloom in the vineyards, surrounded by emerald green hills, and the weather sunny and in the 60's. We decided that the benefits of living in this beautiful place near so many family members would outweigh the loss of our dear friends in Washington and the East.

It was August of 1994 before we headed west. The two most difficult parts of moving were 1) saying goodby to our friends, and 2) having to remove absolutely everything from a residence of 25 years. Susy helped solve both with the brilliant idea of a "house cooling" party, a week before we departed. We sent out over a hundred invitations, saying "you must not bring anything, and you may not leave without taking something." In this way we were able to say goodby to our friends, find a home for all those items that we could neither ship, save, or sell, such as half-filled bottles of liqueurs, old books, and miscellaneous odds and ends.

We took a leisurely 30-day trek westward, stopping to visit some of our favorite sites and visiting old friends en route. We arrived in Napa on September 24, 1994, and the wisdom of our decision has been confirmed over the past eleven years. Washington was an exciting city, and perfect for our careers and for rearing our family, and the Napa Valley has been an ideal place to begin a new life.

One of the joys of returning to California has been frequent family gatherings, which we sorely missed during our years in Washington. As one grows older one appreciates ever more the family get-togethers with our children and with my sisters and spouses, nieces and nephews and their children, and even with three of my original twelve cousins from Dubuque now living in northern California, Jack and Pat Bitter and Ann Bitter Reynolds.

A sad note is that my dear older sister, Patricia, died of congestive heart failure at age 78 in Saratoga on June 22, 2005, which makes us ever more grateful for being close to her these past years. Her love and solicitude for others, doubled in her husband Frank, lives on in her children and grandchildren, the most caring and thoughtful group of people I have ever known.

Through sheer dumb luck, we arrived at a time when the California real estate market was at rock bottom. As a result, with the proceeds of our Washington home we were able to purchase a home in Napa (pop.70,000) at 15 South Newport Drive, and a vacation condominium on the north shore of Lake Tahoe at Tahoe City, just three hours away.

Being big city denizens, we find ourselves frequently in San Francisco, just an hour away, for plays and concerts and to discover a whole new world with our exuberant grandsons.

In the opposite direction, three hours away in this best of all possible worlds, we have the luxury of hiking in the Sierras and for me, skiing at some of the country's finest ski resorts.

Patrick and Myriam were married in Brazil, and to our great delight, moved to California with her sons Dimitri and Yuri, in 1997, and are now located in Monterey. Katy left the law practice to become the director of the tour program at Alcatraz, San Francisco's most popular tourist attraction. In 2003 she married Douglas Olds, a fellow Washingtonian transplanted to San Francisco, and they have presented us with a two delightful grandsons, Rowan Thomas, born April 23, 2003, and Evan Karsten, born December 18, 2005.

We attend classes one day a week at the Fromm Institute for Lifelong Learning, on the campus of the University of San Francisco. As its name implies, Fromm offers daytime courses for retired adults, taught by retired professors. Courses span all the areas one might find in any university, presented in eight-week no-credit sessions for three semesters each year. It has been operating since 1976 and has 1200 enrollees. It is a fine example, I think, of an observation once made by the writer Andrew Solomon: "There is a basic social divide between those for whom life is an accrual of fresh experiences and knowledge, and those for whom maturity is a process of mental atrophy."

Susan, now in her 25th year in the travel business, has a regular clientele in the Napa Valley and is also the volunteer travel coordinator for the Fromm, creating a number of tours and cruises each year for the students, most of whom still love to travel and have the time and where-withal to do so.

For my 75th birthday, Susan treated me to a safari in Tanzania, the second greatest adventure of my lifetime, right behind the Grand Canyon raft trip.

In addition to exploring the nooks and crannies of this amazing state, we were also able to set down some roots in our own community. A local assisted living facility was happy to have me bring my "Romantic Composers of the 19th Century" series to their residents once a month.

My sister Mary Lu and I became volunteers with the Napa Valley Museum's "trunk program" for the local elementary schools. We were costumed as *Californios*, the first settlers in this area during the Rancho Period when all of California was part of Mexico, in the 1840's. With artifacts from the museum we portrayed life as it was in those days, and had great fun presenting our skit to avid fourth graders. We did this for six years until, to our dismay, Mary Lu and Stan decided to take up residence in Brookings, on the south coast or Oregon. Fortunately, they return to Napa rather frequently.

Susan served for six years on the board of the historic preservation group in Napa county, and I regularly conduct walking tours of historic Napa. Susan also helped to organize the Napa Valley Arts and Culture Alliance, a coalition of more than two dozen non-profit groups active in the fields of music, dance, theater, the fine arts, the culinary arts, and historic preservation, whose purpose is to assist each other and to make it known that there is more to this valley than fine wine and great restaurants.

At the other end of the scale there is also poverty and hardship in this area, as in any community. With a number of selfless and dedicated volunteers we created a program called the "Inside Out Network" to assist families of persons incarcerated in the Napa County jail, to connect them to the many private and public agencies that provide assistance in health care, housing, jobs, and the like for these innocent family members.

One strives for balance in one's life. For more than 25 years, thanks primarily to the inspiration and leadership of our great Washington friends, Gerry and Elizabeth Quinlan, Susan and I have been members of the Society of St. Francis de Sales, devoted to the teachings of that great saint, a bishop and doctor of the Church, who lived in the Savoy area of France in the 17th century.

In his many letters and homilies, and particularly in his famous *Introduction to the Devout Life,* Francis was one of the first to teach that a devout spiritual life not the sole prerogative of the monk in the monastery or the hermit in the desert. If the ultimate purpose in life is union with God's love, each of us on our journey can strive for that union in our everyday performance of our own "duties of state," be they as fireman, lawyer, homemaker, or whatever. We need not flee from the world; we are called to live in the world. As such, our relationships are part of our journey to God. Thus our friendships, work, leisure, and social gatherings, can all be means of achieving our ultimate goal, union with God, as well as a reflection of God's love for us.

Toward this end, St. Francis emphasizes what he calls the "little virtues," joy, patience, humility, affability, simplicity, generosity of spirit. He points out that great opportunities to serve God seldom arise, but little ones are frequent.

His words of four hundred years ago have great resonance today. It seems to us a good rule of life, especially in view of all the great blessings from God we have already received.

A friend who owns a winery here in the Napa Valley told us that when he purchased the property several years ago he hired his brother, a Pennsylvania farmer, to come out and manage the vineyard. On arrival, his brother said, "Jim, I know a lot about raising corn, but I don't know much about growing grapes, and this soil doesn't look too good." Jim explained to him that rocky soil is good, because the vines have to struggle in order to produce big, juicy grapes.

A year later the brother reported, "Jim, they ain't strugglin'. They're happy as clams!"

That's pretty much the way we feel. We ain't strugglin' and we're happy as clams.

#

978-0-595-38358-0
0-595-38358-0

Printed in the United States
45632LVS00004B/76-204